Contents

CD-ROM

The accompanying CD-ROM contains:

- Task files for completing the exercises
- Suggested answers
- Practice assignments.

Heinemann Learning to Pass Advanced ECDL AM4

Spreadsheets

Using Office 2000

Jennifer Johnson

www.heinemann.co.uk
✓ Free online support
✓ Useful weblinks
✓ 24 hour online ordering

01865 888058

Heinemann

Inspiring generations

Heinemann Educational Publishers
Halley Court, Jordan Hill, Oxford OX2 8EJ
Part of Harcourt Education

Heinemann is the registered trademark of
Harcourt Education Limited

Text © Jennifer Johnson, 2004

First published 2004

09 08 07 06 05 04
10 9 8 7 6 5 4 3 2 1

British Library Cataloguing in Publication Data is available
from the British Library on request.

ISBN 0 435 45585 0

Designed by Artistix, Thame, Oxon

Typeset by TechType

Cover design by Tony Richardson at the Wooden Ark
Printed in the UK by Thomson Litho Ltd

Acknowledgements
Every effort has been made to contact copyright holders of material reproduced in this
book. Any omissions will be rectified in subsequent printings if notice is given to the
publishers.

Dedication
My work is dedicated to
Victor Emanuel Johnson and Jane Elizabeth Johnson
Without you there would be no me.
Thank you.
Jennifer

Introduction

The Advanced ECDL Spreadsheet Module is for those who have already completed the core ECDL qualification or have intermediate spreadsheet skills. You do not need to have studied or passed core ECDL to take the individual advanced modules.

Unlike core ECDL, which requires you to take modules that cover a selection of software packages, Advanced ECDL is more specialised: you study each module separately; the modules are also tested and certificated separately. The Advanced qualification syllabus develops spreadsheet skills that are not required for ECDL.

This book assumes that you have spreadsheet skills at or above ECDL or intermediate level, and covers the additional skills that are required to enable you to pass the advanced test. Included with the book is a CD-ROM that contains the files you will need for the various exercises.

Each part of the Advanced ECDL syllabus is covered in a sequential order by category. The tasks, within which there are sometimes related topics, have been presented to you in a way that enables you, initially, to learn individual skills. In this way, you can progress quickly through tasks that you are competent at. Some topics are also integrated into later tasks, to give you the opportunity to refresh and test your learning.

CD-ROM

To access the files on the CD-ROM:

1. Insert the CD into your CD-ROM drive.

2. The CD-ROM will run automatically.

Some machines may not support autorun and so the CD ROM will not start automatically. If this is the case:

1. Go to 'My Computer' and double-click on your CD-ROM drive.

2. The CD-ROM should now run automatically.

If it does not run, but instead displays a list of the files on the CD-ROM, then:

Double-click on the folder called 'ECDL_Spreadsheets' and then on the file called 'index.htm'. This will start the user interface screen.

Note: it is best to copy the files onto your computer or network but if you are running the program from the CD-ROM, you must have the CD-ROM in the drive (including when you are trying to exit).

Note on screenshots
The screenshots shown in this book show the Office 2000 version of Excel run on the Windows XP operating system. The same windows on your computer might look slightly different; however, the content and menus will be the same as long as your system is running Office 2000.

Glossary

Before you start: Spreadsheet terms used in this book

default: option(s) already selected by an application.

drag and drop: using the mouse pointer to move an object around the screen.

icon: the graphics on a toolbar button.

object(s): this can be any element of the spreadsheet environment such as a cell, command button or toolbar object. It can also be any element of the chart environment, such as the title, legend, axes or plot area. Chart objects are also known as chart areas.

point: resting the mouse pointer on a screen object.

Screen Tips is a secondary help system that displays a short description of a toolbar button when the mouse pointer is above the button. Screen Tips is a default setting, enabled when your Office application is installed.

system: the computer's operating system.

toolbar button: individual commands contained as part of a toolbar.

Other useful information

Cell or range

- **cells C3:F3** and **cell range B4:B23** both refer to a **range:** the **range operator** has been used.
- the colon (**:**) indicates that a range is being referenced, even if this is not explicitly stated.

The terms **click** and **select cell(s)** are used interchangeably throughout the book. You are required to make the named cells(s) or command button the **active object**.

Highlighted cell(s) are the **active cell(s)**. These are cells that have been **clicked** or **selected**:

 Single highlighted cell

 Range of highlighted cells

Collapsing Windows

Several windows now have Collapse Window icons on the right of text or list boxes that are used to select or enter data.

The Collapse Window icon

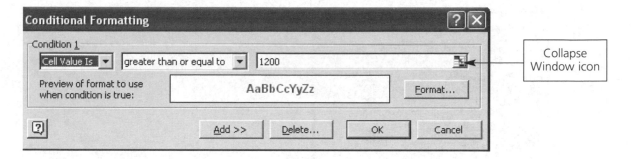

The Collapse Window icon in a menu box

Un-collapsing Windows

Click the Un-Collapse dialog icon to restore the Window.

The Un-collapse Window icon

Example of a collapsed window

If you are unable to access the **Un-Collapse Dialog Icon** press the **Esc** key on the Keyboard to **restore** the window

Office 2000 clipboard toolbar

The Office 2000 clipboard can hold up to 12 separate pieces of data, including text, text graphics or figures, which you can paste/paste special into the document you are creating. The clipboard toolbar can be used between any Office applications you have installed on your system. To view the clipboard:

1. Point to **Toolbars** from the **View** menu.

2. On the sub-menu click **Clipboard**.

Example of an empty Office clipboard

To use the Office clipboard, click on the place in your document where you want the data to go and click the relevant item on the clipboard to paste/paste special this into your document.

The clipboard supports Screen Tips. To see a fragments of the text contained in the item rest your mouse pointer over it.

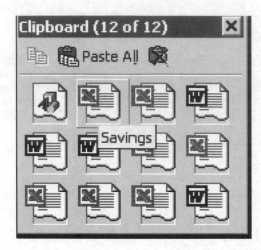

Example Office clipboard with Screen Tip visible

If you are unable to find the Clipboard toolbar, look up **Clipboard** in the Help system.

Section 1: Editing

1.1 Using named ranges

In this section you will cover the following **named range** topics:

- Identifying the name box.
- Creating named ranges via the name box.
- Edit a named range.
- Deleting a named range.

The name box

The **name box** is located to the left of the formula bar above column A and the **Select All** button. It displays the current location of the cursor, depending on the selection or the type of calculation being used, such as a Function.

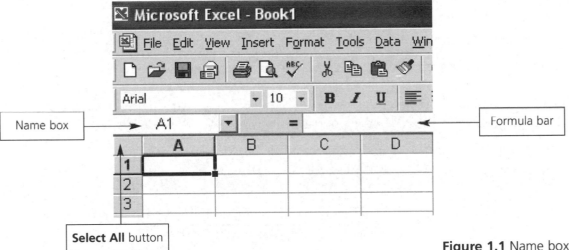

Figure 1.1 Name box – position

In Figure 1.2 a single cell, A2, is the active cell.

Figure 1.2 Name box – single cell

In Figure 1.3 a named range called **PCode** is the active range.

Figure 1.3 Name box – named range

Figure 1.4 indicates that the **IF** function window is active and that an IF function is either being entered or edited in the active cell. Once the function has been entered, the name box will again display the cell address of the active cell where the function has been entered.

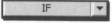

Figure 1.4 Name box – IF Function active

1 – Creating a named range

Method

1 Highlight the cell or range of cells using the mouse.

2 Click in the name box.

> Name box selected and waiting for a new name to be keyed in

B1		=	Product	
	A	B	C	D	E
1		Product	Amount	Selling	Cost
2		Mangos	500	1.95	0.78
3		Pears	250	3.50	1.40
4		Oranges	750	6.22	2.49
5		Pineapple	75	2.50	1.00
6		Nectarine	150	103.00	41.20
7		Lemons	149	125.00	50.00

> Range highlighted B1:E7

Figure 1.5 Creating a named range

3 Key in a name for the range, e.g. **WestOne**.

4 Press the Enter key.

Note: ensure that you press the Enter key or the range may not be created.

Info

If the **name range** has been created successfully when you press the Enter key the range will be highlighted and the name will appear in the name box.

A named range is accessible from any sheet in the workbook.

WestOne		=	Product		
	A	B	C	D	E
1		Product	Amount	Price	Cost
2					
3		Apples	1200	0.55	0.22
4		Bananas	935	0.65	0.26
5		Pears	715	0.55	0.22
6		Peas	143	0.40	0.16
7		Peaches	220	0.30	0.12
8					

> Select all button

Figure 1.6 Named range created

Info

If you need to select an entire worksheet quickly click the **Select All** button (see Figure 1.1). The entire worksheet will be highlighted.

2 – Edit a named range

Method

1 Point the mouse at **Name** on the **Insert** menu, then click on **Define** on the sub-menu to open the **Define Name** window.

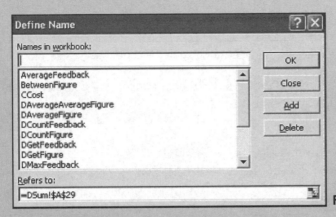

Figure 1.7 The Define Name window

2 Select the range name by clicking on the name, or type the name you want in the name box. The named range syntax will appear in the **Refers to** text box.

3 Edit the syntax as necessary.

4 Click on the **Add** button to add the new range reference value.

5 Click on **OK** to close the **Define Name** window and apply the edited range.

If things go wrong delete the **named range** and repeat the exercise.

3 – Deleting a named range

Method

1 Open the Define Name window.

2 Select the range name by clicking on the name.

3 Click on the **Delete** button.

4 Close the Define Name window.

In the following exercises you will:

- Use the name box to move around a worksheet and to create named ranges.
- Use the name box to create the outline of a spreadsheet using named ranges, and to enter data.
- Edit existing named ranges to include new data in the range.

4 – Use the name box to move to named ranges in the spreadsheet

Method

1 Open the workbook **Staff**.

All files for this section can be located on the accompanying CD-ROM.

2 Select the worksheet **StaffDetails**.

<table>
<tr><td>**Info**</td><td>The name box is used for naming sections of your spreadsheet. It can also be used for moving directly to these named ranges on a worksheet.

The name box will always identify the active cell by displaying the cell reference or named range.</td></tr>
</table>

Figure 1.8 Name box displaying the current active cell

| A1 ▼ | ← | Name box displaying the current active cell |

3   Click on the black arrowhead to the right of the name box to display any named ranges that have been created in the **Staff** workbook (Figure 1.9).

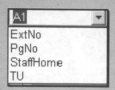

Figure 1.9 Displaying named ranges

4   Select the name **ExtNo** in the name box. (The cursor will move to cell I4, which contains the label **ExtNo**. Cell I4 is now the active cell.)

5   Select each name in the name box to move to the named range within the workbook.

The results on screen should be:

a   Named range **PgNo** references cell J4, which contains the label **PAGERNo.**

b   Named range **StaffHome** references cell A4, which contains the label **PERSONNEL No.**

c   Named range **TU** references cell K4, which contains the label **TRADE UNION.**

6   Close the workbook without saving any changes.

EXERCISE   *5 – Create named ranges*

<table>
<tr><td>**Method**</td><td>

1   Open the workbook **Namecells** and select Sheet1.

The usual outline of this spreadsheet has been amended and named ranges will be used for you to create the new outline and input the data.

2   Create the following named ranges in the cell(s) indicated, using the text in bold as the names for the ranges being created:

B1:H1 – **Title**   B3:B12 – **EnterProducts**
B2 – **Productlabel**   C3:C12 – **EnterAmounts**
C2 – **Amountlabel**   D3:D12 – **EnterPrices**
D2 – **Pricelabel**   E3:E12 – **DisplaysCosts**
E2 – **Costlabel**   F3:F12 – **DisplaysTotals**
F2 – **Totallabel**   G3:G12 – **DisplaysProfit**
G2 – **Profitlabel**   H3:H12 – **DisplaysPercentages**
H2 – **Percentagelabel**   B13 – **GrandTotallabel**

3   Save the workbook.
</td></tr>
</table>

6 – Enter data in named ranges

Method

1 On Sheet1, enter the following emboldened labels using the name box to locate the named ranges to be used:

a **PRODUCE SALES** in the named range **Title**

b **10%** in the named range **Percentagelabel**

c **Product** in the named range **Productlabel**

d **Amount** in the named range **Amountlabel**

e **Price** in the named range **Pricelabel**

f **Cost** in the named range **Costlabel**

g **Total** in the named range **Totallabel**

h **Profit** in the named range **Profitlabel**

i **Grand Total** in the named range **GrandTotallabel**

2 Enter the lists of data below in the named ranges specified:

a Enter the list of Products below in the named range **EnterProducts**	b Enter the list of Amounts below in the named range **EnterAmounts**	c Enter the list of Prices below in the named range **EnterPrices**
Mangos	500	1.95
Pears	250	3.50
Oranges	750	6.22
Pineapple	75	2.50
Nectarine	150	103.00
Lemons	149	125.00
Tomatoes	2500	75.00
Limes	75	69.00
Cherries	4500	29.00
Grapes	762	35.00

3 The title in cells B1:H1 needs some formatting to complete the appearance of the spreadsheet. **Merge** and **centre** the data in the named range **Title**.

Figure 1.10 The completed spreadsheet

	A	B	C	D	E	F	G	H
1		PRODUCE SALES						
2		Product	Amount	Selling	Cost	Total	Profit	10%
3		Mangos	500	1.95	0.78	975.00	390	£2.15
4		Pears	250	3.50	1.40	875.00	350	£3.85
5		Oranges	750	6.22	2.49	4665.00	1866	£6.84
6		Pineapple	75	2.50	1.00	187.50	75	£2.75
7		Nectarine	150	103.00	41.20	15450.00	6180	£113.30
8		Lemons	149	125.00	50.00	18625.00	7450	£137.50
9		Tomatoes	2500	75.00	30.00	187500.00	75000	£82.50
10		Limes	75	69.00	27.60	5175.00	2070	£75.90
11		Cherries	4500	29.00	11.60	130500.00	52200	£31.90
12		Grapes	762	35.00	14.00	26670.00	10668	£38.50
13		Grand Total						

In this section you have created a spreadsheet using the name box.

Save and close the workbook.

7 – Edit named ranges using the define name window

Method

1 Open the workbook **EditNamedRange**.

2 New courses have been added to the **CourseName** worksheet. **Edit** the named range **Courses**, to include cells A1:A10.

3 Two new columns have been added to the worksheet. Adjust the **LeaversAction** named range to include cells A3:I17, and the **Title** named range to include cells A3:I3.

4 New staff have been added to the staff list. Adjust the named range **Staff** to included cells A100:B110.

5 Test all the edited named ranges to ensure that these have been updated.

6 Save and review your work before moving to the next section.

As well as using named ranges, to facilitate creating named ranges, you have used the Define Name window to edit named ranges.

1.2

Using the AutoFormat function

AutoFormats are a template of **fonts**, **font sizes** and **colours** that have been grouped together to provide a quick way of enhancing a spreadsheet. AutoFormats individually are known as **table formats**.

In this section you will cover the following **AutoFormat** topics:

● How to access the AutoFormat window.

● AutoFormat error message.

● Change AutoFormat options.

● Remove an AutoFormat.

1 – Applying AutoFormats

Info

1 Within the spreadsheet list, select a cell to which you want to apply an AutoFormat.

If you do not select a cell within the spreadsheet, the system will not know where to apply the **AutoFormat** and will display the following error message:

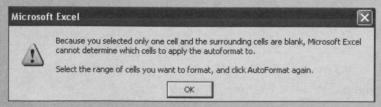

Figure 1.11
AutoFormat window –
table formats

(Click on **OK** to close the message.)

When a cell is selected within a spreadsheet, the system will automatically select the range containing your labels and data.

To view all table formats, use the scrollbar arrows located to the right of the AutoFormat window (Figure 1.12), to move up or down.

2 Click on **AutoFormat** on the **Format** menu.

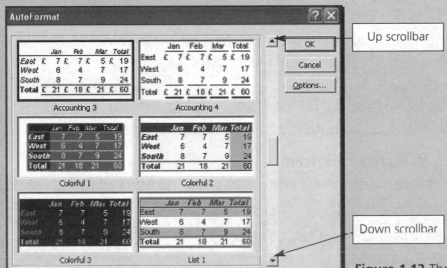

Figure 1.12 The AutoFormat window

3 To apply a format, use the mouse and click on the table format of your choice.

4 Click **OK** to apply the format to the spreadsheet.

In the following short exercises you will apply an AutoFormat to the various worksheets in the **AutoFormats** workbook. All files for this section can be located on the accompanying CD-ROM.

EXERCISE

2 – Using AutoFormats

Method

1 Open the AutoFormat workbook.

2 Select the **Savings** worksheet.

3 Highlight cells A1:B10.

4 Open the **AutoFormat** window.

5 Using the scrollbars, move down until the table format **List 2** is visible.

6 Click on the **List 2** option to select it.

7 Click on **OK** to apply your AutoFormat choice (the window closes).

Info

On this occasion you **selected** the area for the AutoFormat, as there are two blank rows between cells A1:B10.

If you hadn't **selected** the range of cells, AutoFormat would only have applied itself to cells containing data that adjoined the selected cell (see Exercise 3 below).

3 – AutoFormat without selecting cells

Method

1 Select the **SavingsTwo** worksheet.

2 Click cell A1.

3 Apply the List 2 AutoFormat.

Info

The AutoFormat has only been applied to cell A1 as the system was unable to detect the range of cells in the list due to the **blank cell** in row 2.

Note: when creating spreadsheets that you want to use AutoFormat with, blank columns and rows should be avoided.

4 – Repeat AutoFormat

Method

1 Select the **SavingsThree** worksheet.

2 Select cell A2 and apply the List 2 AutoFormat (the AutoFormat will only be applied to cells A1:B8).

3 Select cell A9.

4 From the **Edit** menu, click on: **Repeat AutoFormat**.

Info

The selected AutoFormat is now applied to cells A9:B10.

Rows 9 and 10 are blank and were not originally included as part of the list to apply the AutoFormat to, because they hadn't been **selected**.

5 – AutoFormat options

Info

AutoFormat options are used to control the formatting being applied.

Method

1 To view these in the AutoFormat window, click on the **Options** button.

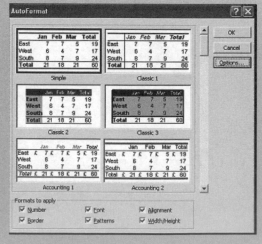

Figure 1.13 The AutoFormat window

2 Close the AutoFormat window.

Task 1.2 Using the AutoFormat function

6 – Using AutoFormat options

Method

1 Select the **SavingsFour** worksheet.

2 Highlight cells A1:B10.

3 Open the AutoFormat window and apply the table format list 2.

4 Click the Options button.

5 Click on the **Alignment** and **Width/Height** tick-box options to deselect them.

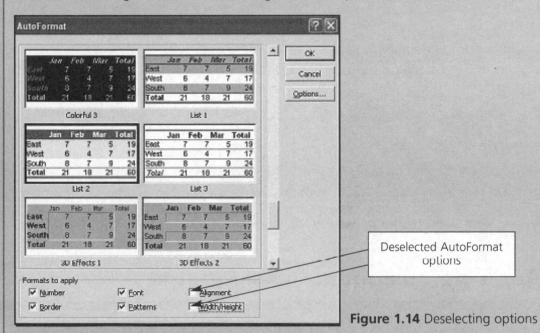

Deselected AutoFormat options

Figure 1.14 Deselecting options

6 Click on **OK** to apply your AutoFormat choice (window closes).

Do not close the workbook.

Info

When the **List 2** table format was applied to the **Savings** worksheet the following formatting was applied:

1 Column A left aligned.
2 The data in cell A2 centred.
3 The width of columns reduced.

Compare this worksheet with the **SavingsFour** worksheet.

Deselecting the **Alignment** and **Width/Height** tick-box options has changed the look of the spreadsheet.

7 – Removing an AutoFormat

Method

1 Click on a cell in the spreadsheet, or highlight the entire spreadsheet.

2 Click on **AutoFormat** on the **Format** menu.

3 Click on the table format **None**.

These steps will remove the applied table format.

4 Remove the Classic 2 AutoFormat from the **SavingsFive** worksheet.

5 Save and close the workbook.

8 – Practice

Task A

Method

1 Open the workbook **Holidays**.

2 Apply a Classic 2 AutoFormat to the spreadsheet in cells C3:H13.

3 Save and close the workbook.

Task B

Method

1 Open the workbook **Bargains**.

2 Apply a Colourful 1 AutoFormat to the spreadsheet.

3 Save and close the workbook.

Review your work before moving to the next main task.

1.3 Applying custom number formats

In this section you will cover the following custom number format topics:

- How to access the Format cells window.
- Create custom number format – figure.
- Create custom number format – figure and text.

Open the **StockOrderFruits** workbook. All files for this section can be located on the accompanying CD-ROM.

The workbook contains one worksheet called **StockOrder**, created by importing a text file. The imported data covers cells A1:F43 and is a list of fruit imports from a company's various outlets in France.

Tasks overview:

- Apply **custom formats** to the Price, Total and Weight columns.
- **Format** the Price and Total columns to French francs, to two decimal places.
- **Sort** the orders so that these can be placed for deliveries back to the outlets.
- **Add** worksheets.
- Selecting multiple worksheets to copy to.
- **Hide** columns.
- Use **Sum** functions to Total columns.

1 – Creating a custom number format for the price column

The figures in the **Price** and **Total** columns on the **StockOrderFruit** worksheet represent French francs and need to be displayed in this format. In this scenario, the computer in the office in which you are working does not have this option by default so you need to create this.

Task A – Create a custom number format

Method

1 Highlight cells E2:E43 (Price column).

2 Click **Cells** from the **Format** menu to open the **Format Cells** window.

3 On the **Number** tab select **Custom** from the **Category** list box on the left.

4 Select the Custom Type code **#,##0.00** from the **Type** list box by clicking on the type example (your selection will be visible in the **Type** text box above). Use the scrollbars to move up or down if you cannot see all types in the list.

Task B – Editing the custom type code to customise it for French francs

Method

1 Click at the end of the selected Type code and press the spacebar once.

2 Add the following custom format **syntax** in the type list box **[$F–40C]** (see Figure 1.15).

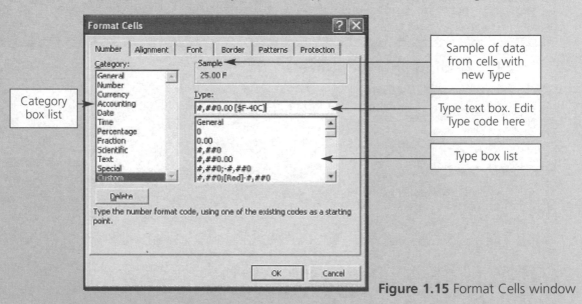

Figure 1.15 Format Cells window

3 Press **Enter** to apply the new Custom code (window closes).

Info

Cells E2:E43 (Price column) will now display the currency as francs (Figure 1.16)

4 Use the Format Painter to copy the currency formatting from cell E2 to the Total column, cells F2:F43.

E
Price
4.50 F
4.50 F
4.50 F
4.50 F
4.50 F
4.50 F
4.50 F
4.50 F
4.50 F
4.50 F
4.50 F
0.60 F
0.60 F
0.60 F
0.60 F
0.60 F
0.60 F
4.50 F

Figure 1.16 The new Custom code

Task C – sorting data

Method

1 Select a cell within the spreadsheet.

2 **Sort** the spreadsheet by the **Item** column – the spreadsheet list has a **Header row**.

The list should be sorted alphabetically with **Ananas** (Pineapples) at the top and **Raisin** (Grapes) at the bottom.

Task D – Adding new worksheets

Method

1 Insert seven new worksheets and **Rename** each one as follows:

1 Ananas
2 Bananes
3 Citron
4 Oranges
5 Pêches
6 Pommes
7 Raisin

Ananas should be the first worksheet in the workbook, followed by **Bananes**, **Citron**, etc. as above, working from left to right, with **StockOrder** the last on the right. To achieve the accent above the 'e' in Pêches, hold down the **Alt** key and type in 0234.

Task E – Selecting multiple worksheets to copy to

Method

1 Click the **Ananas** worksheet name tab, then hold down the **Ctrl** key…

2 **Click** the other seven worksheet name tabs one at a time – do not include the original **StockOrder** worksheet. If you select a worksheet in error, click the worksheet name tab to deselect it.

3 When you have selected all the worksheets, release the **Ctrl** key.

| 19 | | | | | |
| 20 | | | | | |

◄◄ ◄ ► ►◄ / Citron / Oranges / Pêches / Pommes / Raisin /

Figure 1.17 Multiple worksheets selection

4 Paste the current contents of the Clipboard in cell A1 of the **Ananas** worksheet.

The seven new worksheets should now have the same labels in cells A1:E1.

5 Click the **StockOrder** worksheet tab.

6 Copy the **Ananas** list of goods from the **StockOrder** worksheet, cells A2:F7.

7 Paste the current contents of the Clipboard in cell A2 of the **Ananas** worksheet.

8 Copy and Paste the relevant list of goods to the six other worksheets.

Each new worksheet should now only contain data that matches the worksheet name.

Task F – Hide columns

Each worksheet now has a redundant column depending or whether the goods are sold by **weight** or **quantity**.

Method

1 Hide the relevant empty columns, C or D, on each of the new worksheets.

2 Widen columns and/or rows as appropriate, to ensure that all label text is visible.

Do not close the workbook.

2 – Create a custom format for the weight (kg) columns

EXERCISE

Task A

Method

1 Select the **Bananes** worksheet.

2 Highlight cells D2:D7, **Weight (kg)** column:

   a Click **Cells** from the **Format** menu.

   b On the **Number** tab select **Custom** from the Category box list.

   c Select the **Type** code **0** from the list by clicking on the type example. Use the scrollbar arrows to move up or down if you cannot see type in the list.

3 Edit the code to customise this for kilograms:

   a Click at the end of the type code and press the spacebar once.

   b Add the following new custom Type **"kg"**. As the new type is text, this has to be enclosed in double quotation marks – see Figure 1.18.

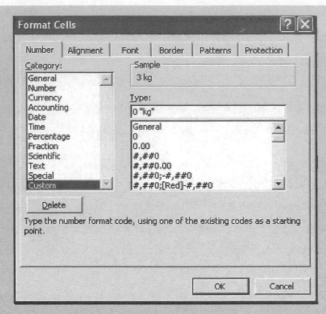

Figure 1.18 Creating a custom format for weight

4 When you have edited the custom **type** code, press **Enter** to apply the code.

Info

The double quotation marks must be input by using **Shift + 2** on the keyboard.

The Weight column list of figures will now display the custom format (kg).

	A	B	D	E	F
1	OrderNo	Item	Weight (kg)	Price	Total
2	7	Bananes	8 kg	4.50 F	36.00 F
3	10	Bananes	8 kg	4.50 F	36.00 F
4	22	Bananes	18 kg	4.50 F	79.20 F
5	1	Bananes	20 kg	4.50 F	90.00 F
6	5	Bananes	81 kg	4.50 F	364.50 F
7	3	Bananes	2 kg	4.50 F	9.00 F

Figure 1.19 kg custom formatting applied to column D

5 Apply the **kg** custom formatting to column D of the following worksheets: **Oranges**, **Pêches**, **Pommes** and **Raisin**.

Info

The choice of how you apply the formatting is up to you, but you could consider:

Choice one
Click **Cells** on the **Format** menu. The new format type will be available under **Custom** on the number tab while the workbook that the new format was created in is open. Use the scrollbar to move up or down to find the new format type.

Choice two
Use the Format Painter to copy the formatting from one worksheet to another.

Task B – Finalising the new worksheets

Method

1 Enter the label **FinalOrder** in cell A8 of all worksheets *except* **StockOrder**.

2 In cell D8 add a **Sum** function, to total the contents of cells D2:D7 on worksheets **Bananes, Oranges, Pêches, Pommes** and **Raisin**, using the syntax:

=SUM(D2:D7)

3 Format column C (**HowMany**) as number, no decimal places, on worksheets **Ananas** and **Citron**.

4 In cell C8 add a **Sum** function to total the contents of cells C2:C7 on each worksheet, using the syntax:

=SUM(C2:C7)

5 In cell F8 of the new worksheets add a **Sum** function to total the contents of cells F2:F7, using the syntax:

=SUM(F2:F7)

That completes the formatting and calculations necessary to place the orders.

It would be nice to be able to see at a glance how much the **total** orders are worth without having to look at each individual worksheet. In a later exercise you will add a **3D Sum function** to consolidate data in adjacent worksheets.

6 Save and review your work.

7 Close the workbook.

EXERCISE ## 3 – Combining two syntaxes

You regularly receive a spreadsheet containing issue numbers and dates shown concurrently. When the data is entered it is represented as **Issue 01/15-07-03**. The computer that processes the data strips out the **text and symbols** and you receive the data in the format shown in Figure 1.20.

The first two digits represent the issue number and the last six digits represent the date of issue. (In Figure 1.20, although there is only one digit displayed for the number, the system knows there is a zero at the beginning but will not display this as it is a negative. However, when the figure is formatted, it will then be displayed.)

Normally you would manually edit each cell to separate the issue number from the date and add the text and symbols. Now that you know how to create a custom number format, you have decided to create one for the data, to save you time formatting each time you receive it.

Figure 1.20 Data received

	A
1	**Issue_Dates**
2	1011102
3	1011102
4	2150901
5	3080501
6	4190702
7	3291003
8	2140401
9	3310103
10	2150302
11	1040402
12	2231202
13	3091101
14	3241003
15	2280702
16	1050502
17	3161202

Method

1 Open the **NewCustomNumber** workbook.

2 Select the **Dates** worksheet. Column A contains a list of issue dates for which you will create a Custom Number Format.

In the previous exercises you created two new Custom Number Formats: one with text and figures, and the other with figures only. Now we need to combine the two.

3 **Combine** two syntaxes to create the new Custom Number Format:

   a Highlight cells A2:A26 on the **Dates** worksheet.

   b Open the **Format Cells** window.

   c On the **Number** tab select **Custom** from the Category box list.

   d Delete the code **General** from the Type text box.

General is the default option when the Format Cells window opens.

e   Enter the following syntax in the Type text box: **"Issue"_"00"/"00-00-00**

4   Press **Enter** to apply the code (window closes).

The data, starting in cell A2, should display as: **Issue 01/01-11-02**

The Custom Number Format construction

The first section of Custom Number Format syntax is enclosed in quotation marks and is treated as text **including** the underscore symbol: this provides the space between the word **Issue** and the **issue number**; the backslash separates the issue number from the **date**.

"Issue"_"00"/"00-00-00

←Test Syntax→ ←Last six→
Figures

The use of zeros for the last six figures, as placeholders in the syntax, ensures that dates such as **01/01/01** are displayed. The hyphens between the zeros tell the system to divide the last six figures into three sections and to place a hyphen on each side of the centre section, in the result.

4 – Demonstrating custom number format construction

1   Enter the following figures on **Sheet2** of the workbook in cell B3: **115072003**

2   Format cell B3 with the new custom format you have just created for the issue date. If you need help with copying the new format you have created, review Exercise 2.

Cell B3 should now display as: **Issue 115/07-20-03**

You have created placeholders for the last six digits – anything before this will be processed with the text portion of the syntax as displayed in cell B3.

3   Save and close the workbook.

5 – Practice

1   Open the workbook **BottleSize**.
2   On the **Size** worksheet, create a custom number format for cells C2:C18 to display the bottle sizes, using the following custom Type syntax: **00 "cl"**
3   Save and review your work before moving to the next section.
4   Close the workbook.

Applying conditional formats

In this section you will cover the following Conditional Formatting options:

- How to access the Conditional Formatting window.
- Creating conditions.
- Adding formatting.
- Adding additional conditions.
- Using operators as part of data to be evaluated against.
- Removing conditional formatting.

Open the **Stationery** workbook. All files for this section can be located on the accompanying CD-ROM.

The workbook contains three worksheets: **Stationery, Payments and Formula**.

One method of obtaining visual feedback from a spreadsheet is to use **Conditional Formatting**. The appearance of the spreadsheet data can be changed, based on the conditions you set, such as font colour, style etc.

1 – Introduction

Task A – Displaying the conditional formatting window

Method

1 Click **Conditional Formatting** on the **Format** menu to open the window.

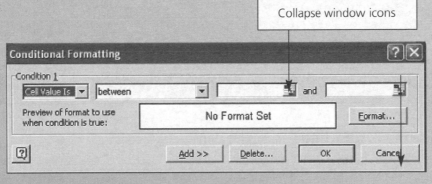

Figure 1.21 Conditional Formatting window

The Conditional Formatting Window Explained

2 The default in the **Condition 1** list box is **Cell Value Is**. Accepting this default option tells the system to evaluate **figures** or **text** in a cell or cells.

3 In the second list box, the default **operator** text is **between**.

4 The third and fourth text boxes (separated by the text **and**) are empty.

Task B – Selecting data for the third and fourth text boxes

Method

1 To use the third and fourth text boxes to select existing data in a worksheet:

   a Click on the **collapse window icon(s)**.

   b Select the cell(s) in the worksheet by clicking on them.

   c Uncollapse the window.

Info

You can also enter data for the third and fourth text boxes via the keyboard.

Note: in the first box, if you change the default to the only other option, **Formula Is**, the system will expect to evaluate and return a **True** or **False** answer based on data or a condition, e.g. a formula.

To use the default operator you must enter/select **dates** or **values** for the third and fourth text boxes so that the system can use these to search and produce results.

2 For example, enter the following in the third and fourth text boxes:

   a The date 01/01/03 in the third text box.

   b The date 09/10/03 in the fourth text box.

Looking at the boxes from left to right, the text would read as:

The Cell Value is between 01/01/03 **and** 09/10/03.

Info

This will instruct the system to use **Condition 1** to search for data in a worksheet between the two dates entered. You could also use this **operator** text to search between two values such as **106** and **958**.

Note: When selected in the second box, the **between** and **not between** operator texts are always followed by **two** default text boxes; all other operators, e.g. **equal to**, have only one **text** box to be completed.

Once you have set the conditions, you will need to create the **format** to be applied when these conditions are met, so as to give visual feedback in the spreadsheet.

Task C – Conditions formatting

Method

Click on: the **Format** button to open the Format Cells window. Here you can set the formatting for **Font**, **Borders** and **Patterns**.

Task D – Adding another Condition to the same cell

Method

1 Return to the Conditions Formatting window (if the Format Cells window is still live, click on **OK** or **Cancel**).

2 Click on the **Add** button (an extra, **Condition 2**, section will appear).

2 – Creating a Condition

Method

1 Select cell C4 on the **StationeryOrder** worksheet.

2 Open the Conditional Formatting window.

3 Accept the default **Cell Value Is** under **Condition 1**.

4 Click the dropdown arrow next to the default **between** option, and change this to **less than** (the window will now change to offer you just one other option to complete).

5 Collapse the Conditional Formatting window and use the mouse to select cell D4.

6 Uncollapse the window.

7 Click the **Format** button to open the **Format Cells** window.

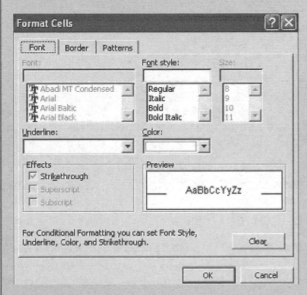

Figure 1.22 Format Cells window

If the **Font** tab is not the active one when the window opens, click on the tab to select it.

8 Select the following:

    a Font style **bold**

    b Colour **red**.

9 Click on **OK** to close the Format Cells window.

Info

In the Conditional Formatting window, a preview is shown of how the data will look when the condition is true (Figure 1.23).

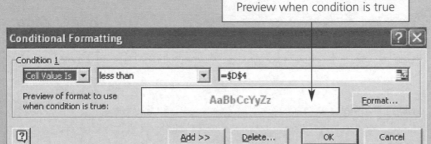

Figure 1.23 Preview of format

10 Click on **OK** to close the Conditional Formatting window.

The contents of cell C4 should change to **bold** and **red**.

11 Highlight cells C5:C23.

12 Select **Repeat Conditional Formatting** from the **Edit** menu, to apply the Conditional Formatting you have created in cell C4 to any cell in the highlighted cells that match the condition.

The Conditional Formatting construction

Info

What you have just said to the system is, if cell **C4** is **less than** cell **D4**, format the contents of cell **C4** as **bold and red**.

A number of conditions can be set in the Conditional Formatting window by clicking the **Add** button when another row is displayed.

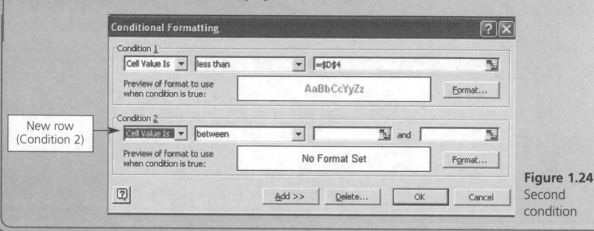

New row (Condition 2)

Figure 1.24 Second condition

EXERCISE

3 – Adding to a created condition

Method

1 Select cell C4 on the **Stationery** worksheet.

2 Open the Conditional Formatting window.

3 Click on **Add**.

4 Accept the default **Cell Value Is** for Condition 2.

5 Click the dropdown arrow next to the **between** option and change this to **greater than.**

6 Select cell D4.

7 Open the **Format Cells** window.

8 Select font style **bold** and colour **teal**.

9 Close the Conditional Formatting window.

Info

Again, what you are telling the system is, if the value in cell **C4** is **greater than** cell **D4**, then format the contents of cell **C4** as **bold and teal**.

10 Highlight cells C5:C23.

11 Select **Repeat Conditional Formatting** from the **Edit** menu, to apply the second Conditional Formatting you have created in cell C4 to any cell in the highlighted cells that match the condition.

4 – Formatting labels in the workbook

Method

1 Merge and centre the title Stationery List across cells B1:E1. The Merge and Centre toolbar button [icon] is on the Formatting toolbar.

2 Change the font size to 14 point and embolden the title.

3 Embolden all labels.

4 Save the workbook.

Select the **Payments** worksheet in the **Stationery** workbook.

On this worksheet the payments for stationery orders are monitored. A number of conditions apply to these orders and payments, and you will use Conditional Formatting to highlight these.

Spreadsheet construction – overview

1 Cell **B1** contains the **date** by which payments should be made.

2 Cells **B3:B5** contain the **additional** charges.

3 Cells **A8:H28** contain the worksheet **Data** and **Labels**.

4 Payment conditions applying to the spreadsheet are that the **department head** must **clear** any **Grand Total** order over £1,200 in **column G**.

5 – Evaluating data in the workbook

In order to be able to **spot check** that clearance has been agreed, apply conditional formatting to **column G** to format the contents of any cell that contains a figure **greater than** £1,200.

Method

1 Select cell G9.

2 Open the **Conditional Formatting** window.

3 Accept the default **Cell Value Is** under Condition 1.

4 Click the dropdown arrow next to the default **between** option, and change this to **greater than or equal to.**

Info

In the first two exercises you collapsed the Conditional Formatting window and used the mouse to select cell content as the data to be evaluated against. In this exercise you will **enter data** to be evaluated against.

5 Key in the figure **1200** as the data to be evaluated, against the figures in cells that meet the condition.

6 In the Format Cells window, select a font style of **bold** and a colour of **teal**.

7 Click on **OK** (you are returned to the Conditional Formatting window, where a preview is shown of how the data will look when the condition is true, see Figure 1.25).

8 Click on **OK** to close the window.

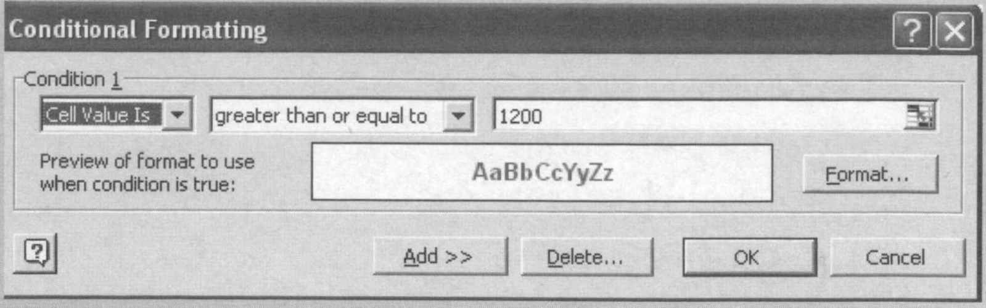

Conditional Formatting   ? ✕

┌─ Condition 1 ──┐
│ [Cell Value Is ▼] [greater than or equal to ▼] [1200   ▦] │
│   │
│ Preview of format to use   ┌──────────────────┐   │
│ when condition is true: │   AaBbCcYyZz   │ [Format...] │
│   └──────────────────┘   │
│ [?]   [Add >>] [Delete...]   [OK]   [Cancel]   │
└──┘

Figure 1.25 The completed Conditional Formatting window

Cell **G9** contains the figure **292.50** and therefore the font style and colour *will not* change to **bold** and **teal**.

Info

9 Highlight cells G10:G28 and select **Repeat Conditional Formatting** from the **Edit** menu, to apply the **Conditional Formatting** you have created in the cell **G9** to the highlighted cells. (The contents of cells **G11, G15, G18, G20 and G26** should change to **bold** and **teal**.)

EXERCISE

6 – Monitoring payment dates

In order to chase late payments or claim early payment discount you need to monitor payments received against the due payment date in cell B1.

To see **at a glance** when payments were made, create the following Conditional Formatting in the **Date Payment Received** column.

Method

1 Select cell H9.

2 Open the Conditional Formatting window.

3 Accept the default **Cell Value Is** under Condition 1.

4 Click the dropdown arrow next to the **between** option, and change this to **less than or equal to**.

5 Select cell B1.

6 Open the **Format Cells** window.

7 Select font style **bold** and colour **blue**.

8 Click on **Add**.

9 Accept the default **Cell Value Is** under Condition 2.

10 In the second box, click the dropdown arrow and select **greater than**.

11 Select cell B1.

12 In the **Format Cells** window, select font style **bold** and colour **red**.

13 Close the Format Cells and the Conditional Formatting windows.

14 Highlight cells H10:H28.

15 Select **Repeat Conditional Formatting** from the **Edit** menu, to apply the Conditional Formatting you have created in cell H9 to the highlighted cells.

Info

The two conditions that you have set ask the system to do the following to the contents of the cells:

o If the dates in cells **H9:H28** are less than cell **B1**, format the contents of cells **H9:H28** as **bold and blue**, otherwise...

o Format the cells as **bold and red** because they do not meet the conditions.

Do not close the workbook.

7 – To find the average value of the grand total column at a glance

Method

1 Select the **Formula** worksheet.

2 Highlight cells G9:G28.

3 Open the Conditional Formatting window.

4 Select **Formula Is** under Condition 1.

5 Enter the following formula in the second text box:

   =(AVERAGE($G$9:$G$28))>700

6 In the Format Cells window select font colour blue.

7 Close the window.

8 Close the Conditional Formatting window.

The formula's instruction is: if the average value of the Grand Total column is **greater than 700** change the font colour to blue.

All values in column G should have a blue font applied.

8 – Remove conditional formatting

Method

1 Highlight the cell(s) containing the conditional format(s).

2 Open the Conditional Formatting window.

3 Click the **Delete** button to open the **Delete Conditional Formatting** window (Figure 1.26).

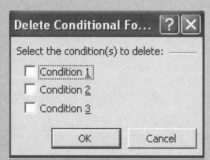

Figure 1.26 Delete Conditional Formatting window

4 Click the tick-box Condition number that you want to delete.

5 Click on **OK** to close the window.

6 Click on **OK** to close the Conditional Formatting window.

The selected condition(s) will be removed from the highlighted cell(s).

9 – Removing conditional formatting – practice

1   Open the **OldConditions** workbook.
2   Delete the following conditions:
    a   On the **Bargains** worksheet, **delete** Condition 1 from cell E3:E16.
    b   On the **Country** worksheet, **delete** Condition 2 from cell D9:G9.
3   Save and review your work before moving to the next section.

1.5   Using Paste Special

Paste Special options are applied in a number of different ways and situations. You can use **Paste Special** options to paste underlying data such as formulas, or to link data outside of a worksheet.

Paste Special option topics:

- How to access the Paste Special dialogue window.

- How to use Paste Section option **Paste**:

  - Formula
  - Values
  - Formats
  - Comments
  - Validation
  - Without Borders
  - Column Widths

- How to use Paste Section option **Operation**:

  - None
  - Add
  - Subtract
  - Multiply
  - Divide

- How to use other options in the Paste Section window:

  - Skip Blanks
  - Transpose
  - Paste Link

In the following sections you will cover the sequence of commands to carry out each **Paste Special** option, followed by a short exercise that can be repeated as often as required to gain the skills necessary to carry out the task.

You will use a mixture of **Edit** menu and **shortcut** (right click) options to carry out tasks. Once you develop a preferred method of accessing **Paste Special** options, use this once you understand the task.

Paste Special option – Paste

In this section you will cover Paste Special options, topics 1 and 2.

To access Paste Special options, the clipboard must contain data that can be pasted.

The default **paste** option when the Paste Special dialogue window opens is **All**. This option will **paste** any **data, formulas, formatting**, **comments** etc. that are within the *original* data being copied.

1 – Copy and paste special a formula: shortcut option

Method

1 Right click the cell containing the formula.

2 From the pop-up menu click **Copy**.

3 Right click the cell where you want to **Paste** the formula.

4 From the pop-up menu click Paste Special to open the Paste Special dialogue window.

Note the various **Paste Special** option buttons, tick-boxes and the **Paste Link** button you will be working with.

Figure 1.27 Paste Special dialogue window

5 Click the **Formulas** option button.

6 Click on **OK** to close the window.

The formula *without the spreadsheet* should now be **pasted** in the new location.

You will use the above sequence of commands in steps 1 to 5 in the second exercise. **Review the steps again**.

Open the workbook **PasteSpecialOne.** All files for this section, including the word processing documents used in the chart exercise, can be located on the accompanying CD-ROM.

The **Start** worksheet contains the data you will be working with in several exercises with **Paste Special** items.

Take some time to look at the other worksheets in the workbook, and to view the data you will be using to work with in conjunction with the data in the **Start** worksheet.

EXERCISE

2 – Copy and Paste Special a formula with underlying functions

Task A

Method

1 Click the **Start** worksheet when you are ready.
2 **Copy** and Paste Special the formula in cell D7 on the **Start** worksheet to cell D7 on the **Formulas** worksheet.

The formula bar should contain the syntax **=SUM(D3:D6)** when cell D7 on the **Formulas** worksheet is selected.

Task B

Method

1 Paste Special the formula in cell B1 on the **Start** worksheet to cell B1 on the **Formulas** worksheet.

The formula bar should contain the syntax **=PROPER(A1)** when cell B1 on the **Formulas** worksheet is selected.

In Exercise 2, selecting the **Formulas** option copied the **underlying function** from cells on the **Start** worksheet without **text** entered or **values** produced by the original function.

Info

Paste Special options give you the choice of **what to copy** from existing worksheet contents.

Note: remember to **Save** the workbook regularly.

Values represent **data** entered in worksheet cells. Selecting the **Values** option button copies data, which can be figures or text, without the underlying function or formatting being copied.

EXERCISE

3 – How to copy values: edit menu option

Method

1 Highlight the cell(s) containing the value(s) you want to copy.

2 Click on **Copy**.

3 Click the cell where you want to **Paste** the value(s).

4 Click on Paste Special from the **Edit** menu to open the Paste Special dialogue window.

5 Click on the **Values** option button.

6 Click on **OK** to close the window.

EXERCISE

4 – Practice

Copy and Paste Special the values in cells A1:H7 on the **Start** worksheet to cell A1 on the **Values** worksheet, using steps 1 to 6 above.

Note: the values should be **pasted** in the new location, *without the underlying formulas.* Extend columns if all data cannot be clearly seen in cells.

Select cell D7 or B1 on the **Values** worksheet.

Info   In Exercise 2 you copied underlying functions from these cells on the **Start** worksheet. The underlying function should not be visible in the formula bar when either cell is selected, as these should not have been pasted when you select the Paste Special option **Values**.

Info   **Formats** represent the types of effects that are added to **data** or **cells** in a worksheet, such as font styles, colour and number, and date formats.

EXERCISE   ## 5 – How to copy formats: edit menu option

Method
1 Highlight the cell(s) containing the formatting you want to copy.

2 Click on **Copy**.

3 Click on the cell where you want to **Paste** the formatting.

4 Click on Paste Special from the **Edit** menu to open the Paste Special dialogue window.

5 Click on the **Formats** option button.

6 Click on **OK** to close the window.

EXERCISE   ## 6 – Copy and Paste Special formats

Copy and Paste Special the formatting in cells C2:H7 on the **Start** worksheet, to cell C2 on the **Formats** worksheet.

Info   The **formatting**, without the spreadsheet contents, will be **pasted** in the new location.

Method
The only visible formatting on the **Format** worksheet will be the borders. To test that other formatting has been copied enter the following:

1 The text **Thursday** in cell F2. The text entered should automatically display a red font colour and bold italic style.

2 The figure **4589** in cell E4. The figures entered should automatically display as currency 2 decimal places in the cell (**£4,589.00**).

3 The Date **16 Jan 03** in cell G6. The date entered should automatically display the date format **dd/mm/yyyy**, which represents 16/01/2003. If your date appears in the format **dd/mm/yy**, your system default formatting has been applied.

4 The text **Monday** in cell C2. The text entered should automatically display an italic style.

5 The text **Tuesday** in cell D2. The text entered automatically should display a bold and underlined style.

Info   **Comments** are small messages you add to cells to pass on information or act as a reminder about the contents of a spreadsheet.

7 – How to copy comments: shortcut option

Method

1 Right click the cell containing the comment.

2 From the pop-up menu click **Copy**.

3 Right click the cell where you want to **Paste** the comment.

4 From the pop-up menu click Paste Special to open the Paste Special dialogue window.

5 Click the **Comments** option button.

6 Click on **OK** to close the window.

8 – Practice

Method

1 Copy and Paste Special the comments in cells C2:H7 on the **Start** worksheet, to cell C2 on the **Comments** worksheet.

9 – Practice

Method

Paste Special the comment in cell B1 on the **Start** worksheet, to cell B1 on the **Comments** worksheet.

The comments, *without the spreadsheet*, will be pasted in the new locations. To view the comments, rest the mouse over cell D6 or E3.

10 – How to copy validation rules: shortcut option

Method

1 Right click the cell containing the **Validation Rules**.

2 From the pop-up menu click **Copy**.

3 Right click the cell where you want to paste the Validation Rules.

4 From the pop-up menu click Paste Special to open the dialogue window.

5 Click on the **Validation** option button.

6 Click on **OK** to close the window.

11 – Practice

Method

Copy and Paste Special the **Validation Rules** in cells G3:G7 on the **Start** worksheet to cell G3 on the **Validation** worksheet.

The Validation Rules, *without the spreadsheet*, will be pasted in the new location.

12 – Testing validation rules

Method

1 Select cell G3 on the **Validation** worksheet and key in the text **Spreadsheet.**

2 Press **Enter**.

An error message will be displayed (Figure 1.28). This is because the **Validation Rule** set for the cell, is that a minimum of three and a maximum of six text characters can be entered.

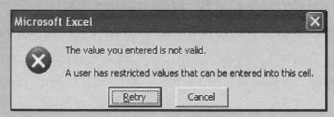

Figure 1.28

3 Click on **Cancel** to close the message box and to remove the text entered.

The following validation rules have been set for cells G4:G7:

- Cell G4 will only accept text that is a minimum of two and a maximum of three characters in length.
- Cell G5 will only accept decimal figures between 2 and 6.
- Cell G6 will only accept a date between 01/01/2003 and 05/01/2003.
- Cell G7 will only accept a time between 18:25:00 and 19:00:000.

4 Test the validation rules created, by entering invalid data in cells G4:G7 on the **Validation** worksheet, to verify that these copied cells work effectively. Use the examples below as a guide:

Cell ref	Example – **invalid** data	Example – **valid** data
G4	**Most**	**Yes**
G5	**7**	**4**
G6	**12/12/2002**	**03/01/2003**
G7	**17:30**	**18:45**

13 – Copying a spreadsheet without the borders: edit menu option

You may have a spreadsheet that contains borders. You want to copy the spreadsheet **without** the borders, to use in another task.

Method

1 Highlight the spreadsheet contents.

2 Click **Copy**.

3 Click a new cell location.

4 Click Paste Special on the **Edit** menu, to open the Paste Special dialogue window.

5 Click the **All except borders** option button.

6 Click on **OK** to close the window.

14 – Practice

1 Copy and Paste Special the data in cells C2:H7 on the **Start** worksheet, to cell C2 on the **Borders** worksheet. The spreadsheet contents, without the borders, will be pasted in the new location.

2 Widen the columns if all data in the cells cannot be seen clearly.

15 – Copying column widths: shortcut option

You may have created some custom column widths that you want to use on other worksheets. Instead of recreating the widths, you can use Paste Special to copy these.

1 Highlight the cells containing the column widths you want to copy.

2 Click **Copy**.

3 Right click the cell where you want to paste the column widths.

4 From the pop-up menu click Paste Special to open the dialogue window.

5 Click the **Column widths** option button.

6 Click **OK** to close the window.

16 – Practice

1 Copy and Paste Special the column widths in cells C2:H7 on the **Start** worksheet to cell C2 on the **Widths** worksheet. The column widths, *without the spreadsheet*, will be pasted in the new location.

2 Note the width of column D, and compare this with the **Start** worksheet.

3 Save and review your work before moving to the section on Paste Special option **Operation**.

Paste Special option – operation

The default **Operation** option when the Paste Special dialogue window opens is **None**. This option will **Paste** any **data, formulas, formatting, comments** etc. that are in the *original* data being copied, but not any underlying Operations options unless these are specifically selected.

The other **Operations** are **Add**, **Subtract**, **Multiply** and **Divide**. You can use these operations to consolidate data from several spreadsheets.

17 – Use paste special option, operation

Task A – Using Add

Method

1 Copy and paste cells D2:E6 on the **Start** worksheet into cell A1 on the **Operation** worksheet.

The original labels and data will be pasted into cells A1:B5 on the **Operation** worksheet:

One	Two
2	96.8
3	75.6
6	72.6
9	82.9

2 Right click cell A1 on the **Operation** worksheet and click Paste Special from the pop-up menu.

3 Click the **Add** option button.

4 Click **OK** to close the Paste Special window.

One	Two
4	193.6
6	151.2
12	145.2
18	165.8

Look at the data in cells A2:B5; each cell is now twice the original value. The **Add** Operation allows the figures in the cells to add the same value again to the original values:

Each cell is now twice the original value.

Info

The **Add** Operation allows the figures in cells to add the same value again to the original value.

Task B – Using Subtract

Method

1 Right click cell A1 on the **Operation** worksheet.

2 Click Paste Special from the pop-up menu.

3 Click the **Subtract** option button.

4 Click on **OK** to **close** the Paste Special window.

One	Two
2	96.8
3	75.6
6	72.6
9	82.9

Look at the data in the table for cells A2:B5. Each cell now contains its original values. The **Subtract** Operation has removed one set of figures, so that only the original values remain.

Data for cells A2:B5, *after* **Subtract** Operation:

5 Delete the contents of cells A1:B5 on the **Operation** worksheet.

Task C – Using Multiply

Method

1 Copy and Paste Special cells D2:E6 on the **Start** worksheet, into cell A1 on the **Operation** worksheet.

2 Right click cell A1 on the **Operation** worksheet.

3 Click the **Multiply** option button in the Paste Special window.

4 Close the Paste Special window.

One	Two
4	9370.24
9	5715.36
36	5270.76
81	6872.41

Look at the data in cells A2:B5. Each cell has multiplied the original figure in the cell by itself, e.g. 2x2 =4; 3x3=9; 6x6=36 and 9x9=81.

Data for cells A2:B5, after **Multiply** Operation:

Task D – Using Divide

1 Right click cell A1 on the **Operation** worksheet, then click Paste Special from the pop-up menu.

2 Click the **Divide** option button.

3 Close the Paste Special window.

Look at the data in cells A2:B5. Each cell has divided the figure in the cell by its original value, e.g. 4/2=2; 9/3=3; 36/6=6 and 81/9=9.

Data for cells A2:B5, after **Divide** Operation:

One	Two
2	96.8
3	75.6
6	72.6
9	82.9

The Paste Special dialogue window contains three other options: the **Skip Blanks** and **Transpose** tick boxes, and the button **Paste Link**.

Skip blanks and transpose

As these are tick-boxes you can use these options in conjunction with any of the option buttons such as **Add** or **Values**.

Cells C7 and H3:H7 on the **Start** worksheet contain no data but have borders. You only want to copy the cells that contain data from the worksheet. To achieve this you can use the Paste Special option **Skip Blanks**.

18 – Using other options in paste special

Task A – Skip Blanks

1 Copy cells C2:H7 on the **Start** worksheet.

2 Right click cell C2 on the **Blanks** worksheet and click **Paste Special** from the pop-up menu.

3 Click the **Skip Blanks** tick-box.

4 Close the Paste Special window.

Example of **Skip Blanks**:

Zero	One	Two	Round	Validation	Blanks
58	2	96.8	97	OneTwo	
314	3	75.6	76	One	
95	6	72.6	73	4	
623	9	82.9	83	02/01/2003	
	20	327.9	328	18:27:00	

All formatting, data, formulas and validation cells that contain data have been pasted.

Cells that are blank have been ignored. Even the formatting has been ignored and has not therefore been copied to the new location.

5 Extend columns if all data cannot be clearly seen in cells.

Task B – Transpose

Method

Transposing data in a spreadsheet reorganises the data into columns and rows.

1 Copy cells C2:H7 on the **Start** worksheet.

2 Right click cell C2 on the **Transpose** worksheet and click **Paste Special** from the pop-up menu.

3 Click the **Transpose** tick-box.

4 Close the Paste Special window.

Transpose example:

Zero	58	314	95	623	
One	2	3	6	9	20
Two	96.8	75.6	72.6	82.9	327.9
Round	97	76	73	83	328
Validation	OneTwo	One	4	02/01/2003	18:27:00
Blanks					

5 Extend columns if all data cannot be clearly seen in cells.

Describe what happened to the data in cells C3:H7 after you placed a tick in the **Transpose** box.

Task C – Using the paste link button

Info

As the name suggests, you use this button to link data together, such as the contents of cells.

You may have data on one worksheet that you want to link to another worksheet. Using the **Paste Link** button will achieve this, and will ensure that when cell data is altered, the changes are reflected in the linked cells.

Method

1 Copy cells C2:H7 on the **Start** worksheet.

2 Paste Special the data in cell C2 on the **PasteLink** worksheet.

3 Click the **Paste Link** button in the Paste Special window.

4 Click any cell **in the range** C2:H7 on the **PasteLink** worksheet. Note the linking syntax in each cell: **=Start!G3**.

5 Click cell C7 (the cell value is zero at the moment as no data has been added in the original worksheet).

6 Select the **Start** worksheet.

7 Enter the function **=sum(c3:c6)** in cell C7 on the **Start** worksheet then press Enter.

8 Select the **PasteLink** worksheet.

Has the function you have just entered on the **Start** worksheet updated the data in cell C7 on the **PasteLink** worksheet?

If your answer is **No** retrace your steps.

Using the **Paste Link** button you have created a link between cells C2:H7 on the **Start** and **PasteLink** worksheets. Any data entered in the original worksheet **Start** should be updated in the linked cell on the **PasteLink** worksheet.

19 – How to paste special worksheet data or charts into another application

EXERCISE

Method

1 Highlight the **data** or **chart**.

2 Click on **Copy**.

3 Open your word processing application.

4 Open a specific word processing document if relevant.

5 Click **Paste Special** on the **Edit** menu to open the dialogue window.

6 If you are pasting **data**:

   a Click **Microsoft Excel Worksheet Object** as the **Source data**.

   b Click on **OK** to Paste Special the data into the word document (window closes).

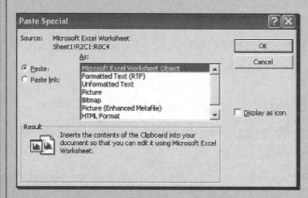

Figure 1.29 Paste Special window for data

7 If you are pasting a **chart object**:

   a Click **Microsoft Excel Chart Object** as the **Source data**.

   b Click on **OK** to Paste Special the chart into the word document (window closes).

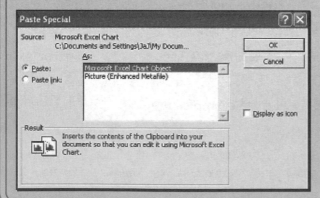

Figure 1.30 Paste Special window for charts

Task 1.5 Using Paste Special

20 – Practice

Method

1 Copy cells C1:D5 on the **Chart** worksheet.

2 Paste Special the data (using the instructions above) into the word processing document **PasteSpecialData.doc**.

3 **Centre** the data under the **Title** in the word processing document.

4 **Save** the file as MyPasteSpecialData.

5 **Print** a copy of the file if you have access to a printer.

6 Close the word processing document and application.

21 – Practice

Method

1 Copy the chart **Test Paste Special** on the **Chart** worksheet.

2 Use the instructions above to Paste Special the chart into the word processing document **PasteSpecialChart.doc**.

3 **Centre** the chart under the **title** in the word processing document.

4 **Save** the file as **MyPasteSpecialChart**.

5 **Print** a copy of the file if you have access to a printer.

6 **Close** the word processing document and application.

Info

Getting immediate help in the Paste Special window:

o Click the **question mark** symbol on the Paste Special title bar and then, in the Paste Special window, click the option that you would like to see a brief description of.

o Open any **Help** facility available in your application and key in the **option text** shown in the Paste Special window.

In this section you have used Paste Special options **Skip Blanks**, **Transpose** and **Paste Link**.

Save and review your work before moving to the main task.

Paste special data example   Paste Special chart example

One	Two
25	45
17	27
33	12
75	86

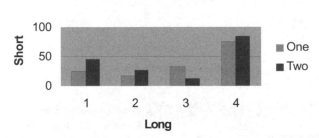

Import and delimit a text file

Data that needs to be used in a spreadsheet is often created or stored in a text file by large mainframe computers as this economises on system resources such as memory and space on the hard drive.

In this section you will learn the basic steps to import a text file into a spreadsheet application and manipulate the imported data.

1 – How to import a text file

Method

1 **Open** your spreadsheet application.

2 Click **Open** on the **File** menu.

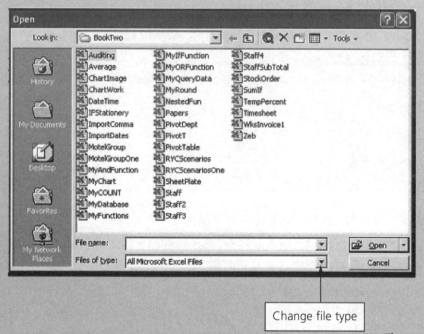

Change file type

Figure 1.31 The Open File window

Note: you can also start the **Text Import Wizard** by pointing to **Get External Data** on the **Data** menu and clicking **Import Text File** on the sub-menu to open the Import Text file window. While the name of the open window is changed, the sequence that follows remains the same.

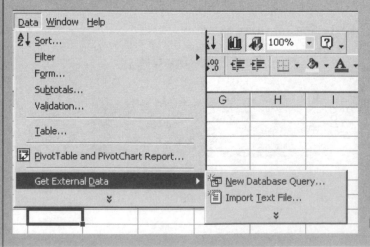

Figure 1.32 Get External Data

3 In either window, navigate to the folder where you have saved the text file you want to import.

4 To view files with a ***.txt** extension, in the window: **Change** the **Files of type** option from **All Microsoft Excel Files** (or however your spreadsheet package files are named) to **Text Files**, to see a list of text files in the selected folder.

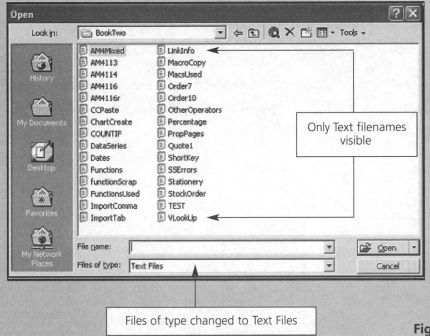

Only Text filenames visible

Files of type changed to Text Files

Figure 1.33 Viewing text files

5 Click the **File name** to select the file.

6 Click the **Open/Import** button to start the **Import Text File Wizard**. The wizard has three steps to import a file.

The Text Import Wizard – Step 1 of 3

Info

Here you need to supply some information about the make up of your file so that the system understands how to import the data contained in the file.

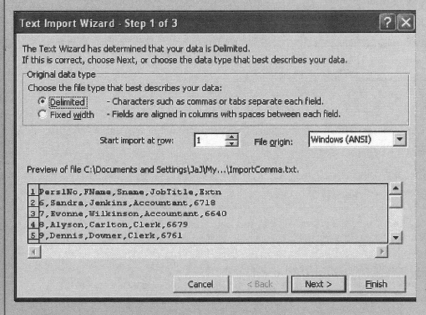

Figure 1.34 Text Import Wizard: Step 1

The wizard will read the file you have selected for import and make some assumptions about the contents for the **Original data type** import option.

Original data type

This option refers to how the text (fields) in the file is laid out. The wizard offers a choice between **Delimiter** and **Fixed width** for the **Original data type** option.

Delimiter

A **Delimiter** is a marker that indicates where a **field** starts and ends when importing data.

If you select the **Delimiter option** this tells the system that the **fields** in your file are separated by one of the following delimiters:

- Tab key (→)
- Comma (,)
- Colon (:)
- A **Space** inserted by using the spacebar on the keyboard.

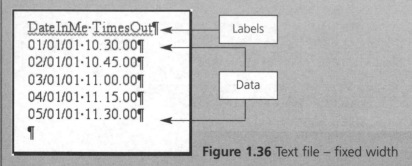

Figure 1.35 Text file delimiter – using tab key to separate text (fields)

Fixed width

This option tells the system that the **fields** in your file are all items of the same length, aligned in columns and separated by spaces. In Figure 1.36 below, the two columns have eight characters and a space between the labels and data.

DateInMe·TimesOut¶ ← Labels
01/01/01·10.30.00¶ ←
02/01/01·10.45.00¶
03/01/01·11.00.00¶ ← Data
04/01/01·11.15.00¶
05/01/01·11.30.00¶ ←
¶

Figure 1.36 Text file – fixed width

If the system recognises the layout of your text file it will select an **Original data type** option for your file. If the system has chosen the wrong option change this by selecting the appropriate **Option** button.

In the example below, taken from Step 1 of 3, the wizard, having read the file that was being imported, determines that **Delimited** is the **Original data type** – which is correct.

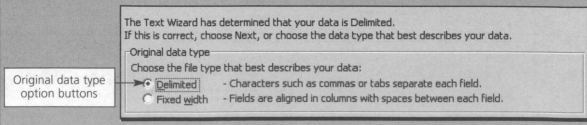

Original data type option buttons

The Text Wizard has determined that your data is Delimited.
If this is correct, choose Next, or choose the data type that best describes your data.

Original data type

Choose the file type that best describes your data:

○ Delimited — Characters such as commas or tabs separate each field.
○ Fixed width — Fields are aligned in columns with spaces between each field.

Figure 1.37 The Text Wizard determines the Original data type

Task 1.6 Import and delimit a text file

Importing files

If you did not create the file you are going to import, check the following before attempting to import!

- The file data type.
- Specifically, which part of the file needs to be imported, if you are not importing all data contained in the file.
- The environment the file was created in (e.g. Windows (ANSI)).
- Is a custom delimiter in use?

Other options in Step 1 of 3 of the Text Import Wizard

Figure 1.38 Start import at row – spin buttons

If, for example, out of 20 rows, you only need to import rows 5 to 20, use the spin buttons to change the number displayed to 5 – the starting point.

File origin

This means the operating system that the file was created in. On a Windows system when the wizard opens and recognises a Windows file, the default in the list box is **Windows (ANSI)**.

To change **File origin** options, select an option from the list box.

Figure 1.39 Change File origin options

If your file was created in another system and has not been recognised, you can select from the following:

- **Macintosh** – an alternative operating system to the Windows generation of operating systems.
- **MS-DOS (PC-8)** – one of the predecessors to Windows (ANSI).

Preview of file

Displays contents, filename, and path to the storage location on the computer.

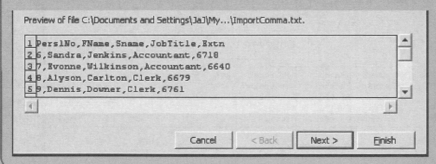

Figure 1.40 Preview of file

7   If the data you see in the **Preview of file** is not as expected, click **Cancel** to close the text import wizard, then restart it and select an alternative file.

The Text Import Wizard – Step 2 of 3

In Step 2 you select the specific delimiter that is contained in your file. In the example below the system has suggested **Tab** as the delimiter.

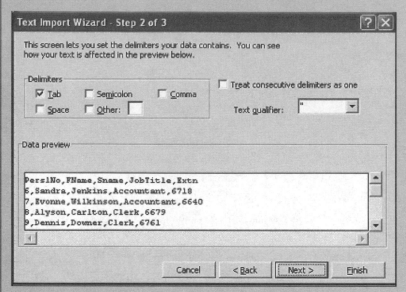

Figure 1.41 Text Import Wizard: Step 2

Commas delimit the file being imported. To change the delimiter option suggested, click the appropriate tick-box.

If the delimiter is non-standard, in the **Other** text box in the **Delimiter** section (Figure 1.42) enter the delimiter you want to use via the keyboard. In the Data preview area, you will then see a preview of the data and how this will be imported.

Figure 1.42 Import example with comma delimiter selected

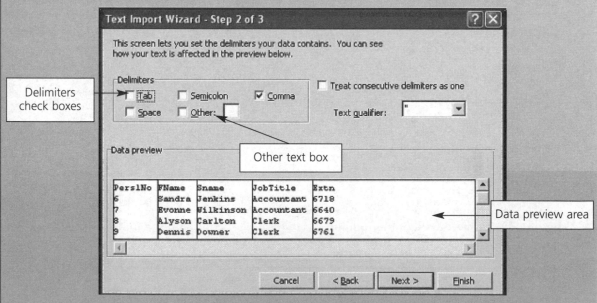

Select the **Treat consecutive delimiters as one** box if your delimiter has more than one character.

The Text Import Wizard – Step 3 of 3

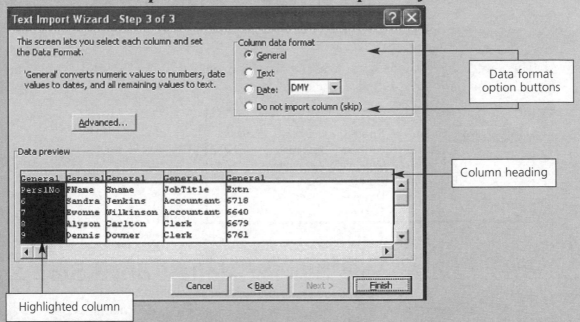

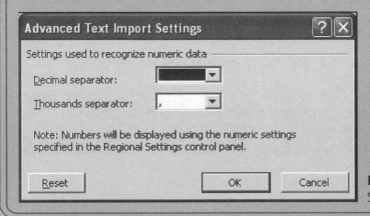

Highlighted column

Data format option buttons

Column heading

Figure 1.43 The Text Import Wizard: Step 3 of 3 – Column data format option buttons

The data format option offered when Step 3 opens is the default called **General**.

The other options are **Text** and **Date**.

If the data you are importing has a specific format you can set this here by clicking the column heading to highlight the column and then select a data format.

The **data format** option buttons also have a list box from which you can select a format type for the date display such as **YMD.**

Selecting the option **YMD** would display the date **01/11/01** as **Y**ear, **M**onth and **D**ay.

If you do not want to import a particular column, highlight the column and select the **Do not import column (skip)** option button.

To open the Advanced Text Import Settings window, click the Advanced button (Figure 1.44) in Step 3 of the Wizard.

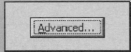

Figure 1.44 Advanced button

If you have custom **Decimal** and/or **Thousand** separators in a text file, click on the **Advanced** button (Figures 1.43 and 1.44), and set the separators in the **Advanced Text Import Settings** dialogue window (Figure1.45), so that they will be recognised when the file is imported.

Figure 1.45 Advanced Text Import Settings

8 After setting the custom separators, click **OK** to close the settings window.

9 To import the text file click the **Finish** button. The text file will be imported into your spreadsheet application.

The spreadsheet will only contain one sheet tab. The name of the default sheet tab will reflect the name of the text file being imported.

	A	B	C	D	E
1	PersINo	FName	Sname	JobTitle	Extn
2	6	Sandra	Jenkins	Accountan	6718
3	7	Evonne	Wilkinson	Accountan	6640
4	8	Alyson	Carlton	Clerk	6679
5	9	Dennis	Downer	Clerk	6761
6	10	Gor	Thannette	Clerk	6761

Figure 1.46 An imported text file

The Text Import Wizard – alternative Step 2 of 3

Used if the system is unable to determine how a text file is delimited.

In Step 2 of 3 of the Text Import Wizard you will be presented with suggested **column breaks**, and the option to set the field widths yourself.

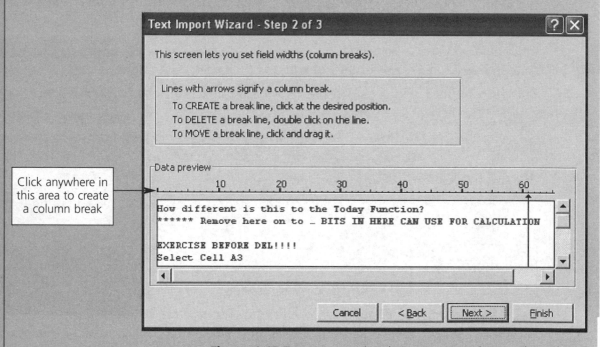

Click anywhere in this area to create a column break

Figure 1.47 Text Import Wizard: Step 2 – creating a column break

Column Breaks:
- To **create** a column break, **click** anywhere on the ruler in the data preview area to insert an arrow as a marker.
- To **move** a column break arrow, **click and drag** the arrow left or right to a new location.
- To **delete** a column break arrow, **double click** the arrow. You can also **drag and drop** the column break arrow down towards the command buttons in the window. The column break arrow will be deleted.

Task 1.6 Import and delimit a text file

2 – Saving an imported text file in a spreadsheet format

1 Click **Save As** from the **File** menu.

2 Ensure that you change the **Files of type** to **Excel Files** (or however your spreadsheet package files are named).

3 Enter a name for the file.

4 Click **Save**.

The imported text file will be saved in a **spreadsheet format**.

3 – Importing and formatting a fixed width text file

All files for this section can be located on the accompanying CD-ROM.

Task A – Importing the file

1 **Open** your spreadsheet application.

2 **Open** the text file **Shoes** to start the Import Wizard.

In Step 1 of the Import Wizard, the defaults selected should be as follows:

○ The **Original data type** is **Fixed width**.
○ **Start import at row – 1**.
○ The **File origin** is **Windows (ANSI)**.

If the options are not as above, **select** them then click the **Next** button.

Step 2 of the Import Wizard

The Import Wizard, having read the contents of the file **Shoes**, should have made the following assumptions:

○ Original data type is **Fixed width**.
○ Guess at **column breaks**.

The system feels it is has had to guess at the **column breaks** in the text file, and so the **alternative Step 2** window, with suggested **column breaks**, and the option to set these widths yourself, is presented.

The text file you are importing has a space on either side of the word 'is'

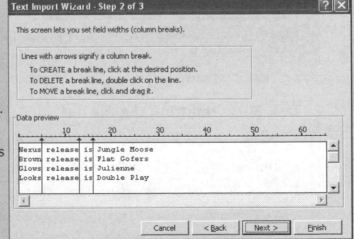

Figure 1.48 Import Wizard alternative Step 2 with suggested column breaks

in the row of data. The system has determined that the space on either side of the word, along with the other spaces in the row, is a separate **column break** from the text.

The word **is** belongs with the text in the **second** column break, which should read as '**release is**'.

3 Delete the column break after the word **release** (Figure 1.48).

The data preview area (Figure 1.49) shows the **column breaks** necessary, at points 5 and 16 approximately, to import the file accurately.

Figure 1.49 Column breaks for Shoes text file

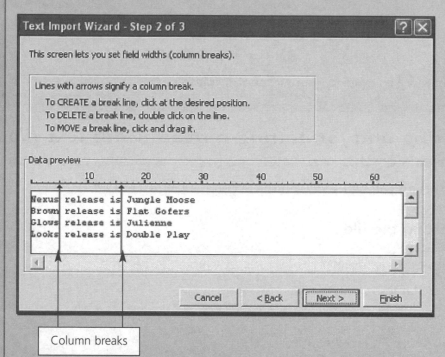

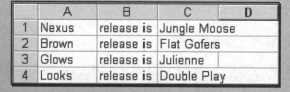

4 In the alternative Step 2 of the Wizard, click the **Finish** button to accept all other default options in Step 3, and to **import** the text **file**.

	A	B	C	D
1	Nexus	release is	Jungle Moose	
2	Brown	release is	Flat Gofers	
3	Glows	release is	Julienne	
4	Looks	release is	Double Play	

Figure 1.50 The imported text file Shoes

The file will be imported based on the information you supplied or accepted in each stage of the Wizard.

Task B – Formatting the file data

Method

1 Extend column C if all data cannot be seen clearly in the cells.

2 Highlight row 1 and **Insert** a new row.

3 In cells A1:C1 respectively, enter the following labels:

- **Company**
- **Text**
- **Shoe Name**

4 Embolden all Labels in cells A1:C1.

5 Save the imported text file in a **spreadsheet format** with the filename **Shoes**.

	A	B	C
1	Company	Text	Shoe Name
2	Nexus	release is	Jungle Moose
3	Brown	release is	Flat Gofers
4	Glows	release is	Julienne
5	Looks	release is	Double Play

Figure 1.51 Completed Shoes file

Save and review your work before moving to the next section.

In this section you have imported a text file and delimited by **space**. To facilitate importing the text file, you have also amended the default alternative **Import Wizard Step 2 Column Breaks**, for the file.

4 – Practice

In this exercise you import a text file and save this in a spreadsheet format. The imported data will then be used in later exercise.

Method

1 Open a new workbook.

2 **Import** the text file **Dates.txt**. Accept all the text import **defaults** offered by the Text Import Wizard, by clicking the **Finish** button in Step 1 of 3.

3 The imported text file contains one column of data in **column A** on the worksheet.

4 **Save** the workbook as **ImportDates** in a **Spreadsheet** format.

5 **Insert** eight new **rows** at the top of the worksheet.

6 **Enter** the following **Labels** in cells B9:D9: **DAY, MONTH, YEAR**.

	A	B	C	D
9	Data April - Nov	DAY	MONTH	YEAR
10	01/04/2000			
11	01/04/2000			
12	01/04/2000			
13	01/04/2000			
14	01/04/2000			
15	01/04/2000			
16	01/04/2000			
17	01/04/2000			
18	02/04/2000			
19	02/04/2000			
20	02/04/2000			
21	02/04/2000			
22	02/04/2000			
23	02/04/2000			

Figure 1.52 The ImportDates file

7 **Save** and close the file.

Creating and importing a text file

Info

Spreadsheets are able to handle file formats, especially if these have been created with delimiters.

Delimiters

Delimiters are usually inserted in one of the following formats:

Tab key (→), Comma (,) and also the spacebar.

To get a feel for text files that you will be importing, **create** the following **text file**. Use a plain text editor such as **Notepad** to create the file; this will ensure that the file has the (**txt**) file extension.

EXERCISE 5 – Creating a comma delimited text file

Method

1   Open your Text Editor. Take care to observe the following protocol, and enter the text from the **Example File**, shown in the box on the right:

   a   When creating the file contents, do not use the **spacebar** to separate one piece of text from another, use a **comma** instead.

   b   At the end of a line of text, use only the **Enter** key to start a new row.

2   Save the file as **ImportComma**.

3   Close the file.

Example File:

```
PersNo,FName,Sname,JobTitle,Extn
6,Sandra,Jenkins,Accountant,6718
7,Evonne,Wilkinson,Accountant,6640
8,Alyson,Carlton,Clerk,6679
9,Dennis,Downer,Clerk,6761
10,Gor,Thannette,Clerk,6761
```

If necessary, review Exercise 1 before going on to the next exercise.

EXERCISE 6 – Importing files: practice

Task A

1   Import the text file **ImportComma** (the name of the file indicates the type of delimiter you need to select in the Text Import Wizard).

The imported data should cover the cells A1:E6 if the file has been created correctly, and the delimiters set accordingly.

2   Save **ImportComma.txt** in a spreadsheet format, but retain the original filename of **ImportComma**, ensuring that the file extension is of a spreadsheet format.

3   Save and close the file.

Task B

1   Import the text file **ImportTab** (the filename should give you a clear indication of the delimiter to select in the Text Import Wizard dialogue steps).

The imported data should cover the cells A1:E6.

2 Save the file as **FinanceStaff**, in a spreadsheet format.

3 Close the file.

Task C

1 Import the text file **ExportOne**. The file delimiter is **Commas**.

The imported data should cover the cells A1:F9.

2 Save the file as **Bookings**, in a spreadsheet format.

3 Close the file.

To aid your understanding of text files, you have now created and imported a text file and saved this in a spreadsheet format.

> ## Display Tasks

1.7 Freeze and unfreeze panes

Freezing row and or column titles provides a way of ensuring that data you need to see or constantly refer to when working with a spreadsheet is always available.

You need to select the correct cell, column or row, to ensure that the data you always want to see is contained within a freeze.

All files for this section can be located on the accompanying CD-ROM.

EXERCISE 1 – Apply the Freeze Panes command

Method

1 Open the workbook **StaffFreeze**.

2 Select the **StaffDetails** worksheet.

3 Select cell A1 on the worksheet **StaffDetails**.

4 Click **Freeze Panes** from the **Windows** menu.

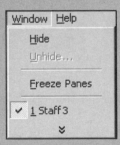

Figure 1.53 Window menu

After applying the Freeze Panes Command your worksheet should now look like the example in Figure 1.54. Notice the **lines** that have appeared between columns **C** and **D**, and rows **8** and **9**.

Figure 1.54 Freeze Panes applied

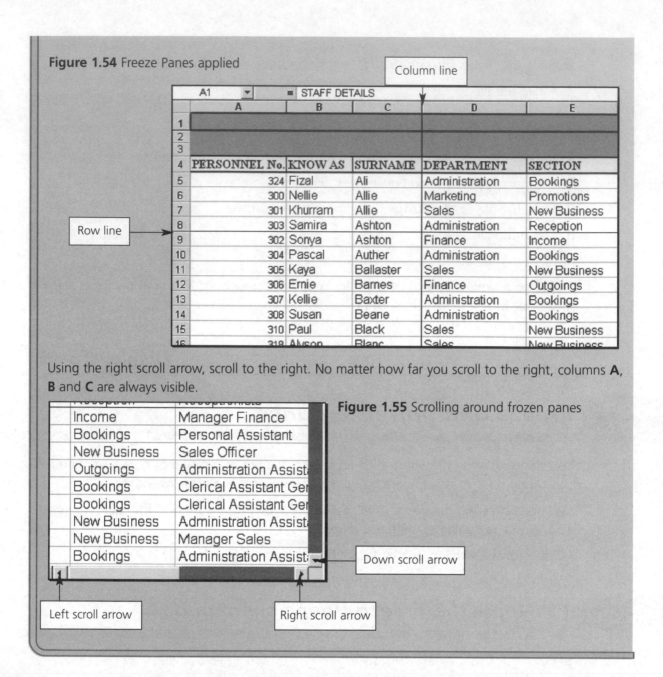

Column line

	A	B	C	D	E
1					
2					
3					
4	PERSONNEL No.	KNOW AS	SURNAME	DEPARTMENT	SECTION
5	324	Fizal	Ali	Administration	Bookings
6	300	Nellie	Allie	Marketing	Promotions
7	301	Khurram	Allie	Sales	New Business
8	303	Samira	Ashton	Administration	Reception
9	302	Sonya	Ashton	Finance	Income
10	304	Pascal	Auther	Administration	Bookings
11	305	Kaya	Ballaster	Sales	New Business
12	306	Ernie	Barnes	Finance	Outgoings
13	307	Kellie	Baxter	Administration	Bookings
14	308	Susan	Beane	Administration	Bookings
15	310	Paul	Black	Sales	New Business
16	318	Alyson	Blanc	Sales	New Business

A1 = STAFF DETAILS

Row line

Using the right scroll arrow, scroll to the right. No matter how far you scroll to the right, columns **A**, **B** and **C** are always visible.

Figure 1.55 Scrolling around frozen panes

Reception	Receptionists
Income	Manager Finance
Bookings	Personal Assistant
New Business	Sales Officer
Outgoings	Administration Assista
Bookings	Clerical Assistant Ger
Bookings	Clerical Assistant Ger
New Business	Administration Assista
New Business	Manager Sales
Bookings	Administration Assista

Down scroll arrow

Left scroll arrow

Right scroll arrow

EXERCISE

2 – Practice

Method

1 On the **PubSales** worksheet select cell A2.

2 From the **Window** menu select **Freeze Panes**.

Use the scroll arrow to move to the right. What was the view this time? Did all cells move to the right?

3 Cell A1 on the **StaffDetails** worksheet has had the format **Merge** and **Centre** applied to cells A1:K1. These cells are therefore treated as one cell.

4 Unfreeze the worksheets **PubSales** and **StaffDetails**.

Task 1.7 Freeze and unfreeze panes

Unfreeze panes command

Click **Unfreeze Panes** from the **Windows** menu.

Figure 1.56 Window menu – Unfreeze Panes

3 – Practice

Task A – StaffDetails

Method

1   Click cell A2 on the **StaffDetails** worksheet and apply the Freeze Panes command.

2   Scroll to the right of the worksheet.

Can you see columns A, B or C when you scroll to the right?

3   Unfreeze panes on the **StaffDetails** worksheet.

Task B – PubSales

Method

1   Click cell A1 on the **PubSales** worksheet and apply **Freeze Panes**.

2   Scroll to the right of the worksheet.

Can you see the Columns A, B or C when you scroll to the right?

Info

Yes. **Merge** and **Centre** formatting has been applied to cells A1:G1 and these are therefore treated as one cell.

3   Click cell F14.

4   Use the keyboard shortcut **Ctrl+Home** to move Home (cell A1).

Note: after carrying out Step 4, if cell A1 is the active cell, then the Freeze Panes command was not correctly applied to it in the first part of the task.

Info

Using the keyboard shortcut **Ctrl+Home** with Freeze Panes alters 'Home' to cell C11.

Cell **D9** is the first cell outside the Freeze Panes area and should now be the active cell after using the keyboard shortcut **Ctrl+Home**.

5   Unfreeze panes on the **PubSales** worksheet.

6   Press **Ctrl+Home**.

Info

Using the shortcut **without** Freeze Panes will move the cursor to cell A1, which now becomes the active cell (again).

4 – Practice

Method

1 Click cell E5 on the **PubSales** worksheet and apply **Freeze Panes**.

2 Scroll to the right of the worksheet. What can you see?

Info

On this worksheet, **Freeze Panes** is not really any help if E5 is used as the starting point for the freeze.

Which columns and/or rows freeze or scroll, is determined by **How** and **Where** the Freeze Panes command is applied.

3 Unfreeze all panes on the **PubSales** worksheet.

4 Save and close the workbook.

5 – Practice

Method

1 Open the workbook **FreezePractice**.

2 On the **Computers** worksheet, freeze row 1.

3 On the **Accessories** worksheet, freeze columns A and B, and row 1.

4 Save and close the workbook.

Save and review your work before moving to the next main task.

1.8   Hide and unhide elements in a worksheet

You can customise your worksheet to display specific rows and/or columns.

This is a way of hiding data that may not be needed at the time or has become redundant and will be removed when you recreate the spreadsheet.

Open the workbook **StaffHide1**. All files for this section can be located on the accompanying CD-ROM.

1 – Unhide columns

Method

1 Select the worksheet **HideUnhide**.

2 Highlight a range of columns that *includes* the hidden columns C and D (e.g. highlight columns B:E by clicking and holding the mouse on column header B, drag the mouse over columns B:E, then release the mouse).

3 Point to **Column** on the **Format** menu, then click **Unhide** from the sub-menu (the hidden columns will then be visible).

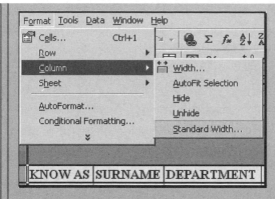

KNOW AS **SURNAME** **DEPARTMENT**

Figure 1.57 Hide/Unhide menu

4 **Unhide** columns C and D on the **HideUnhide** worksheet.

2 – Hide adjacent columns

Method

1 On the **HideUnhide** worksheet, highlight columns C and D by clicking and dragging the mouse over the column heading Letters.

2 Point to **Column** on the **Format** menu, then click **Hide** on the sub-menu (the selected columns will be hidden).

3 – Hide non-adjacent columns

Method

1 Highlight column G.

2 Hold down **Ctrl** while clicking the column headers A and J.

3 Release the **Ctrl** key.

4 Point to **Column** on the **Format** menu, then click **Hide** on the sub-menu (the selected columns will be hidden).

Do not close the workbook.

To unhide column A you cannot use the unhide column procedure shown in Exercise 1, because column A has no other columns to the left of it.

Before unhiding column A we need to look at, and understand, cursor shapes.

Understanding cursor shapes

Info

Position the mouse pointer on the gap to the left of the column B header. The mouse pointer will change shape from a **thick white cross** to a **black double-headed arrow** . Drag the column B header to the right of the screen to expose column A.

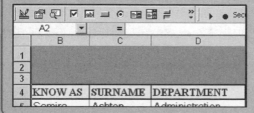

Figure 1.58

Unhide column A if you have not done so already.

Cursor Shapes

The **thick white cross** ✜ is the standard cursor shape, displayed when clicking a cell, highlighting a row, a column, or a range of cells e.g. cells A9:F9.

Rest the mouse pointer on the gap between the column A and B headers. The pointer will change shape and become a **black double-headed arrow**. When the cursor assumes this shape, column width and row height can then be extended.

The shape of the mouse pointer, and the area of the window it is active in, gives you a visual clue to the type of tasks you can perform.

When the pointer changes to an **I Beam** ⌶ what type of task can you perform in a spreadsheet?

Rest the mouse pointer over the **formula bar** or **name box** for a clue.

(The formal name for the **I Beam** mouse pointer is **Text Select**.)

EXERCISE

4 – Hide adjacent rows

Method

1 Highlight rows 7, 8 and 9 on the **HideUnhide** worksheet by clicking row header 7 or 9 and dragging the mouse pointer down or up to select the row.

2 Point to **Row** on the **Format** menu, then click **Hide** on the sub-menu (the selected rows will be hidden).

EXERCISE

5 – Hide non-adjacent rows

Method

1 On the **HideUnhide** worksheet, highlight row 13.

2 Hold down the **Ctrl** key while clicking row headers 16 and 18.

3 Release the **Ctrl** key.

4 Point to **Row** on the **Format** menu, then click **Hide** on the sub-menu (the selected rows will be hidden).

EXERCISE

6 – Unhide rows

Method

1 On the **HideUnhide** worksheet, highlight a range of rows that includes one row **before** the first hidden row (7) and one row **after** the last hidden row (18).

2 Point to **Row** on the **Format** menu, then click **Unhide** on the sub-menu.

The highlighted hidden rows will now be visible.

7 – Hide/unhide shortcut menu

Method

1 Highlight row or column.

2 Right click the highlighted row or column.

3 From the pop-up menu, click **Hide** or **Unhide**.

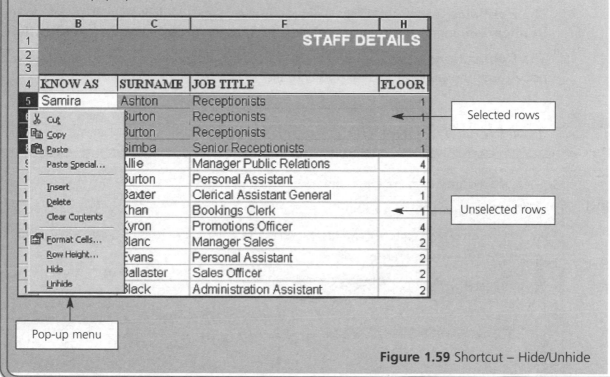

Figure 1.59 Shortcut – Hide/Unhide

8 – Practice

Task A

Method

1 Select the **StaffLeaveCalc** worksheet.

2 Hide all staff that work in the Sales Department: rows 6, 10, 15, 20, 23, 27, 30, 32, 36 and 39.

Task B

Method

1 Open the workbook **HidePractice**.

2 On the **Computers** worksheet, hide rows 2, 5, 6, 8, 11, 12, 15, 16, 17, 18, 19, 20 and 24.

3 On the **Accessories** worksheet, hide columns F, J and N.

Save and review your work before moving to the next section.

Hide and unhide worksheets

Open the workbook **StaffHide2**. All files for this section can be located on the accompanying CD-ROM.

Select the **PubSales** worksheet.

The **PubSales** worksheet tracks newspaper and magazine deliveries. The data in the **Publication** and **Price** columns is linked to a hidden worksheet called **Publications**.

The **Publications** worksheet is used to store a list of newspapers, magazines, their current prices, and the publication day for each title.

1 – How to unhide a worksheet

Method

1 On the **Format** menu point to **Sheet**.

2 Click **Unhide** on the sub-menu.

You will be presented with the **Unhide** window. The window will contain a list of any worksheets in the workbook that have been hidden.

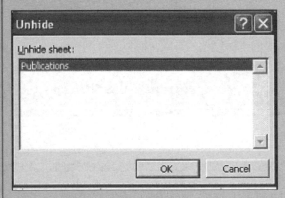

Figure 1.60 Unhide window

3 **Click** the name of the worksheet you want to unhide.

4 Click **OK** to open the worksheet and to close the **Unhide** window.

5 If you have not done so already, **unhide** the Publications worksheet.

Task A

Method

1 Add the following data to the **Publications** worksheet:

Publication	Cost	Publish Day
PC Advisor	3.99	Tuesday
New Woman	1.99	Monday
Computer Active	0.99	Friday

2 Save the workbook.

3 Print a copy of the **Publications** worksheet.

3 – How to hide a worksheet

Method

1 Select the sheet you want to hide.

2 On the **Format** menu, point to **Sheet**.

3 Click **Hide** on the sub-menu.

The worksheet will be hidden.

4 – Practice

Method

1 Hide the **Publications** worksheet.

2 Hide the **HideUnhide** worksheet.

3 Hide the **StaffLeaveCalc** worksheet.

The **StaffDetails** and **PubSales** worksheets will be the only visible worksheets in the StaffHide2 workbook.

4 Save and close the workbook.

Open the workbook **HideSheetPractice**.

You share this workbook with other staff members who prefer to look at figures; you prefer to work with charts.

5 – Unhiding/hiding

Task A – Unhiding

Method

1 Unhide the following worksheets:

  a Expenses.

  b Income Chart.

  c ProfitLoss Chart.

Task B – Hiding

Method

1 Hide the following worksheets:

  a Expenses.

  b Income Chart.

  c ProfitLoss Chart.

Save and close the workbook.

Save and review your work before moving to the next section.

Open the workbook **StaffSubTotalling**. All files for this section can be located on the accompanying CD-ROM.

1 – Preparing the data before applying subtotal features

Task A

Method

1 Select the **PubSales** worksheet.

You use this worksheet to monitor publication sales to your customers. The spreadsheet you are working with covers cells A1:F75 of the worksheet.

2 Enter the following formula, which will multiply the column **How Many** by the column **Price**, in cell G3 of the **PubSales** worksheet: **=(E3*F3)**

3 Copy the formula to cells G4:G75.

Normally after you have calculated the price, you manually go through the spreadsheet and total the final bill based on the house number.

You have been on a course where you were introduced to the topic subtotalling.

Today, instead of manually preparing the final bill, you have decided to use the **PubSales** worksheet data to practice using features provided in subtotalling.

Info

You should ensure that each column has distinctive labels and that the columns you want sub-totals produced for have been sorted together to group them, if more than one criterion is to be used:

○ Your spreadsheet has distinctive labels in cells **A2:G2** ✓.

○ Your spreadsheet is not sorted to group together the **House No.** and **Publication** columns ✗.

Task B – Sorting data

You want to produce a final bill based on each customer's **house number** and the **publications** they have purchased in that **week**.

Method

1 Select cell A3 and from the **Data** menu, click on **Sort**.

2 Select the following criteria:

   a Sort by **House No.**

   b Then by **Publication**.

If your system has not detected that the list has a header row, click the **Header row** option button to select it.

3 Click **OK** to accept all other default options and to close the window.

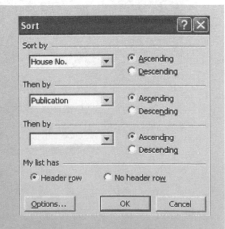

Figure 1.61 Sort window

The data on the worksheet is now sorted and displayed by **House No.** and **Publication**.

At the end of each week you will need to send customers a bill for the deliveries, which normally takes you some time to produce manually. You have been told that if you use the **sum** function feature in sub-totalling, this will produce the figure for each house number and speed up the task.

2 – Applying an automatic subtotal to the total column

Method

1 Select cell A3.

2 Click **Subtotals** from the **Data** menu.

The system will make an assessment of the data contained in your list and offer a suggestion to use the subtotal function, **Sum**.

On this occasion the suggestions are: **At each change in:** House No. **Use function:** Sum. **Add subtotal to:** Total.

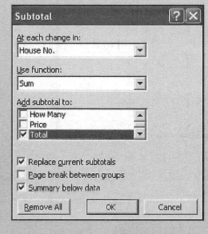

Figure 1.62 Subtotal window with suggested options

3 Click **OK** to accept the suggestions. Current subtotals will be replaced and the new subtotal placed below the data.

These **Subtotal** options provide a **total** at the end of the deliveries for each individual house number, and a **Grand Total** at the end of the spreadsheet.

4 Print a copy showing the subtotals if you have access to a printer.

Figure 1.63 Part of the Subtotal spreadsheet

85	14 Total						£5.65
86	15		Yes	Evening Standard	5	£0.35	£1.75
87	15		Yes	Independent	5	£0.65	£3.25
88	15	Thursday		Racing Weekly	1	£1.25	£1.25
89	15	Friday		TV Weekly	1	£0.90	£0.90
90	15 Total						£7.15
91	Grand Total						£113.62
92							

Changing the view of a subtotal spreadsheet

Info

If you only want to see or print your subtotal spreadsheet, click the **minus** icons on the left of the spreadsheet to hide the data and display only the subtotals.

The **minus** and **plus** icons are part of the **Outline Symbol** group of icons that includes the **Row Level** icons.

When clicked, **Minus** outline symbols will change to **Plus** symbols (See Figures 1.64 and 1.65).

Figure 1.64 Changing the view of a subtotal spreadsheets

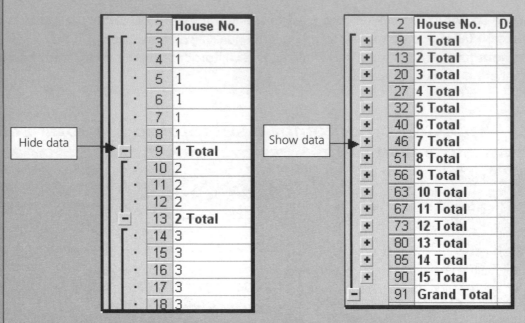

You can also use the **row level** icons to change the view of a subtotal spreadsheet. Here there are only three levels of data, so only three row levels are currently available.

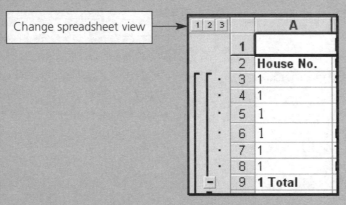

Figure 1.65 Using row level icons

The current subtotal spreadsheet contains three row levels of data, grouped as:

a Details row and subtotals.

b Subtotals and Grand Total.

c Grand Total.

If you select row level number 1, your spreadsheet will only display the **Grand Total**. Level number 2 displays **Totals plus Grand Total**, and number 3 **All data** on the spreadsheet.

Practice changing the view of your subtotal spreadsheet using the **row level** icons.

EXERCISE   3 – Count a subtotal

Method

How many papers are delivered to each house number?

1 Open the **Subtotal** window and change entry in the **Use function:** box to **Count**.

Do not change any other options.

Task 1.10 Applying subtotalling functions

2 Close the window.

The **Grand Count** should be **73**. If not, re-check that you followed the method correctly, as the sub-total has not been applied accurately.

4 – Removing subtotals from the PubSales worksheet

Method

1 Click cell A3.

2 Click **Subtotals** from the **Data** menu, to open the Subtotal window.

3 Click the **Remove All** button.

The subtotals will be removed and the Subtotal window will close.

4 Save the workbook.

5 – Updating subtotals

What is the **maximum** amount each house number spends per week?

Method

1 Select cell A3 and open the Subtotal window.

2 Create the following **Max** subtotal:

   a At each change in: House No.

   b Use function: Max.

   c Add subtotal to: Total.

This subtotal replaces the current subtotals and should now appear below the data.

The **Grand Max** should be **£3.50** if the subtotal as been applied as specified.

3 Remove the subtotals from the **PubSales** worksheet.

4 Save and close the workbook.

6 – Practice

Method

1 Open the workbook **SubTotalTwo**.

The workbook represents the wine sales for a company called **Barnes**.

You will only be working with the **Type** column, to produce subtotals.

2 On the **Sum** worksheet, select cell A3 and apply the following subtotals:

A	B
a At each change in: Type	**a At each change in:** Type
b Use function: Sum	**b Use function:** Average
c Add sub-total to: Total Price	**c Add sub-total to:** Total Price
This **replaces** the current sub-total and should now appear below the data.	This **should not** replace current sub-totals, and should appear below the data.

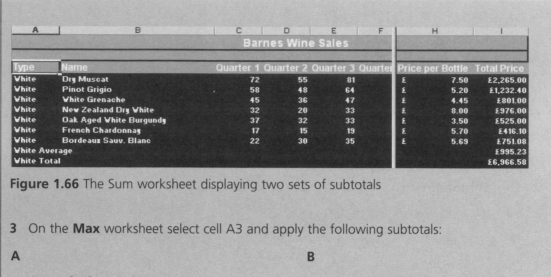

Figure 1.66 The Sum worksheet displaying two sets of subtotals

3 On the **Max** worksheet select cell A3 and apply the following subtotals:

A

a **At each change in:** Type
b **Use function:** Max
c **Add sub-total to:** Total Price

This **replaces** current subtotals and should place these below the data.

B

a **At each change in:** Type
b **Use function:** Min
c **Add sub-total to:** Total Price

This **should not** replace current subtotals and should appear below the data.

Sheet3 in the workbook contains another copy of the spreadsheet you have been working with. You can use this copy to experiment with subtotalling features.

Save and review your work before moving to the next section.

1.11 Using data tables

A data table enables you to evaluate several pieces of information at the same time against a static set of facts and figures.

For example, you may want to buy a new computer. Having visited the hardware shop, the sales assistant has advised you that the interest rate on the price of the computer will depend on the time of year that you purchase the system. You need to work out which month to choose so that you can budget your income.

The system you have decided on is priced at **£5000**. A one-input data table could help you to decide when would be the best period in which to purchase your computer. The interest rates for the next six months are shown in the table to the right:

No **down payment** is necessary for the purchase of the computer.

You will pay for the cost of the computer over 36 **months** – this is known as the **Term**.

The **cost amount** of the computer you have decided to purchase is **£5000**.

Month	Rate
January	2.5%
February	4.00%
March	5.05%
April	9.00%
May	10.00%
June	12.50%

1 – One-input data tables

Task A – Preparing the spreadsheet

Method

1 Open your spreadsheet application and enter the following data:

   a **In cell C2**: enter the label **Computer Purchase Analysis** (which explains the purpose of the data table). Extend the cell so that the entire text in the label is visible.

   b **In cell C4**: enter the label **Down Payment**.

   c **In cell D4**: enter the label **None**, as you will not be making any down payments on this occasion.

   d **In cell C5**: enter the label **Interest Rate**.

   e **In cell D5**: leave blank. This will be the input from your data table once you have completed the necessary steps.

   f **In cell C6**: enter the label term, **Months** (which represents 'nper').

   g **In cell D6**: enter the term figure **36** (which represents 3 years).

   h **In cell C7**: enter the label **Purchase Price**.

   i **In cell D7**: enter the Purchase Price, **5000** (which represents the **pv** argument).

2 Save the file as **DataTable**.

Task B – Formatting

Method

1 Ensure that cell D6 is formatted as **Number**, **General**.

2 Format cell D7 as **currency**, two decimal places.

3 Right Align cells D4:D7.

Task C – Creating the data table area

Method

1 In cell C10 enter a label for the data table called **Monthly Payments**.

2 Enter a label for each month:

   a In cell A12 enter the label **January**.

   b Use the **Fill Handles** to fill in the series February to June in cells A13:A17.

3 In cells B12:B17 enter the Interest Rate figures from the 6 month table above.

   Note: ensure that the percentage sign (%) is added after each figure, so that the system is aware of the type of calculation you are requesting.

4 Format cells C11:C17 as **currency**, two decimal places.

5 Format cells B12:B17 as **percentage**, two decimal places.

Task D – The calculation

Method

1 In cell C11 enter a function to perform the calculations for you.

For this calculation we need the **PMT** function. This function calculates payments made at regular intervals at fixed interest rates, such as for the computer you wish to purchase.

The PMT syntax construction

=PMT(rate,nper,pv,fv,type)

- The **rate** argument is in cell **D5** – the input cell for your data table.
- The **nper** argument is in cell **C6** – the length of the repayment.
- The **pv** argument is in cell **D7** – the amount borrowed to buy the computer system.

You will accept any system defaults for the two other arguments **fv** and **type**.

2 Enter the following function in cell C11 (you can enter the function directly in the formula bar or use the Function Wizard): **=PMT(D5/36,D6,-D7)**.

Function construction

The data table **divides** the contents of cell **D5** by **36**, then **looks** in cell **D6**, and **subtracts** the contents of cell **D6** from cell **D7**. This calculation computes the various repayments each month, based on the interest rate for the month in which you purchase the computer system.

Task E – Set the data table

Cells B12:B17 contain the various interest rates.

1 Highlight cells B11:C17 using the mouse.

Cell C11 contains the formula to perform the calculation.

Cells C12:C17 will contain the results.

2 Select **Table** from the **Data** menu to open the **Table** window.

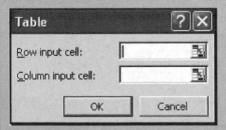

Figure 1.67 Table window

The data (the various interest rates) is in a **column**.

3 From the Table window select Column input cell by clicking on the Collapse Window icon 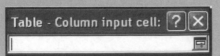. (The Table window will minimise and allow you full access to the spreadsheet, to select the column input cell. This cell provides the system with information on the construction of your data table.)

Figure 1.68 Minimised data table

The cursor is in the input area, so you could key in the cell reference directly, but to ensure accuracy, select the input cell by clicking on it.

4 Select cell D5 using the mouse. (The table column input will now contain an **absolute** reference to the designated cell.)

Absolute references are identified by the dollar sign **($)** preceding each part of the cell reference. You would have to remember to key these in if you entered the cell reference manually.

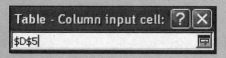

Figure 1.69 Keying values into minimised data table

5 After selecting the column input cell, click the **Un-collapse window** icon. The Table window will maximise for you, to confirm your column input cell.

6 If the input is correct, click OK (Table window closes).

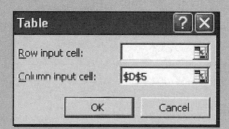

Figure 1.70 Table window with values keyed in

The data table will now be filled with various options so that you can make an informed decision on when to buy your new system.

7 Format the data table as follows:

a Apply separate borders to the data table and analysis areas.

b Fill all non-data entry areas within the borders with shading – Grey 40%.

c Fill the two title areas with a colour of your choice.

	A	B	C	D
1				
2			Computer Purchase Analysis	
3				
4			Down Payment	None
5			Intrest Rate	
6			Term(Months)	36
7			Purchase Price	£5,000.00
8				
9				
10			Monthly Payments	
11				£138.89
12	January	2.05%		£140.36
13	February	4.00%		£141.76
14	March	5.05%		£142.52
15	April	9.00%		£145.41
16	May	10.00%		£146.14
17	June	12.50%		£147.99

Figure 1.71 The completed data table

System options

If you find that calculating the data table is taking a lot of resources from your computer or a network of computers, adjust the following properties when you create your table:

1 Select the **Tools** menu, **Options**, **Calculation** tab (Figure 1.72).

2 Under the **Calculation** options, select the **Automatic except tables** option.

When you have selected the **Automatic except tables** option, you can calculate a data table by:

a Pressing the **F9** function key on the keyboard or

b Selecting the **Tools** menu, **Options**, **Calculation** tab. Click on the **CalcNow** button.

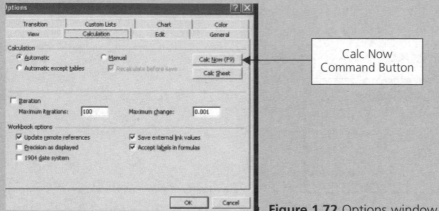

Figure 1.72 Options window – Calculation tab

Important points to note about how a data table functions

1 The boundaries of the data table:

a Is the data table a **row** or **column** input?

b Where is the precise location of the input cell?

2 When tested, you will be asked to create a data table from a specific range of cells; no indication is given of where the input cell is. But if you are able to recognise the data table **type**, the input cell location will be easily recognisable.

3 If you see the following formula in the Formula Bar, but no data in the data table, then you have located the data table boundaries, but not the input cell: {=TABLE(,D5)}

EXERCISE **2 – Practice**

You have decided that you can afford to purchase your new computer system, but wonder how much interest you will pay overall, depending on which month you decide to buy.

Method

1 Copy the contents of cells A1:D17 and paste this into cell A1 of the next available sheet in the workbook. This should ensure that all cells occupy the same area on the new sheet, and that all cell references remain the same. Ensure that all data in the cells can be seen; adjust column widths as appropriate.

Note: the underlying data syntax for the table calculations will not be copied with the spreadsheet. Delete the contents of cells C12:C17.

2 Recreate the data table calculations in cells C12:C17, following the steps in Exercise 1.

3 Add the label **Total Interest** to cell D10, and widen the column so that all the text is visible.

4 Format cells D11:D17 as **Currency**, two decimal places.

In cell D11 you need to enter a formula that multiplies (**Payments** by **Term**), then subtracts (the **Loan Amount**).

The first **payment** figure is in cell C11, cell D6 represents the **term**, and cell D7 the **loan amount**.

5 Enter the following formula syntax in cell D11: **=(C11*$D$6)-$D$7**.

6 Copy the formula to cells D12:D17.

7 Use the Format Painter to blend new cells with your existing formatting.

8 Save your work.

You now have a data table that not only shows you your monthly payments, but also the total interest for the period.

3 – Two-input data tables

To get an overall picture of interest **and** term requires a two-input table using column and row input values, and one formula.

Task A

1 Select a new worksheet in the workbook **DataTable**, and enter the following labels in the cells indicated:

   a C2: **Computer Purchase Analysis**

   b C4: **Down Payment**

   c D4: **None**

   d C5: **Interest Rate**

   e C6: **Term(Months)**

   f C7: **Purchase Price**

Ensure that the entire label texts are visible in all cells.

2 Make the entry **2.05%** in cell D5. This cell is still the column input for your data table, but on this occasion it contains a value.

3 Enter the value **12** in cell D6. This will be the row input for your data table, and will also contain a value.

4 Enter the purchase price **2000** in cell D7.

5 **Enter: a** the following figures in cells B9:F9:

2.05%	4.00%	5.05%	9.00%	10.00%	12.50%

   b Enter these percentages in cells A10:A15:

6
12
24
36
48

6 Format cells A10:A15 as **percentage**, two decimal places.

Info

Cell A9 will contain the function that will carry out the calculation on the row and column input data.

a single formula needs to read a row and a column of data, and produce a result.

The formula is the same as the PMT function, but with an additional function called **ABS**, used to create a **nested** function.

For this task, the syntax for the PMT function used earlier, looks like this: **=PMT(D5/12,D6,-D7)**

The syntax for the nested function looks like this: **=ABS(PMT(D5/36,D5,D6))**

The **ABS** function differs from the PMT function because it is used to return the absolute value of a number, and belongs to the Math & Trig Function catalogue.

7 Enter the following function syntax in cell A9: **=ABS(PMT(D5/36,D5,D6))**

8 Highlight cells A9:F15 and create the data table using the following cells for the input to the data table:

   a **D6**: Row input

   b **D5**: Column input

9 Format cells B10:F15 as **currency**, two decimal places.

10 Use the Format Painter to format cell A9 as **currency**, two decimal places.

Task B – Formatting the spreadsheet

Method

1 Format cells as follows:

   a **B10:F15**: apply a border, with inside gridlines to cells.

   b **A10:A15**: fill colour – **light turquoise**

   c **B9:F9**: fill colour – **turquoise**

   d **A9**: fill colour – **pale blue**

   e **D5:D6**: fill colour – **pale blue**

   f **C2**: fill colour – **sky blue**

   g Cell range **A9:A15**: apply **left**, **top** and **bottom** borders.

   h **A9**: apply a **right** border.

   i Cell range **B9:F9**: apply a **top** and **right** border.

   j **A9**: centre the cell contents.

   k **A10:A15**: **left align** and **embolden** the cell contents.

   l **B9:F9**: **left align** and **embolden** the cell contents.

   m **C2:D7**: apply a **border**, with no inside gridlines to cells.

Note: have you saved your work recently? Remember to do this frequently.

Data tables

One-input tables

You can use many formulas and input values in a one-input table, but these must refer to the same input cell. (For reference, see Exercise 2.)

Two-input tables

A two-input table relies on one formula and is therefore not as flexible as the one-input table.

Two-input data tables – attention point for exams:

o If you see the following error message in the **formula cell** of a two-input data table, and the table still returns data, check the input cells – there needs to be data in both:

#DIV/0!

Interpretation:

a The formula was divided by zero (0); **b** Reference detected to a blank cell.

---

4 – Practice

The file below can be located on the accompanying CD-ROM.

Background to exercise

o You have borrowed **£150,000** to purchase a house (cell D2).

o The interest rate is **6.50%** (cell D1).

o How much **interest** will you have to pay at this **interest rate**? (cell D3)

Method

1 Open the workbook **DataTableNewHome**.

The **Home** worksheet in the workbook contains the basic outline to create a data table.

2 In cell D3 on the **Home** worksheet, enter the following Sum function syntax to calculate the interest: **=SUM(D2*D1)**

The answer in cell D3 should be **£9,750.00**

3 Re-enter the above function syntax in cell D6 on the **Home** worksheet.

The answer should be the same as in cell D3, i.e. **£9,750.00**

If the **interest rate** changes, how will this affect the interest you pay?

Info

You have **recreated** the function syntax in cell **D6**, to use in creating a data table to look at the variable **interest rates** in cells **C7:C18**.

Now create a data table from cells **C6:D18**, that will calculate relevant **interest** amounts for the **interest rates** in cells **C7:C18**.

Cell **D1** is the **column input cell**.

The results of the data table will be displayed in cells **D7:D18**. At a glance, you will be able to see how any change in **interest rates** affects the **interest** you will have to pay on the **£150,000** borrowed.

Explanation for calculation of the expected result

Cells **C7:C18** contain a variety of **interest rates**, to assess the answer to the question: If the **interest rate** changes how will this affect the **interest** you pay?

a Cell **D1** is the column input cell.

b Cells **D7:D18** will contain the **interest** that you will have to pay, at...

c The **interest rate**, in the corresponding cells **C7:C18**.

4 Save and review your work before moving to the next exercise.

EXERCISE

5 – Practice

Method

1 Open the workbook **DataTableQuestion**.

2 On the **Investment** worksheet, create a data table from cells C5:D21 that will calculate interest amounts for the interest variables in column C.

3 Save and close the workbook.

This concludes the section on data tables.

Save and review your work before moving to the next section.

In this section you have used and created data tables.

Protection Tasks

1.12

Applying a password to a worksheet

Introduction

Protecting your data

Having spent time and effort creating your spreadsheet and getting this to perform as required, your next step should be to think of **protection**.

Mistakes happen quite easily and are not always noticed at the time, so it is as well to be prepared.

Types of Protection

1 Low level protect:

- Protecting existing worksheet contents.
- Preventing new worksheets from being added.
- Preventing existing worksheets from being deleted.

2 Targeted protection:

- Protecting **specific** cells. Recreating data is easier than recreating a formula that may have taken a great deal of time and effort to develop in order to achieve the desired results.

3 Password protection:

- Control of: **a** access to the workbook and, **b** those authorised to make changes to worksheet contents.

4 A mixture of all three types of protection.

This is often necessary, and will depend on the working environment. For example:

- Are your files saved in a secure area? Can others gain access to these?
- Do others need to use the workbook?
- What type of changes do you want others to be able to make to the workbook?

In the following exercises you will learn how to apply various types of protection to meet the needs of different working environments.

EXERCISE *1 – How to protect worksheets*

Method

1 Select the worksheet.

2 On the **Tools** menu, point to **Protection**.

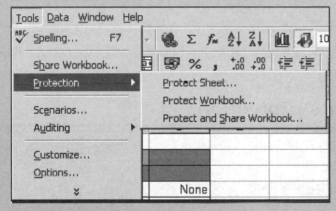

Figure 1.73 Protection menu

3 Click **Protect Sheet** on the sub-menu, to open the Protect Sheet window.

Figure 1.74 Protect Sheet window

When the window opens, all Protect Sheet options are selected by default.

Protect Sheet window options are:

Info

- **Contents**: This option refers to data in cells and to any charts saved in the worksheet.

- **Objects**: This option refers to any graphics in the worksheet, e.g. a chart or company logo.

- **Scenarios**: This option refers to any scenario created and saved as part of the workbook, to analyse data.

4 Deselect any options you do not want to protect. Entering a password is optional.

5 Click **OK** to close the window. (If you have not entered a password the protection steps will end here.)

If you have entered a password, the system will ask you to confirm the password entered.

6 Re-enter the password in the **Confirm Password** window.

Note: be sure to read the **Caution** message supplied by the system, and the advice given about keeping a separate record of passwords used, and that passwords are case-sensitive.

Figure 1.75 Confirm Password window

7 Click **OK** to close the window and apply the selected options.

All workbooks for the following exercises can be located on the accompanying CD-ROM.

EXERCISE *2 – Applying contents protection*

Method

1 Open the workbook **1_Protect**.

The workbook contains two worksheets, **DiscountQtr1** and **DiscountQtr2.**

Background

Worksheet **DiscountQtr1** contains the completed worksheet you use to track your savings in Quarter 1. You have made a copy of the spreadsheet on the **DiscountQtr2** worksheet so that you can update this when new purchases are made.

In order to prevent changes to the contents of the worksheet **DiscountQtr1**, you need to protect it.

If you are unable to complete a step in the following exercise, review the steps in Exercise 1 above.

Method

2 Apply the following protection to the **DiscountQtr1** worksheet:

   a Open the Protect Sheet window.
   b Deselect the **Objects** and **Scenarios** options.
   c Enter the password, **ProtectOne**.
   d Close the window.
   e Re-enter the password **ProtectOne** in the Confirm Password window.
   f Close the window to apply your options.
   g Save and close the workbook.

3 – Testing the applied contents protection

Method

1   Reopen the workbook **1_Protect**.

2   Delete the contents of cell F3 on the **DiscountQtr1** worksheet.

Attempting to delete the contents of a protected worksheet should produce the following error message:

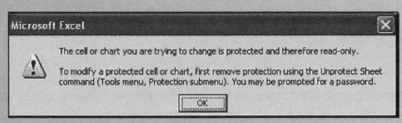

Figure 1.76 Example of Error message

3   Click **OK** to close the error message.

If you **do not receive** the error message, retrace your steps in protecting the worksheet. Protection has not been applied.

4   Close the workbook **1_Protect**.

4 – How to unprotect worksheets

Background

You have noticed a data entry error on the **DiscountQtr1** worksheet in cell B6. In order to amend this error you need to **unprotect** the worksheet to edit the contents of cell B6.

You included a password when protecting the **DiscountQtr1** worksheet. When you remove this you will be able to amend the data entry error in cell B6.

Method

1   Open the workbook 1_Protect and select the worksheet **DiscountQtr1**.

2   Point to **Protection** on the **Tools** menu.

3   Click **Unprotect Sheets** on the sub-menu. (If you have not entered a password, the unprotect steps will end here.)

If you have entered a password, the system will ask you to enter it in the Unprotect Sheet window, to remove protection.

Info

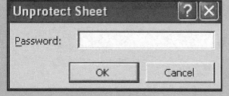

Figure 1.77 Unprotect Sheet window

4   Enter the password.

5   Click **OK** to close the Unprotect Sheet window. You will be returned to the spreadsheet where you can edit or enter data.

5 – *Practice*

Method

If you are unable to complete a step in the following exercise, review the steps in Exercise 5 above.

1 Unprotect the **DiscountQtr1** worksheet.

2 Enter the figure **18.75** in cell B6 on the worksheet.

3 Save the workbook.

6 – *Practice*

Method

1 Protect the contents of the **DiscountQtr1** worksheet, using the original password **ProtectOne**.

2 Save the workbook.

7 – *Testing the applied contents protection*

Method

1 Enter the following data in the **DiscountQtr2** worksheet, to ensure that other worksheets in the workbook **1_Protect** can receive data:

a
In cells B3:B8:

£45.99
£15.99
£9.79
£17.99
£63.50
£4.50

b
In cells C3:C8:

£72.50
£23.70
£14.62
£20.94
£90.85
£8.35

2 Save and close the workbook.

8 – *Protecting practice*

Method

1 Open the workbook **2_ProtectExpenses**.

2 Protect the contents of Sheet2 with the password **03112003**.

3 Save and close the workbook.

Task 1.12 Applying a password to a worksheet

9 – Unprotecting practice

Method

1 Open the workbook **3_UnprotectSales**.

2 Unprotect the **FirstQrt** worksheet (the password is **FirstQrt**).

3 Save the workbook.

4 In the workbook, attempt to delete data in cells, in the worksheets **SecondQrt**, **ThirdQrt** and **LastQrt**, to ensure that they are still protected.

5 **Close** the workbook.

10 – Protecting practice

Method

1 Open the workbook **4_NoPassword**.

2 Unprotect Sheet1 (the worksheet *is not* password protected).

3 Enter the label **Export** in Cell G1.

4 Protect Sheet1 (*do not* enter a password).

5 Save the changes to the workbook.

Review all your work in this section.

Close all workbooks that are open before moving to the next main task.

1.13

Applying a password to specific cells

If you have already completed the **Use data tables** section (Task 1.11), you will have created the workbook **DataTable** and you may want to use this now, or you can use the workbook **DataTableCells**. Both should contain the same data.

All workbooks for this section can be located on the accompanying CD-ROM.

Open the workbook **DataTable** or **DataTableCells**.

Evaluation of work already carried out in the workbook

The worksheet **OneInputTable** contains **labels** and **figures**, and one main **formula**. The percentage figures were entered by you and can be recreated quite easily. The labels are an indication of the type of data that needs to be entered, and where.

On the **OneInputTable** worksheet, the following cells would benefit from **Targeted Cell Protection**:

a **C11** – the PMT formula
b **D5** – the column input
c **C5** – the column input label (interest rate)
d **D6** – the term figure
e **C6** – the term (months) label

On the **OneInputCont** worksheet it would be advisable to protect the same cells as in the **OneInputTable** worksheet, with the addition of cell **D11**, the formula that calculates the Total Interest.

On the **TwoInputTable** worksheet, the following cells would also benefit from Targeted Cell Protection:

Cells **A9**, **D5**, **C5**, **D6** and **C6**.

Protecting cells

This operation is carried out in two parts, as you still need to be able to enter data in certain cells.

If you do not need to enter data in certain cells, then you could go straight to Task B.

EXERCISE **1 – Protecting designated cells**

The lists of cells above contain formulas and labels that you have decided to protect.

You may decide to change the **price** you are evaluating, the **percentages** figures and/or the **month** labels, so you need to ensure that these cells can still receive data entry at a later stage.

Before you begin, create a backup copy of the workbook and save the file as **DataTableBack**.

Task A – How to unprotect cells

Method

1 Highlight cells **A12** through **B17**, and **D7**, on the **OneInputTable** worksheet. These cells need to receive data entry and therefore need to be **unprotected** cells.

Info

To Highlight cells that are not in the same row or column, after clicking the first cell or range of cells with the mouse, hold down **Ctrl** on the keyboard while you click the remaining cell(s).

2 Click cells from the **Format** menu to open the **Format** cells window.

3 Click the **Protection** tab.

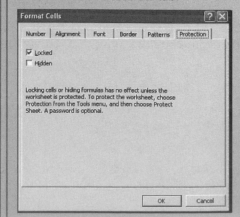

Figure 1.78 Format Cells window – Protection tab

When the **Format Cells** window opens, the **Locked** option will have a tick in the box. Removing the tick will unprotect the cells you have highlighted, and leave all other cells locked.

4 Click the **Locked** option tick-box to deselect this.

5 Click **OK** to close the Format Cells window.

6 Click anywhere on the spreadsheet outside the highlighted cells, to clear them.

Task B – Protecting the worksheets

1 Point to **Protection** on the **Tools** menu.

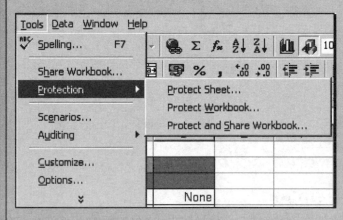

Figure 1.79 Accessing Protection

2 Click **Protect Sheets** on the sub-menu, to open the Protect Sheets window.

Figure 1.80 The Protect Sheets window

3 **Deselect** the **Objects** and **Scenarios** options (ensure that the **Contents** option is selected).

4 Enter the password **contents**, in lowercase text.

Figure 1.81 The completed Protect Sheets window

5 Click **OK** to close the window and to apply your options.

The system will ask you to confirm the password entered.

6 Re-enter the password **contents** in the Confirm Password window (Figure 1.82).

Figure 1.82 The Confirm Password window

Info

Note the Caution message supplied by the system and the advice given about keeping a separate record of passwords used, and that passwords are case-sensitive.

7 Click **OK** to close the window and to apply the selected option(s).

Office 2000 tip

To move between unlocked cells on a protected worksheet, click an unlocked cell, then press the **Tab** key on the keyboard.

2 – Testing the worksheet

Method

1 Check that the following cells **can** receive new data: **B12:B17**, **A12:A17**, and **D7**.

   a Click on each cell individually then press the **Delete** key (the data should be removed in the usual way).

   b **Undo** your changes and **Save** the file on each occasion.

2 Check that the following cells **cannot** receive new data: **C11**, **D5:C5**, and **D6:C6**. Click on cells individually then afterwards press **Delete** each time.

You should receive the following error message, telling you that the cells are protected.

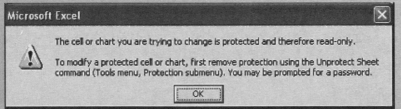

Figure 1.83 Error message

3 – Practice

Method

1 Apply the **protecting cells** procedure to sheets 2 and 3; you decide which cells to unprotect, if any. (Cell protection, and the reasons for it, was covered in Section 1.3.1.)

2 If you are happy with your results, save your work!

Review your work before moving to the next section.

Close the workbook.

4 – How to remove protection

To **unlock** cells you need to **unprotect** the worksheet.

Method

1 Point to **Protection** on the **Tools** menu.

2 Click **Unprotect Sheet** on the sub-menu, to open the **Unprotect Sheet** window.

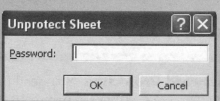

Figure 1.84 Unprotect Sheet window

3 Enter the **password** then click **OK** to close the window.

The worksheet will now be unprotected.

In the following exercises you will practice protecting and unprotecting cells in worksheets.

All steps to carry out the following exercises were covered in exercises 1 to 4. Review these as necessary.

5 – Practice

Method

1 Open the workbook **MyAccounts**.

The following cells on worksheet **Sheet1** can receive data entry:

  a **A1** through **E3**.

  b **B5** through **D11**.

  c **A4** and **A12**.

2 Unprotect worksheet **Sheet1** using the password **accounts**.

3 Change the **formatting** in cells **E4:E12** to **Currency**, two decimal places.

4 Unlock the following cells:

  a **A1** through **E3**.

  b **B5** through **D11**.

  c **A4** and **A12**.

5 **Protect** the worksheet, contents only, using the password **accounts**.

6 **Save** and close the workbook.

6 – Practice

Method

1 Open the workbook **Courses**.

2 **Protect** the **contents** of the following cells from data entry, with the password **simple**:

    a **B1:B2**.   b **D7:D12**.   c **B14:D14**.

3 **Save** and close the workbook.

1.14 Applying a password to a workbook

The highest level of protection is **Workbook Password Protection**. You need to know the password to gain access to the contents of the workbook. To apply password protection to a workbook you need to use the **Save As** command on the **File** menu.

The **DataTableCells** workbook you have been working with would benefit from password protection to control access, after you have added cell protection.

EXERCISE 1 – Adding password protection to the workbook

Method

1 **Open** the workbook **DataTableCells**.

2 Click **Save As** from the **File** menu to open the Save As window.

Figure 1.85 Save As window

3 Click **General Options** from the **Tools** menu to open the **Save Options** window.

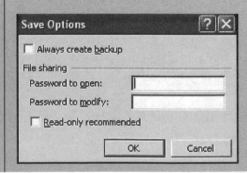

Figure 1.86 Save Options window

Save options explained

Always create backup

Creates a backup copy each time you save the workbook.

Password to open

You must know the password to access the contents of the workbook.

Password to modify

Password to open gives you access to the workbook, but **Password to modify** adds a further degree of protection; unless you know the password you will be unable to modify the contents of the workbook once it is open.

Read-only recommended

Opens a workbook as read-only. This means that users have to save the workbook by a new name if they want to make changes to its contents.

Note: passwords can have a maximum of fifteen characters, can include letters and numbers, and are case sensitive.

To the system, **PASSWORD**, **password** and **Password** are three different passwords. If you forget the password you have used, you will not be able to gain access to the workbook. Keep a separate record of passwords used.

4   In the **Password to open** option (Figure 1.87), enter **system** as the password. This will prevent the file from being opened unless the user knows the password:

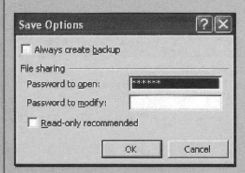

Figure 1.87 Password Save Options

5   Click **OK**.

6   When prompted to confirm the password (Figure 1.88), enter the password **system** again. Remember, passwords are case sensitive.

Figure 1.88 Confirm Password window

7   Click **OK** to close the Confirm Password window (you will be returned to the Save As dialogue window).

8 Click **Save**.

As the file already exists, a system prompt (Figure 1.89) will check that you want to overwrite the existing file.

Figure 1.89 System prompt message

9 Click on **Yes**, to replace the original file (the workbook will remain open on screen).

2 – Test the password protection you have applied

Method

1 Close and reopen the workbook **DataTableCells**.

You will be presented with the **Password** window (Figure 1.90).

Figure 1.90

2 Enter the password **system** and select **OK** to close the **Password** window, and to open the **DataTableCells** workbook.

3 Close the workbook.

All workbooks for this section can be located on the accompanying CD-ROM.

3 – Modify password

You want to manage the process of who can **modify** the contents of the **Accounts** workbook.

Method

1 Add the password **AccessControl** to the **Accounts** workbook using the **Save** option, **Password to Modify**.

2 Close and then reopen the workbook.

When the **Accounts** workbook is reopened you will be presented with the following password window:

Info

If the user does not know the password they will only be able to open the workbook in read-only mode.

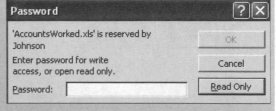

Figure 1.91 Password window

3 Open the workbook in read-only mode.

4 Close the workbook.

4 – Practice

You want to manage the process of who can **open** or **modify** the contents of the **MyCourse** workbook.

Method

1. Add the passwords **FullControl** and **MyKey** to the MyCourse workbook, using the **Save** options **Password to Open** and **Password to Modify** respectively.

2. Save and close the workbook.

3. Open the workbook and test the password options you have applied.

4. Close the workbook.

1.15 Removing a password from a workbook

Method

1. **Open** the workbook using the password(s).
2. Click **Save As** from the File menu.
3. In the Save As window, click **General Options** from the **Tools** menu.
4. In the Save Options window, **Delete** the password(s) entered.
5. Select **OK** to close the Password window.
6. **Save** the file.
7. When prompted to overwrite existing file, select **Yes**.

Do the steps to remove password protection seem familiar? They should be. The steps are very similar to the sequence for adding a password.

All workbooks for this section can be located on the accompanying CD-ROM.

EXERCISE 2 – Practice

Method

1. Remove the password **AccessControl** from the **AccountsWorked** workbook.
2. **Save** and close the workbook.

EXERCISE 3 – Practice

Method

1. Remove the passwords **FullControl** and **MyKey** from the **MyCourseWorked** workbook.
2. **Save** and close the workbook.

Save and review your work before moving to the next section.

Section 2: Data handling

2.1 Sorting data by columns

Lists in a spreadsheet need to be created in organised columns and rows if you want to use the **Sort Menu** option to organise the existing data in the list.

Organised spreadsheet list:

	A	B	C	D	E
1	Name	Surname	Dept	Section	Ext
2	Fizal	Ali	Administration	Bookings	1194
3	Nellie	Allie	Marketing	Promotions	1051

- The **headers row** for this list is in columns A:E or cells A1:E1.
- The organised **data** in cells A2:E3 matches column headers in cells A1:E1.

Unorganised spreadsheet list:

	A	B	C	D	E
1	Name	Surname	Dept or Section	Section or Ext	Ext
2	Fizal Ali		Administration	Bookings	1194
3	Nellie	Allie	Marketing Promotions	1051	

- The **headers row** for this list is in columns A:E or cells A1:E1.
- The unorganised **data** in cells A2:E3 does not match the column headers in cells A1:E1.
- Data in rows 2 and 3 has been placed in columns where it would be difficult to find this in a large spreadsheet.

Using the sort ascending or descending standard toolbar buttons options

If you only have **one** or **two columns** of data in the list that you want to sort and these *do not* have **header rows** you can use the Sort **Ascending** or **Descending** Standard **Toolbar Buttons** to perform a basic sort of the data.

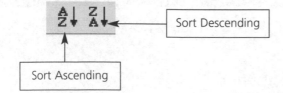

Sort Descending

Sort Ascending

Figure 2.1 Sort Ascending or Descending standard toolbar buttons

1 – Sorting data practice

Method

1. Open your spreadsheet application and enter the following data:

   Row 1 should contain the **labels** in **cells A1 and B1**.

2. **Click** cell A1.

3. **Click** the **Sort Ascending** toolbar button to perform a basic sort of the data in the worksheet, based on the contents of **column A,** the selected column.

NameF	NameS
Sonya	Patel
Samira	Choudry
Khurram	Carter
Kaya	Ballaster
Pascal	Azar
Nellie	Allie

The system did not detect the **labels** in **row one**. These were sorted with the data in **Cells A2:B7** and are now displayed in **row three**.

Open the workbook **BasicSortPractice**. All files for this section can be located on the accompanying CD-ROM.

The **BasicSortPractice** workbook contains three worksheets to help you further understanding using **lists** in a worksheet to sort data.

2 – Sort Ascending practice

Method

1. **Click cell A1**.

2. **Click** the **Sort Ascending** toolbar button to perform a basic sort of the data in the worksheet based on the contents of **column A** the selected column.

3 – Sort Ascending practice

Method

Select the **NoLabels** worksheet:

- Row 1 should contain the following data in cells A1 and B1: Samira Choudry.

- Row 7 should contain the following data in Cells A7 and B7: Khurram Carter.

1. Click cell A1.

2. Click the **Sort Ascending** toolbar button to perform a basic sort of the data in the worksheet based on the contents of **column A** the selected column.

Your results should be:

- **Fizal Ali** first entry in the sorted list cells A1:B1.

- **Sonya Patel** last entry in the sorted list cells A7:B7.

The data has been sorted based on the contents of column A as cell A1 was selected before you **click** the Sort **Ascending** toolbar button.

3 – Sort unorganised data practice

Method

Select the **Unorganised** worksheet.

1 Click cell A1.

2 Click the **Sort Ascending** toolbar button to perform a basic sort of the data in the worksheet based on the contents of **column A** the selected column.

The system will detect that row one contains labels as these were used in exercise two and these will not be sorted with the data.

3 Click the **Sort Descending** toolbar button.

Again the labels are not sorted with the list in cells A2:E3.

As the list is unorganised no amount of sorting, if this was a large list, would find data that you could trust to be accurate.

4 – Sort organised data practice

Method

Select the **Organised** worksheet.

1 **Click cell A1**.

2 Click the **Sort Ascending** toolbar button to perform a basic sort of the data in the worksheet based on the contents of column A the selected column.

Your results should be:

- Fizal Ali.
- Sonya Ashton.

As this list is organised you can use the **Sort Menu** option to organise the existing data in the list by the column labels to produce specific results.

3 Save and review your work before moving to the next section.

4 Close the workbook.

5 – Sort data using Data menu

In this exercise you will practice using the **Sort** command from the **Data** menu.

You can **sort** a list by a maximum of 3 columns in the basic window.

To sort a list of data by a column label such as **Surnames** into alphabetical order in a spreadsheet.

Method

1 Select a cell within the list of data.

2 Click **Sort** from the **Data** menu.

If you do not select a cell in the list before clicking **Sort** you will see the following error message:

Figure 2.2 Sort Error message

Click **OK** to close the message and select a cell within the list *before* clicking **Sort** on the **Data** menu.

Task 2.1 Sorting data by columns

The Sort window

When the Sort window opens:

- If a list has a **header row** and this has not been detected by the system.
  Click the **header row** option button.

- If a list has no header row, the list can be sorted by using the default column header
  reference e.g. column A.

- When you click the black arrowhead next to **Sort by** or **Then by** criteria options, a
  dropdown list of column header or the default column header is available in the
  dropdown list box.

Figure 2.3 Sort window view – A

Figure 2.4 Sort window view – B

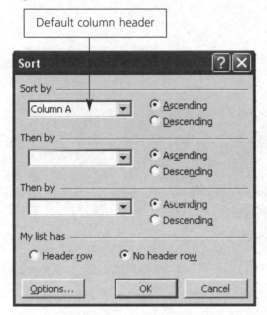

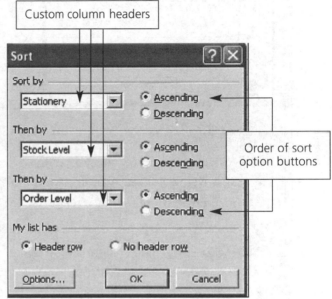

By default, data is sorted in **ascending** order e.g. (**A to Z**) or (**1 to 10**).

Clicking the **descending** option button will sort a list by in reverse order (**Z to A**) or (**10 to 1**).

When you have selected your criteria and order of sort, click **OK** to close the **Sort** window to apply your sort option criteria to the list.

EXERCISE | *6 – Sort by different criteria*

Open the workbook **StaffSort**.

The spreadsheet you are working with covers cells A1:K40 of the worksheet **StaffDetails** and is sorted by the **Surname** column.

You want to group staff by department.

Method

1 Sort the **StaffDetails** worksheet using the following criteria:

- The **Sort by** criteria is **Department**.
- The **Then by** criteria is **Section**.
- The **Then by** criteria is **Supervisor Title**.

Figure 2.5 Completed Sort window

2 Click **OK** to accept the default **Sort Ascending** option and close the window.

Your results should be:

- **307, Kellie Baxter, Administration**, first entry in sorted list.
- **334, Edward Evans, Sales**, last entry in sorted list.

3 **Re-sort** the StaffDetails worksheet by **Personnel No**. using the following criteria:

- The **Sort by** criteria is **Personnel No**.
- The **Then by** criteria is **None**.
- The **Then by** criteria is **None**.

Click **OK** to accept the default **Sort Ascending** option and close the window.

Your results should be:

- **300, Nellie Allie** first entry in sorted list.
- **335, Kia Kyron** last entry in sorted list.

7 – Re-sort data in columns

Task A – Hide columns

Hide columns **A; D; E; F; H; I; J; K**.

Method

1 **Re-sort** the **StaffDetails** worksheet by **Supervisor Title**, using the following criteria:

- The **Sort by** criteria is **Supervisor Title**.
- The **Then by** criteria is **None**.
- The **Then by** criteria is **None**.

Click **OK** to apply the sort and close the Sort window.

Your results should be:

- **Kellie Baxter,** first entry in sorted list.
- **Nisha Patel,** last entry in sorted list.

Task B – Unhide all columns

1 **Re-sort** the **StaffDetails** worksheet by **Personnel No**. using the following criteria:

   o The **Sort by** criteria is **Personnel No**.

   o The **Then by** criteria is **None**.

   o The **Then by** criteria is **None**.

2 Save the workbook.

---

8 – Sort data by multiple columns

To sort the data on StaffDetails worksheet by:

Personnel No.; **Surname**; **Section**; **Department**.

The **least important** column in the sort order is **Surname**.

If you need to sort data by more than three columns you will need to undertake the sort process in two stages.

Task A

Sort the list *first* by **the least important column**.

1 **Sort** the **StaffDetails** worksheet by **Surname** using the following criteria:

   o The **Sort by** criteria is **Surname**.

   o The **Then by** criteria is **None**.

   o The **Then by** criteria is **None**.

2 Click **OK** to accept the default **Sort Ascending** option and close the window.

The **most important** column in the sort order is **Personnel No**.

Task B

1 Sort the list *second* by **the most important column**.

   Re-sort the **StaffDetails** worksheet by **Personnel No**. using the following criteria:

   o The **Sort by** criteria is **Personnel No**.

   o The **Then by** criteria is **Section**.

   o The **Then by** criteria is **Department**.

2 Click **OK** to apply the sort and to close the Sort window.

Note: to sort data by multiple columns you need to prioritise your data and then create the sort in stages. More than 4 columns would need more than two sort stages. You will need to identify what is important at each stage and then include this as the **Sort By** option of stage two of your sort.

3 **Re-sort** the **StaffDetails** worksheet by **Personnel No**. using the following criteria:

   o The **Sort by** criteria is **Personnel No**.

   o The **Then by** criteria is **Section**.

   o The **Then by** criteria is **Department**.

4 Click **OK** to apply the sort and close the Sort window.

5 Save and close the workbook.

9 – Practice

Method

1 Open the workbook **Brandy**.

This workbook records the various types of brandy stocked by **Johnny's Outlet**. You have been asked to use the workbook to produce various lists for the business.

You need to create a **price list** of the types of brandy **Johnny's Outlet** has for sale.

2 **Sort** the list on **Sheet1** of the **Brandy** workbook using the following criteria:

- The **Sort by** criteria is **Price**.
- The **Then by** criteria is **Brandy Name**.
- The **Then by** criteria is **Size**.

Your results should be:

- **Cos U Visier, £8.99**, first entry in sorted list
- **Jean, £85.93**, last entry in sorted list.

3 **Hide** the following columns to create the **price** list: columns B; D; F.

4 **Rename Sheet1** as **PriceList**.

5 Apply the font style bold to cells C3:C24.

10 – Practice

Johnny's Outlet staff are often asked where a particular brand **originates** from and they have to spend time looking this up. In this task you will create a list to assist staff with this question.

Method

1 Sort the list on **Sheet2** of the **Brandy** workbook using the following criteria to create an alphabetical list of producers:

- The **Sort by** criteria is **Producer**.
- The **Then by** criteria is **Brandy Name**.
- The **Then by** criteria is **Size**.

Your results should be:

- **The Pomona, England**, first entry in sorted list.
- **Bulls Light, Spanish**, last entry in sorted list.

2 **Hide** the following columns to create the **producers** list: columns B; C; F.

3 **Rename Sheet2** as **Producers**.

4 Apply the font style bold to cells D3:D24.

11 – Practice

In general the types of brandy stocked in **Johnny's Outlet** are **40% Vol**. They have recently started to stock a variety of brandies of different **Vol**. In order to promote these create the following:

Method

1 Sort the list on **Sheet3** of the **Brandy** workbook using the following criteria to create a **descending** list of **Vol**:

- The **Sort by** criteria is **Vol. (descending)**.
- The **Then by** criteria is **Age (descending)**.
- The **Then by** criteria is **Brandy Name**.

Your results should be:

- **Fruit Brandy, Plum, 45%, Age 4**, first entry in sorted list
- **Red Passion, 16%, Age 6**, last entry in sorted list.

2 **Hide** the following columns to create the **Vol.** list: columns C; D; E.

3 Rename **Sheet3** as **Vol**.

4 Apply the font style bold to cells F3:F24.

12 – Practice

Johnny's Outlet want to promote some of the aged, old brandy that they have in stock.

Method

1 Sort the list on **Sheet4** of the **Brandy** workbook using the following criteria: **Size, Brandy Name, Age, Vol**.

2 The **least important** column in the sort order is **Brandy Name**. Use the following criteria to sort the data:

- The **Sort by** criteria is **Brandy Name**.
- The **Then by** criteria is **None**.
- The **Then by** criteria is **None**.

Your results should be:

- **Amphora**, first entry in sorted list.
- **Uralt**, last entry in sorted list.

3 The **most important** column in the sort order is **Age**. Use the following criteria to sort the data:

- The **Sort by** criteria is **Age**.
- The **Then by** criteria is **Vol**.
- The **Then by** criteria is **Size**.

Your results should be:

- **Prune**, first entry in sorted list.
- **Greek 7 stars**, last entry in sorted list.

4 Rename **Sheet4** as **Age**.

5 Apply the font style bold to cells B3:B24.

6 Save and review your work before moving to the next sorting section.

13 – Practice

Open the workbook **MultiSort**.

The workbook contains details of various Microsoft courses that staff can book. The **Course Title** column currently sorts the data contained in all worksheets. The spreadsheet you will be working with covers cell A1:D14 of all worksheets.

You will sort the data and hide columns, and or rows, to present various views for the Training Manager:

Task A – Courses mapped to the internal certification program

Method

1 **Sort** the list on **Sheet1** of the **MultiSort** workbook using the following criteria:

   Mapped to Certification Program?, Course Title, Booking Number and **Index No**.

2 The **least important** column in the sort order is **Index No**. Use the following criteria to sort the data:

   o The **Sort by** criteria is **Index No**.

   o The **Then by** criteria is **None**.

   o The **Then by** criteria is **None**.

   Your results will be:

   o **1**, first entry in sorted list.

   o **18**, last entry in sorted list.

3 The **most important** column in the sort order is **Mapped to Certification Program?** Use the following criteria to sort the data:

   o The **Sort by** criteria is **Mapped to Certification Program?**

   o The **Then by** criteria is **Course Title**.

   o The **Then by** criteria is **Booking Number**.

   Your results should be:

   o **Index No 11**, first entry in sorted list.

   o **Index No 10**, last entry in sorted list.

4 **Hide** the following columns/rows to create the **Mapped** list:

   o Columns E; F; G.

   o Rows 15 through 20.

   o Rename **Sheet1** as **Mapped**.

14 – Practice

Task B – Courses awaiting allocation of exam number view

Method

1 Sort the list on **Sheet2** of the **MultiSort** workbook using the following criteria: **Booking Number, Exam Number, Software Version Covered** and **Course Description**.

2 The **least important** column in the sort order is **Course Description**. Use the following criteria to sort the data.

- The **Sort by** criteria is **Course Description**.
- The **Then by** criteria is **None**.
- The **Then by** criteria is **None**.

Your results will be:

- **11**, first entry in sorted list.
- **3**, last entry in sorted list.

3 The **most important** column in the sort order is **Exam Number**. Use the following criteria to sort the data:

- The **Sort by** criteria is **Exam Number**.
- The **Then by** criteria is **Booking Number**.
- The **Then by** criteria is **Software Version Covered**.

Your results should be:

- **Index No 1**, first entry in sorted list.
- **Index No 10**, last entry in sorted list.

4 **Hide** the following columns/rows to create the **Mapped** list:

- Columns A; C; G.
- Rows 2 to 14 inclusive.
- Rename **Sheet2** as **NeedExamNumber**.

Task C – Courses awaiting a course description view

Method

1 Sort the list on **Sheet3** of the **MultiSort** workbook using the following criteria: **Course Description**, **Software Version Covered**, **Course Title** and **Mapped to Certification Program?**

2 The **least important** column in the sort order is **Mapped to Certification Program?** Sort the data by the **Mapped to Certification Program?** column.

Your results will be:

- **11**, first entry in sorted list.
- **10**, last entry in sorted list.

3 The **most important** column in the sort order is **Course Description**. Sort the data by the following criteria:

- **Course Description**.
- **Software Version Covered**.
- **Course Title**.

Your results should be:

- **Index No 11**, first entry in sorted list.
- **Index No 3**, last entry in sorted list.

4 **Hide** the following columns/rows to create the **Description** list:

- Columns C; D; E.
- Rows 8 through 20.

5 Rename **Sheet3** as **Description**.

Save and review your work before moving to the next section.

To facilitate sorting data by multiple columns you have also looked at the makeup up of a list necessary to use the **Sort window**, used **basic sorting** facilities, and hidden columns and rows to present your completed list for use.

Sheet4 in the workbook contains a copy of the data you have been working with that you can use to practice the task item **Sort data by multiple columns** for experiential learning.

2.2   Custom sorting data

In this section you will cover the following custom sort topics:

- Fill Handle
- Fill Series
- **Months** and **Days Series**
- Create and use a custom list
- Use an existing custom list.

Info

The Fill Handle

You have probably used the **Fill Handle** in your spreadsheet application to copy data such as **text**, **numbers** and **formulas** between adjacent spreadsheet cells. The **Fill Handle** can also be used for entering known **series**.

Months and days series

The **Month** and **Day** lists series usually come as part of a spreadsheet package.

If a **month** of the year or a **day** of the week is entered, the Fill handle can be used to automatically enter the rest of the series that has been saved in a custom list.

EXERCISE

1 – Sort using the Fill Handle

Method

1 **Open** a new workbook.

2 In **Cell A2** enter the label **March**.

3 Position your mouse on the bottom right corner of the cell containing the label **March** to access the Fill Handle.

Figure 2.6 Accessing the Fill Handle

The mouse pointer will change shape and become a **small black cross** ┼ . This cursor pointer is know as **Precision Select**.

4 Use the mouse pointer to drag the **Fill Handle** down **five** cells to fill in the **series April** to **September** down a single column in the worksheet. This procedure is called using the Fill Handle.

The **Fill Handle** could also been used to drag across **five** cells to fill in the series April to September across a row in the worksheet.

While you are dragging observe each month appearing on the right of the cells.

Figure 2.7 Using the Fill Handle

When you release the mouse, cells A2:A8 will contain all the months from March through to September.

5 Enter the label **Monday** in cell B1 on your worksheet, then use the **Fill Handle**, to complete the series of **days** in row 1.

6 Enter the label **Monday** as shown in cell B2 of your worksheet, then use the **Fill Handle**, to complete the series of **days** in row 2.

Note how the **Fill Handle** copies the text case-format that you have entered.

Figure 2.8 Case-format retained

	A	B	C	D	E
1	Monday				
2				Friday	
3					

Figure 2.9 Case-format not retained

	A	B	C	D	E
1	Monday	Tuesday	Wednesda	Thursday	Friday
2	monday				
3					
4				friday	

If a **series** has been saved in a custom list, the **Fill Handle** will fill the known series, and is *not case sensitive* as demonstrated here; the **Fill Handle** will copy the original format entered.

7 **Close** the workbook without saving your changes.

EXERCISE

2 – Applying a custom sort

Method

1 Open the workbook **StaffCustomSort**. All files for this section can be located on the accompanying CD-ROM.

2 **Unhide** the worksheet **StaffLeaveCalc**.

You have created the worksheet **StaffLeaveCalc** to track the start period of leave for staff in your section and need to group months together.

Each time you sort the list by the **Start Month**, column (See LH column below), the list is sorted and presented in alphabetical order like Example Two (right).

What you need here is a **Custom Sort** to resolve the default alphabetical ascending order of the spreadsheet application.

Example One	Example Two
START MONTH	START MONTH
January	April
February	August
March	December
April	February
May	January
June	July
July	June
August	March
September	May
October	November
November	October
December	September

Sorting data

Before you apply a custom sort you should sort the data to group the same months together.

3 Select cell A4 and **open** the **Sort** window.

4 Select the **Sort by** criteria **START MONTH**.

5 Click the **Options** button to open the **Sort Options** window.

Figure 2.10 Sort window

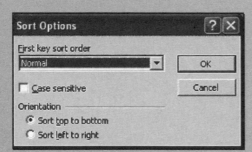

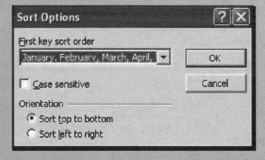

Figure 2.11 Sort Options window

The options selected when the window opens are:

o First key sort order is **Normal** by default.
o Orientation is **Sort top to bottom** by default.

You need to change the First Key sort order option to instruct the system to sort in month order and not the default alphabetical order.

6 Click the black down arrow to the right of the **first key** box and select the **sort order** that displays the months of the year, in chronological order and the first letter capitalised (Figure 2.12).

Figure 2.12 Change First key sort order

7 Accept all other default options by clicking the **OK** button to confirm your sort options and to close the Sort Options window.

8 Click **OK** to close the Sort window.

The column **START MONTH** is now sorted chronologically by month ascending.

	A	B	C	D	E
1			STAFF DETAILS		
2					
3					
4	PERSONNEL No.	START MONTH	KNOW AS	SURNAME	DEPARTMENT
5	300	January	Nellie	Allie	Marketing
6	301	February	Khurram	Allie	Sales
7	317	February	Lana	Haffenden	Administration
8	319	February	Marie	Doreau	Administration
9	329	February	Marcel	Bogle	Administration
10	302	March	Sonya	Ashton	Finance
11	318	March	Alyson	Blanc	Sales
12	320	March	Angie	Coker	Finance
13	331	March	Colin	Cranford	Sales
14	332	March	Akida	Simba	Administration
15	333	March	Crystal	Williams	Finance
16	334	March	Edward	Evans	Sales
17	306	April	Ernie	Barnes	Finance

Figure 2.13 New First key sort order

9 Save and review your work before moving to the next section where you create your own **Custom List** that will then be available to use for **Custom Sorts** and automatic **Fill Series** features of spreadsheets.

10 Close the workbook.

3 – Accessing existing custom lists

Method

1 Open your spreadsheet application.

2 Select **Options** on the **Tools** menu.

3 Select the **Custom Lists tab**.

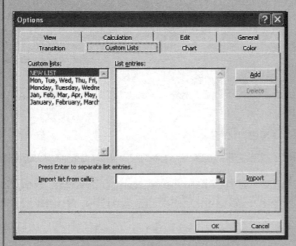

Figure 2.14 Options window – Custom Lists tab

The section **Custom Lists** displays the current lists available for use with the Fill Handle; you used the day list in exercise 1 and the month list in Exercise 2.

4 Close the **Options** window by clicking **OK**.

4 – Accessing and using fill series

Info

When a series has been created, the series exist in the same way as a macro you have created. The series is available for use if you know they exist and how to access them with the **Fill Handle**.

The **Fill Series** exists for **series** that have not been created and stored as part of your spreadsheet package or for a custom series you want to apply at that time.

To enter a Fill Series using the right mouse button, i.e. button, enter the first series, e.g. 4.

Method

1 Using the right mouse button drag down to cover the number of cells you want to fill, release the mouse button and from the pop-up menu click **Fill Series**.

Info

If you enter a random figure the system will fill these in logically, e.g. if you enter **4** and drag over 5 cells the numbers filled in will fill 5 to 9.

2 Enter the number **25** in cell A1.

3 Using the right mouse button, drag down to cover cells A2:A17 then release the right mouse button.

Figure 2.15 Fill Series

4 Click **Fill Series**.

The series should fill the numbers **26** to **41**.

5 **Close** the workbook without saving your changes.

5 – Create a custom list (series)

The organisation you are currently working for has four sales teams: **North, South, East** and **West**. The sales Teams are always referenced in the order (**series**) **North, South, East and West**.

Data for each team is entered regularly, as referenced. It would be useful to be able to key in **North** and then use the **Fill Handle** to fill in the rest of the series.

When a **Custom List** is created, the list is available for **Custom Sorts** and the automatic **Fill Series** features of spreadsheets.

In this exercise a Custom List is created for the sales teams, represented by **North**, **South**, **East** and **West**.

Method

1 **Open** a new workbook and enter the following **data** in cells A1:D1.

| North | South | East | West |

2 Select **Options** on the **Tools** menu.

3 Select the **Custom Lists** tab. On the custom lists tab you have two options for entering new lists:

Info

Option 1
Import the list directly from entries in cells via the **Import list from cells** text box. You can enter the cell address directly via the keyboard, or use the collapse window icon to minimize the Options window and use the mouse to select the cells.

Option 2
Enter the list via the keyboard in the List Entries text box (ensure that the spacebar is used to separate list entries), then click **Add** to add the new list to the **Custom lists** section.

Using option 1, the collapse icon method, will give you an opportunity to see how the cell references are written for future reference, if you decide to create a Custom List at a later stage manually via the keyboard.

4 Collapse the Options window and use the mouse to select cells A1:D1.

Figure 2.16 Collapse window

5 Maximise the window.

Info

When cells are selected using the collapse icon method with the mouse pointer, the cell reference is shown as an absolute reference.

Example cell reference: **$A$1:$D$1**.

6 Click the **Import** button.

Info

The list will be imported from the cells and become a custom list.

The entries in the new custom list will be displayed in the Custom List and List entries sections of the **Options** window.

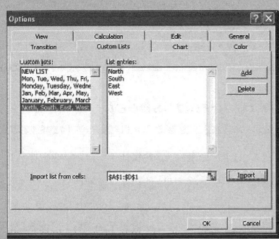

Figure 2.17 Options window with new Custom List

7 Click **OK** to close the window.

8 Open the Options window to check your new entries.

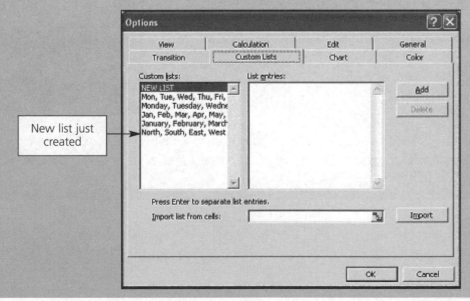

New list just created

Figure 2.18
Checking new List
Options

9 Test out your new list. Enter North in any cell, using the AutoFill Handle to fill the series with South, East and West. Is the list you have just created also available for sort options?

10 Open the Sort window.

11 Click the Options button.

12 Click the black down arrow to display the options available for the first key sort order.

13 Your new list should be displayed.

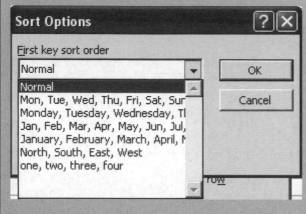

Figure 2.19 Sort Options window

13 Click Cancel to close the Sort Options window.

14 Close the Sort window.

15 Save and close the workbook.

6 – Apply a custom list to a spreadsheet

In this exercise you will use the custom list you have just created.

Method

1 **Open** the workbook **NewCustomSort** and select **Sheet1**.

2 Select cell A3 and open the **Sort** window.

3 Select the **Sort by** criterion **Team**.

4 Click the **Sort** options button.

5 Select the (new) **First key sort order** North, South, East and West.

6 Close the **Sort Options** and **Sort** windows.

Column B of the worksheet will now be sorted by the name of the team.

Figure 2.20 Spreadsheet with new Custom List applied

Year	Team	Figure
2000	North	800
2001	North	1500
2002	North	2500
2000	South	300
2001	South	1000
2002	South	200
2000	East	500
2001	East	2000
2002	East	100
2000	West	600
2001	West	2000
2002	West	700

Info

Creating your own custom lists can give you more flexibility using a workbook.

7 **Save** and close the workbook.

Method

1 Open the workbook **StaffCustomSort**.

2 Select the **PubSales** worksheet.

3 Select cell A3 and open the **Sort** window. Select the following criterion as **Sort by Day**.

4 Open the **Sort Options** window.

5 Change the **First key sort order** to the **sort order** that displays the days of the week, in chronological order, first letter capitalised (Figure 2.21).

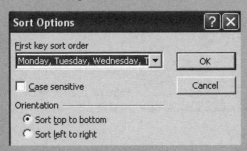

Figure 2.21 Days of the week Sort Options window

6 Click **OK** to accept all other default options and to close the window.

7 Close the Sort window.

Column B of the worksheet will now be sorted in chronological order by the days of the week.

Active window object – A

Question Which object in the Options window is the active object?

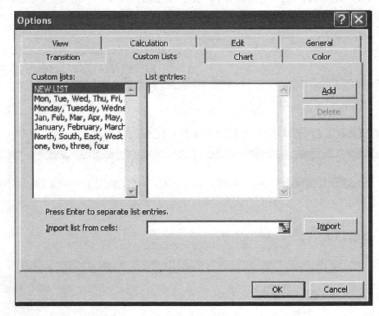

Figure 2.22 Active window object – A

Answer: **List entries** list box.

Question: Why?

Answer: a Text message **Press Enter to separate list entries visible**.
b I Beam cursor flashing in List entries list box.

Active window object – B

Question: Which **object** in the Options window is the **active** object?

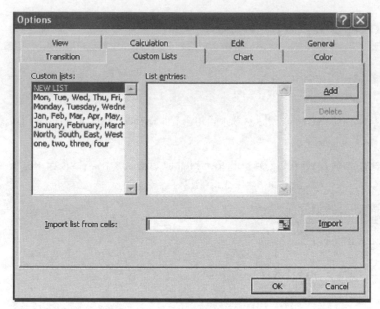

Figure 2.22a Active window object – B

Answer: Import list form cells text box.

Question: Why?

Answer   **a** Press enter to separate **list entries** text message not visible.

             b I Beam Cursor flashing in **Import list from cells** text box.

As well as custom sorting data, you have also used the task item **unhide worksheets**.

To facilitate performing custom sorts you have created and used a custom list.

> *Querying/Filtering Tasks*

2.3   *Filtering data to produce a query*

Open the workbook **StaffFiltering**. All workbooks for this section can be located on the accompanying CD-ROM.

EXERCISE   *1 – To filter data in a list*

Method

1   Select cell A4 from within the list.

2   Point to **Filter** on the **Data** menu.

3   Click **AutoFilter** on the sub-menu.

Info

AutoFilter arrows will attach to each column label.

PERSONNEL No. ▾	KNOW AS ▾	SURNAM ▾	DEPARTMENT ▾	SECTION ▾
301 Khurram	Allie	Sales	New Business
305 Kaya	Ballaster	Sales	New Business

Figure 2.23 List with AutoFilter arrows displayed

4 Click an arrow to display the list contents for an individual column.

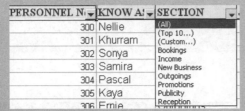

Figure 2.24 Column displayed

5 To **Filter** the list, select the item New Business by clicking on it.

Your list will then filter your selection, and only data that meets the filter criteria will be visible on screen.

EXERCISE

2 – Removing an AutoFilter

When a column is the active column the AutoFilter arrow changes colour on screen to indicate this.

Active column **Ext No.**

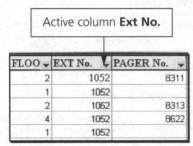

Figure 2.25 The active column

Info

To display all records in a filtered list you can use one of 2 methods:

1 Point to **Filter** on the **Data** menu, click and Show All from the sub-menu.

2 Click the **AutoFilter** arrow of the column used as the filter, then select **All** from the dropdown list.

Either action will redisplay all the data on the worksheet.

Method

1 Display all records on **StaffDetails** worksheet.

2 Select a cell within the list.

3 **Point** to **Filter** on the **Data** Menu.

4 Click **AutoFilter** on the sub-menu, to remove the AutoFilter arrows.

Figure 2.26 AutoFilter deselected   Figure 2.27 AutoFilter selected

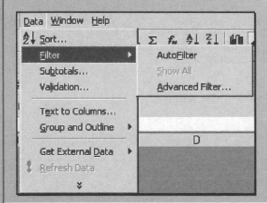

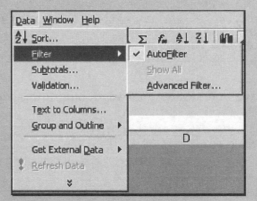

The AutoFilter arrows attached to each column label will be removed.

- Select **cell A1**.
- Remove **AutoFilter**.

3 – Basic filtering

Task A

Method

Two members of staff have been allocated the wrong extension number on the **StaffDetails** worksheet.

1 Select cell A4 and apply AutoFilter.

2 Filter the list by **Ext No 1052**.

3 Change the old extension numbers for the members of staff listed below to the new extension number:

Personnel No.	Surname	Old Ext No.	New Ext No.
331	Cranford	1052	**1072**
305	Ballaster	1052	**1071**

4 Remove the **Ext No**. filter.

Task B

Method

Filter the list by the **Section** Income.

Question: Who are the three people who work in the **Income Section**?

Answer: **Sonya Ashton, Angie Coker** and **Steve Coxford**.

1 Remove the **Section** Filter.

Task C

Method

Filter the list by Trade Union (**Y**).

Question: How many members of staff have declared that they are members of a trade union and work in the Bookings section?

1 Click the AutoFilter arrow on the **Section** column and select **Bookings** from the options presented.

2 Click the AutoFilter arrow on the **Trade Union** column and select **Y** from the options presented.

Solution: Remove the filter from the **Section** and **Trade Union** columns.

Save and review your work before moving to the next section.

4 – Create a single or multiple criteria query

Open the workbook **QueryDatabase**.

In this task you will use a **Data Form** to look at and query data in a spreadsheet.

Info

You can use a Data Form to scroll through the data contained in a spreadsheet. The following explores this option:

1 Select cell A4.

When you select a cell within the list this tells the Data Form the boundaries of the data on the spreadsheet.

2 Click **Form** from the **Data** menu.

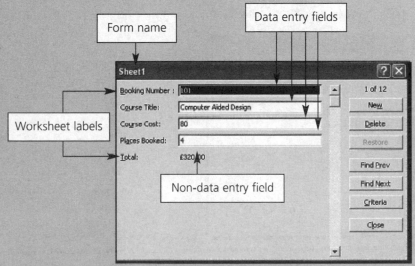

Figure 2.28 Data Form

The Data Form has picked up many characteristics from the spreadsheet, for example:

o The **Form Name** is **Sheet1**, taken from the worksheet where the data is stored.

o The **range** of the **labels** in the spreadsheet; it has used these to identify each **column** on the form.

o The **cells** that should be used for **data and non-data entry**; it has presented these accordingly in the Data Form.

3 Click the **Find Next** button on the Data Form to scroll through the data in the spreadsheet.

5 – Enter a new booking using the data form

Method

1 Click the **New** button on the **Data Form** and enter the following data:

o **121** for the Booking Number
o **Using the VBA Editor** as the Course Title, and **123.50** as the Course Cost
o Places Booked are 4.

2 Press **Enter** to enter the data onto the spreadsheet.

To view the data you have just entered, click the **Find Prev** button on the Data Form.

The record you have just entered should be displayed in the Data Form.

3 **Save** the workbook.

6 – Querying records with the data form

You can also use the Data Form to query data to find records that match a given criterion. Find all courses that cost less than 90.

Info

The **less than** Operator is represented by the following symbol <.

Method

If you have closed the Data Form, use the instructions above to open it again.

1 Click the **Criteria** button (you will be presented with a blank Data Form to enter the criteria).

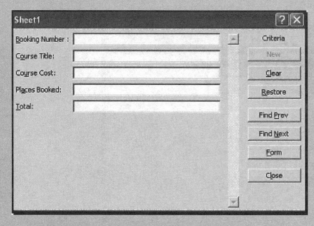

Figure 2.29 Blank Data Form

2 Enter the following criterion in the **Course Cost** text box: **<90**.

3 Click the **Find Next** button.

The Data Form should indicate that **9** of your 21 records **meet** the Criterion.

Info

To move through and view these records use the **Find Next** and **Find Prev** command buttons to move backwards and forwards through the records.

4 Close the form when you have finished viewing records.

The Data Form is useful should you want to see a complete **Row** of data at a glance (Figure 2.30).

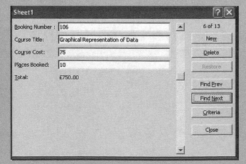

Figure 2.30 Data Form

Task 2.3 Filtering data to produce a query

Querying data using advanced options

In this task you will use **Custom AutoFilter** to query data in a spreadsheet.

Custom AutoFilter allows you to search by criteria in the same way as a Data Form.

1 – Query data in a spreadsheet

Task A

Method

1 Select cell A4.

2 Point to **Filter** on the **Data** menu, then click **AutoFilter** from the sub-menu.

Info

The system places a dropdown arrow on each column so you can filter the list by the criteria required, based on the contents of the list.

	A	B	C	D	E
1		Courses			
2					
3	Booking Numbe ▼	Course Title ▼	Course Cost ▼	Places Booke ▼	Total ▼
4	101	Computer Aided Design	£80.00	4	£320.00
5	102	Computer Art	£100.00	5	£500.00
6	103	Database Concepts	£700.00	10	£7,000.00
7	104	Fire Officers	£99.00	4	£396.00
8	105	First Aid	£155.00	4	£620.00
9	106	Graphical Representation of Data	£75.00	10	£750.00
10	107	Networking	£2,000.00	7	£14,000.00
11	108	Operating Systems	£1,500.00	7	£10,500.00

Figure 2.31 Autofilter

3 Click the **Arrow** next to the **Places Booked** label and select the number **4**.

	A	B	C	D	E
1		Courses			
2					
3	Booking Numbe ▼	Course Title ▼	Course Cost ▼	Places Booke ▼	Total ▼
4	101	Computer Aided Design	£80.00	4	£320.00
7	104	Fire Officers	£99.00	4	£396.00
8	105	First Aid	£155.00	4	£620.00
13	110	VDU Assessors	£200.00	4	£800.00
16	113	Mail Merge	£23.50	4	£94.00

Figure 2.32 Filtered results

The worksheet will automatically be filtered and display six records that have four people booked on them.

Info

The black arrow next to the Places Booked label has changed colour to indicate that this column is the **criterion** the list has been **filtered** by.

Task B – Display all records on Sheet1 worksheet

We will try the same Criterion (**<90**) with **AutoFilter** as we used in the **Data Form**.

To use the **is less than** operator as in the Data Form, a **Custom AutoFilter** needs applying.

1 Click the arrow next to the **Course Cost** column.

2 From the list of options, select **Custom** to display the **Custom AutoFilter** window.

The **Custom AutoFilter** window is where you can set **Criteria** that require the use of **Operators** displayed in text format.

Figure 2.33 Default Custom AutoFilter window

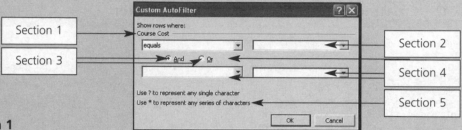

Section 1

As you selected the **Custom** option via the **Course Cost** column, the **Custom AutoFilter** window includes the column **Label**.

Section 2

In row one the **default** operator when the window opens is **equals**.

From this dropdown list box, you select the type of operator you want to use.

In the text box to the right you select or enter the criterion for the operator to assess against.

Section 3

The default function when the window opens is **And**.

If you only enter a single criterion to search by, in row one you do not need to change the default option.

If you search by two criteria, you will need to make a decision about how you want to search:

o Using the default function **And** would combine the two criteria entered in section two and four i.e. greater than 200 **and** less than 400.

o Selecting the **Or** function would ask the function to use both criteria for the calculation i.e. equals £100 **or** equals £62.50.

Section 4

Row two has no **default** operator when the window opens.

In the first dropdown list box you select the type of operator you want to use.

In the text box to the right you select or enter the criterion for the operator to assess against.

Section 5

Using wildcards

When you are searching text in a spreadsheet you can use two default wildcards to help you search for data.

Here are examples of two default wildcards available in the Custom AutoFilter window:

The question mark (**?**) and the asterisk (*****).

The question mark **wildcard** is used to represent a single character within words or data being queried that the words or data may have in common.

Example of wildcard syntax: **??D?**.

The above combination of the wildcard and text letter (D) will display all text with 4 or less characters with D as the third letter.

The asterisk wildcard is used in a similar way.

Example wildcard syntax: **I***.

This will display any text starting with the letter I.

Task C – Creating a query with custom AutoFilter.

Method

1　Click the arrow next to the course **Course Cost** column.

2　Open the **Custom AutoFilter** window.

3　Select **less than** from the first list box under the **Course Cost** label.

4　Enter 90 as the figure in the second (top right hand) list box.

Info

You could have selected a figure that already exists in the worksheet, in the second list box but the figures available are not what you want to work with at this stage.

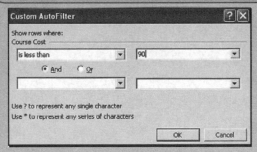

Figure 2.34 Completed Custom AutoFilter window

After setting the criteria, select **OK** to apply them and to close the Custom AutoFilter window.

The nine records returned are the same as the nine returned with the Data Form.

	A	B	C	D	E
1		Courses			
2					
3	Booking Numbe	Course Title	Course Cost	Places Booke	Total
4	101	Computer Aided Design	£80.00	4	£320.00
9	108	Graphical Representation of Data	£75.00	10	£750.00
12	109	Text Processing	£69.50	10	£695.00
14	111	VDU Users	£55.00	20	£1,100.00
15	112	Word Processing	£69.50	10	£695.00
16	113	Mail Merge	£23.50	4	£94.00

Figure 2.35 Returned Records

Custom AutoFilter displays all records that meet the criteria in the filtered spreadsheet.

Info

Custom AutoFilter allows you to use more than one criterion on a single column.

EXERCISE *2 – Custom Autofilter within a range*

Method

Use the Custom AutoFilter window to display rows where:

Course Cost is greater than **90**
And
is less than **150**.

When the query filter is applied this should return 3 records, **Computer Art**, **Fire Officers** and **Using the VBA Editor**.

1　**Display** all records.

2 Remove the AutoFilter.

Each of the Query methods you have covered has its own benefits

Data Forms

- The Data Form can only handle a maximum of 32 Fields but has the ability to show a complete record that meets the criteria specified.

- Data Forms can use all **cells** that should be used for **data entry** to enter criteria against, but is limited by the number of fields in a spreadsheet.

- In a **Data Form**, records are only visible one at a time.

- Data Forms can also find records but the criterion is single for each record.

- The Data Form is unable to process this type of criteria e.g.
  Cost Course >90.00 <150.00

- You can use the Data Form to **add and delete** records.

- If the worksheet data is wide using a Data Form saves you scrolling or using Freeze Panes for columns and rows.

AutoFilter

- AutoFilter is single criterion.

- Operators cannot be selected.

- All data found that meets the criteria is displayed.

- You can filter by all columns to find specific data.

Custom AutoFilter

- Enables you to use two criteria on a single field.

- All data found that meets the criteria is displayed.

- Operators can be selected.

- You can use wildcards as part of the filter.

Save and review your work before moving to the Query practice section.

3 – Practice

In the following exercises you will use a **Data Form** or **Custom AutoFilter** to query the data in a spreadsheet.

Open the workbook **CreateQueryPractice**. You will be working with the **Booking** worksheet.

- Row 1 of the worksheet contains the spreadsheet title **Courses**.

- Row 2 of the worksheet contains the spreadsheet **Column Labels**.

- The spreadsheet covers cells A2:A46.

- The spreadsheet data is contained in cells A3:A46.

4 – Create a single criterion query using a wildcard in the custom AutoFilter window

Task A

Method

1 Apply **AutoFilter** to your list.

2 Open the Custom AutoFilter window via the **Courses Title** column.

3 Select the **begins with** Operator.

4 Enter the following criterion **?D**.

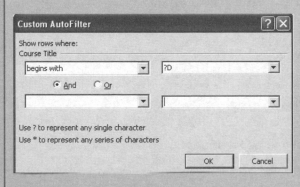

Figure 2.36 Completed Custom AutoFilter window

5 Close the Custom AutoFilter window to accept the default **And** Function option.

The above combination of the wildcard and text letter should display all **course names** in the **Course Title** column that have the letter **D** as the second letter.

Your results should be, by booking number:

Results			
110	111	134	135

6 **Display** all records in the spreadsheet.

Task B

Method

1 Open the Custom AutoFilter window via the **Courses Title** column.

2 Select the **begins with** Operator.

3 Enter the criterion **I***.

4 Close the **Custom AutoFilter** window to accept the default **And** Function option.

The above combination of text letter and wildcard should display all **course names** in the **Course Title** column starting with the letter **I**.

Your results should be, by booking number:

Results				
100	122	129	130	141

5 **Display** all records in the spreadsheet.

5 – Create a query using a data form

Task A – Create a single criterion query using a data form

Method

How many courses in the spreadsheet cost more than £1000?

1 Select a cell within the list.

2 Open the Data Form.

3 Click the **Criteria** button.

4 Enter the following criterion in the **Course Cost** text box: >1000.

5 Click the **Find Next** button.

Your results should be, by booking number:

Results				
107	108	123	124	131

6 Scroll through the Data Form to view all returned records.

Task B – Create a multiple criteria query using a data form

Method

How many courses in the spreadsheet cost more than £1000 and have less than 4 places booked?

1 Open the Data Form.

2 Click the **Criteria** button.

3 Enter the following criterion in the **Course Cost** text box: >1000.

4 Enter the following criterion in the **Places Booked** text box: <4.

5 Click the **Find Next** button.

Your results should be, by booking number:

Result
124

6 Close the Data Form.

6 – Create a query using the custom AutoFilter window

Task A – Create a single criteria query using the custom AutoFilter window

Method

How many courses in the spreadsheet have more than 10 places booked?

1 Apply AutoFilter to your list (if you removed these for the Data Form exercises).

2 Open the Custom AutoFilter window via the **Places Booked** column.

3 Select the **is greater than** Operator.

4 Select the number **10**.

5 Close the Custom AutoFilter window to accept the default **And** Function option.

Your results should be, by booking number:

Results					
111	115	117	118	122	125
126	127	129	130	132	133
134	135	136	137	138	139
140	141	142	143		

Task B – Create a multiple criteria query using the custom AutoFilter window

Method

How many courses in the spreadsheet have more than 10 but less than 15 places booked?

1 Open the Custom AutoFilter window via the **Places Booked** column. Row 1 should contain the first search criterion applied in exercise Task A.

2 In Row 2, select the **is less than** Operator and the number **15**.

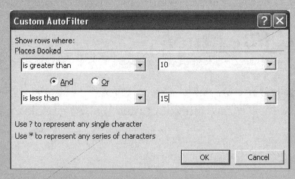

Figure 2.37 Completed Custom AutoFilter window

3 Close the Custom AutoFilter window to accept the default **And** Function option.

Your results should be, by booking number:

Results			
117	126	127	137

4 **Display** all records in the spreadsheet.

7 – Create a multiple criteria query using the custom AutoFilter window

EXERCISE

Method

How many courses in the spreadsheet have 7 or 100 places booked?

1 Open the Custom AutoFilter window via the **Places Booked** column.

2 In Row 1, select the **equals** operator and the number **7**.

3 In Row 2, select the **equals** operator and the number **100**.

4 Click the **Or** Function option button.

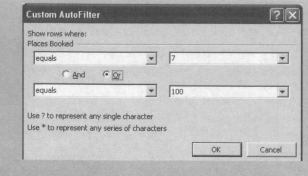

Figure 2.38 Completed Custom AutoFilter window

5 Close the Custom AutoFilter window.

Your results should be, by booking number:

Results			
107	108	128	135

6 Display all records in the spreadsheet.

7 Remove the AutoFilter.

Save and review your work before moving to the next section.

2.5 Using the Advanced filter tool

Open the workbook **AdvancedImportDates**. All workbooks for this section can be located on the accompanying CD-ROM. The workbook contains a list of sales dates imported from a text file.

A random sample of sales data is required for audit purposes.

Background

You have been left the following information and instructions to complete the task by your manager using **Advanced Filter** to gain hands-on experience of this workbook tool.

Advanced Filter options offer a quick way to view what is referred to as a subset of data by extracting only the data that meets a given criterion. The worksheet you will search contains **1015 Rows** of information.

To use Advanced Filter you need to set up a criteria area at the top of the workbook in row 1 and enter the data you want to search for in row 2. As the spreadsheet is large (cells B10:D1024) and you are not able to see all data, having the criteria area at the top of the workbook is an advantage.

In Exercises 1 to 3 you will practice the process of extracting data using the Advanced Filter tool. These exercises can be repeated as necessary.

In Exercise 4 you extract the data required for audit purposes and save these to individual worksheets.

In Exercise 5 you extract data based on various questions about greyhounds managed by the kennels **Your Pick,** using commands for the **Advanced Filter** tool that you have already worked through.

1 – Advanced filter option – Filter the list, in-place: practice

EXERCISE

Method

1 On the **AdvanceFilter** worksheet, **Copy** and **Paste** the labels in cells B9:D9 to cell A1.

Example labels:

DAY	MONTH	YEAR

2 In cell A2 enter the number **4**.

3 Set up an Advance Criteria search:

   a Click cell A9.

   b Point to **Filter** on the **Data** menu, then click **Advanced Filter** on the sub-menu to open the **Advanced Filter** window.

Figure 2.39 Filter menu   **Figure 2.40** Advanced Filter window

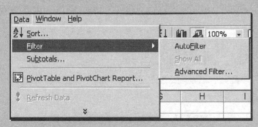

Info

The Advanced Filter window – options

Action section
The **Filter the list**, **in-place** option will be selected, as this is the default option.

If you wanted to filter a list and copy this to another area of your spreadsheet you would select **Copy to another location**. If you select this option, the **Copy to** option, which is currently disabled in the example, is enabled for Data Entry.

4 On this occasion accept the default option **Filter the list, in-place**.

List range

Info

You can enter the **List Range** via the keyboard for the **Filter the list, in-place** option, or use the collapse dialogue icon to minimise the window and select the range using the mouse.

As you have selected cell A9 before opening the Advanced Filter window, the range Cell A9:D1024 has been selected by the system as the **List Range** to be searched and data extracted from.

Note: if you enter the List Range for a list via the keyboard, include the dollar sign ($), as part of the cell reference, to create an absolute reference.

5 Accept the default **List Range** selected by the system.

Criteria range

The **Cell label(s)** and the **Data** define a criteria range.

You set up a criteria area at the top of the workbook in row 1 and enter the data you want to search for in row 2.

6 Use the collapse window icon to select cells $A$1:$A$2 or enter this via the keyboard as the **criteria range** argument.

7 Select **OK** to apply the **Filter** and to close the Advanced Filter window.

You should have **48 Records Filtered** in answer to your criteria question 'Display all individual sales transactions that took place on the **4**th day in any month or year in the **criteria range** argument (cells A1:A2) contained in cells A9:D1024'.

2 – Removing a filter

1 Point to **Filter** on the **Data** menu, then click **Show All** on the sub-menu (this action will redisplay all records in the list after a filter).

2 **Remove** the filter.

3 **Save** the workbook.

3 – Advanced filter option – copy to another location: practice

1 In cell A2 enter the number **4** if this has been deleted.

2 In cell B2 enter the number **11**.

Setting up an Advance Criteria search

3 Click cell A9.

4 Open the Advanced Filter window then:

   a Click the Action option button **Copy to another location**.

   b Select or enter the cells $A$1:$B$2 as the **criteria range** argument.

   c Select or enter cell G1 as the **Copy to** argument.

   d Click on **OK** to apply the **Filter** and to close the Advanced Filter window.

You should have **28 Records Filtered**. On the 4th day of the 11th month in any year, 28 sales transactions took place based on the **criteria range** argument.

5 **Select** columns **G to J** inclusive and **delete** data contained in these columns. In the next exercise you will cut and paste copied data into new worksheets.

6 **Save** the workbook.

In Exercise 1 when the Action option **Filter the list, in-place** was used, all rows that did not meet the **criteria range** argument were hidden. To view all rows, you pointed to **Filter** on the **Data** menu and clicked **Show All** on the sub-menu.

In Exercise 3 when the Action option **Copy to another location** was used, rows were copied to a new location.

Note: when you use this option you must delete the copied list if you do not want to save this in the location it was copied to.

If you are not ready to attempt Exercise 4 work through Exercises 1 and 3 again.

4 – Copy (data) to another location

Method

In this exercise you will copy data to cell G1 on the **AdvancedFilter** worksheet and move these to individual worksheets.

Your manager has asked you to extract and copy the following data from cells A9:D1024, and to save these on individual worksheets:

Dates (criteria) to be extracted:

Day	Month	Year
29	4	2000
19	7	2000
7	4	2001
3	11	2001

The workbook has two empty worksheets. You will extract **four** sets of data.

1 **Insert** two new worksheets.

2 **Rename** the four empty worksheets as detailed below. The worksheet names match the data to be extracted in the example above but in the month portion of the worksheet name, use text for clarity.

3 Rename the worksheets:

   a 29April2000

   b 19July2000

   c 07April2001

   d 03November2001.

4 **Save** the workbook.

5 Enter the Criteria arguments. **Select** the **Advanced Filter** worksheet:

   a In cell A2 enter the **Day** argument **29**.

   b In cell B2 enter the **Month** argument **4**.

   c In cell C2 enter the **Year** argument **2000**.

6 Set up an Advance Criteria search:

   a Click cell A9.

   b Open the **Advanced Filter** window.

c Click the Action option button **Copy to another location**.

d Select or enter cells $A$1:$C$2 as the **criteria range** argument if this is not the default when the window opens.

e Click the **AdvanceFilter** worksheet tab and select or enter cell G1 as the **Copy to** argument if this is not the default when the window opens.

f Select **OK** to apply the **Filter** and to close the Advanced Filter window.

7 Move copied data that matches the criteria:

a **Cut** and **Paste** the copied data in cells G1:J9 into cell A1 on the worksheet **29April2000**.

b **Extend** columns to ensure that all data can be seen in cells if necessary.

c **Save** the workbook.

d Click cell A2 on the **AdvanceFilter** worksheet.

8 From the table that follows, create Advanced Filter criteria arguments **A to C**.

Note: by default, when you select the **Copy to** argument, the system will offer you the last location used in a workbook as the cell or range in which to place data you are moving. For this exercise, click the **AdvanceFilter** worksheet tab and enter or select cell G1 as the **Copy to** argument.

Criteria Arguments	Day	Month	Year	Save to Worksheet
A	19	7	2000	19July2000
B	7	4	2001	07April2001
C	3	11	2001	03November2001

Info

o Where to enter the criteria arguments is covered in Step 5.

o Setting up an Advance Criteria search is covered in Step 6.

o Cutting and Pasting the extracted data to the relevant worksheets is covered in Step 7.

Info

Within the completed workbook there should be the original worksheet **AdvanceFilter**, and four new worksheets containing the data for audit, as shown below:

1 The original worksheet **AdvanceFilter** containing all data.

2 Data on worksheet **29April2000** should cover cells A1:D9.

3 Data on worksheet **19July2000** should cover cells A1:D11.

4 Data on worksheet **07April2001** should cover cells A1:D17.

5 Data on worksheet **03November2001** should cover cells A1:D16.

9 **Hide** column A on the following worksheets:

a 29April2000.

b 19July2001.

c 07April2001.

d 03November2001.

10 Review your work.

Save and close the workbook when you are ready to move to the next exercise in this section.

Task 2.5 Using the Advanced filter tool

5 – Practice

Method

In this exercise you will extract data based on various questions about greyhound managed by the kennels **Your Pick,** using the Advanced Filter tool.

1 Open the workbook **DogQuery** and select the **Data** worksheet.

2 **Insert** three new rows at the top of the worksheet.

3 **Copy** and **Paste** the labels in cells A5:E5 to cell A1 (this will create the criteria area **labels** in cells A1:E1). **Criteria** (questions) will be entered in cells A2:E2 as appropriate.

4 Click cell A5.

Note: when you open the Advanced Filter window, always accept or select the following options for tasks in this exercise:

    a Action: Copy to another location.

    b List range cells A5:E29.

    c Criteria range: enter as specified for each question.

    d Copy to cell H1 (any data found).

5 **Cut** and **Paste** the data copied to cell H1:L1 (after closing the Advanced Filter window) to a new worksheet.

6 Copy the labels in row one of the **Data** worksheet to each new worksheet to identify cell contents.

7 Save workbook.

8 Create the following Advanced Filter Queries:

    o Q1 How many dogs have the owner ID no. **A01**?

    o Q2 How many times does the name **Lady** appear in the **Name** column?

    o Q3 How many dogs does the owner with the **SName Taj** have at the kennels?

    o Q4 How many dogs have a **Name** that starts with the letter **S**?

    o Q5 How many owners have a **SName** that starts with the letter **O**?

9 Save and review your work.

Practice question

How many greyhounds belong to the **owner** with the identification number (**IDNo**) **A01**?

1 Enter **A01** in cell D2 on the **Data** worksheet.

2 Use the Advanced Filter window to filter the list in place.

Your results should be, by dog ID number: **1, 11** and **23**.

In this section you have used advanced query/filter options and used the task item **Hide columns**.

Save and review your work before moving to the next section.

Linking data in worksheets

Open the workbook **IntroLinking**. All student files for this section can be located on the accompanying CD-ROM.

In this workbook you keep a record of sales and sales staff names. Sales staff in each division are constantly changing.

The **StaffAndSales** worksheet contains **sales** and **staff names**.

The **Sales** worksheet contains sales.

The **Salesperson** worksheet contains **staff names**.

You have decided to learn how to link data within and between worksheets to cut down on data entry tasks. In the following exercise you will practice two methods of linking data in worksheets.

EXERCISE

1 – Using the formula bar to link data within worksheets

Method

Basic instructions for linking data on the same worksheet.

1 Click the cell you want to use to link to data. Click cell B3 in the **StaffAndSales** worksheet.

2 Enter an **operator** for the system to use to process the data: you want cell B3 to be **equal to** the contents of another cell. Enter the **equal to** operator = via the keyboard.

3 Click the cell containing the data you want to link to, in this case **cell I3** on the **StaffAndSales** worksheet.

4 Press **Enter** to create the linking formula.

5 Reselect cell B3 and view the linking syntax in the Formula Bar.

Info

Linking syntax example: **=I3**.

6 If you have not done so already, use the instructions above to link cell B3 on the **StaffAndSales** worksheet with data contained in **Cell I3**.

7 Repeat the above procedure to enter sales staff names in cells B4:B6 for the North Group.

EXERCISE

2 – Using the paste link button to link data within worksheets

You can review **Paste Link** commands in the **Format Painter** instructions in the Data Tasks in Editing Section 2.

Info

To link cells you can also use the Paste Special option **PasteLink**.

1 copy cell J3 on the **StaffAndSales** worksheet.

2 **Right** click cell B11 on the **StaffAndSales** worksheet, then click **Paste Special** from the pop-up menu.

3 Click the **Paste Link** button in the **Paste Special** window.

4 Repeat the above procedure to enter sales staff names in cells B12:B14 for the **South** Group.

When you link data using the **Formula Bar** it is possible to use the **Fill Handles** to copy the data, because the cell reference used here is a **relative** reference.

Relative reference example: **=I4**.

When you use the Paste Link button the system inserts an **absolute** reference. If you use the **Fill Handles** to copy the data, you will have to edit the cell reference as necessary.

Absolute reference example **=$I$4**.

5 Using one of the above methods enter the salesperson data for the **East** and **West** groups on the **StaffAndSales** worksheet.

6 To ensure that the linking syntaxes are working, edit the following cells to add the names of new staff members:

   a In cell I3 replace **Nellie** with **Constance**. Cell B3 should reflect this change.

   b In cell J6 replace **Raymond** with **Yolanda**. Cell B14 should reflect this change.

   c In cell K5 replace **Edward** with **Noel**. Cell B21 should reflect this change.

   d In cell L6 replace **Marie** with **Ernie**. Cell B30 should reflect this change.

7 **Save** the workbook.

8 Review your work.

3 – Practice

Open the workbook **DataTableLink**. The file can be located on the accompanying CD-ROM. This is a back-up of the workbook **DataTableNewHome**. (You used the workbook to create and use a one input table.)

In the original exercise you entered the function syntax in cell D3 to multiply the *sum borrowed* by the *interest rate* and then re-entered this in cell D6 to create the Data Table.

1 Select the **Home** worksheet and **Delete** the function in cell D6.

(All cells in the range D7:D18 will **display** as £0.00 after you delete the function.)

If you select a cell in the range 7D:D18 the Formula Bar will display the following syntax: **=TABLE(,D1)**.

The Data Table parameters are still available if you **link** this to the function that creates the values.

2 Using the most appropriate **linking** method from the previous exercises, link cell D6 to cell D3 on the **Home** worksheet, to recreate the Data Table contents.

Hint: absolute cell reference.

Changing the way you carried out the original exercise has the following benefits:

o You will not have to make changes in two places, therefore you have cut down on data entry tasks.

o The chance of introducing errors into the spreadsheet has been reduced.

o Ensures that data changed in one place is reflected in another place.

o It has linked two **task items** together.

Review your work before you move to the next linking Task.

3 Close the **DataTableLink** workbook when you have completed the exercise.

2.7 Linking data between worksheets

This procedure is the same as for linking **within** a worksheet, with the extra requirement that you have to include the name of the worksheet where the data is contained that you want to link to.

3 – Using the formula bar to link data between worksheets

EXERCISE

Method

1 If it has been closed, open the workbook **IntroLinking**.

2 **Click** the **cell** you want to **use** to link to data cell B3 on the **Sales** worksheet.

3 Enter an **operator** for the system to use to process the data. You want cell B3 to be equal to another cell's contents, so enter the **equal to** operator = via the keyboard.

4 **Click** the worksheet tab containing the cell you want to link with: **Salesperson**.

5 **Click** the **cell** you want to link with: **A3** on the **Salesperson** worksheet.

6 **Press Enter** to create the linking formula.

7 If you have not done so already, use the instructions above to link cell B3 on the **Sales** worksheet with data contained on the **Salesperson** worksheet in cell A3.

1 – Outcome

EXERCISE

o Cell B3 on the **Sales** worksheet should contain the name **Nellie**.

o The **Formula Bar** should display the following **equal to** linking syntax when cell B3 is selected: **=Salesperson!A3**.

Linking syntax explained

The **equal to** operator instructs the system to make the linked cell content equal to the cell this is linked to.

Salesperson represents the **worksheet name** where the original data is contained. The exclamation mark (**!**) separates the **worksheet name** from the **reference address of cell A3**. This enables the system to process your request to link the two cells on separate worksheets to display the same data.

You can repeat the above procedure to enter sales staff names in cells B4:B6 for the **North** group on the sales worksheet, or use the **Fill Handles** to copy the data, as the cell reference used here is a relative reference and the staff names in cells A3:A6 on the **Salesperson** worksheet are organised in the same order as the **Sales** worksheet.

8   Link the sales staff names in **Cells B11:B14** for the **South** group.

2 – Use paste special options to link data between worksheets

EXERCISE

In this exercise you will use Paste Special option **Paste Link**, to link the sales staff names on the **Salesperson** worksheet to the **Sales** worksheet.

Method

1   Select the **Salesperson** worksheet.

2   **Copy** the data in cell C3.

3   **Right** click cell B19 on the **Sales** worksheet and click **Paste Special** from the pop-up menu.

4   Click the **Paste Link** button to link the data between the worksheets.

The name **Akida** should appear in cell B19.

5   Repeat the above procedure to enter sales staff names in cells B20:B22 for the **East** group and cells B27:B30 for the **West** Group.

Info

If you decide to use the **Fill Handle** you will need to edit the cell reference as **Paste Link** uses an absolute reference.

6   To ensure that the linking syntax that was used is working, edit the cells below, in the **sales** worksheet, by adding the names of the following new staff members:

A3:A6	B3:B6	C3:C6	D3:D6
Kellie	Pascal	Joanne	Christine
Susan	Marcel	Paul	Billy
Wendy	Shena	Steve	Sean
Lana	Fran	Angie	Colin

Any changes made to the **data** in cells A3:D6 on the **Salesperson** worksheet should be reflected on the **Sales** worksheet.

Review your work before moving to the next section.

7   Save and close the workbook.

3 – Practice

EXERCISE

Open the workbook **StaffLinkBetween**. All student files for the following exercises can be located on the accompanying CD-ROM.

A review of staff job descriptions has resulted in the renaming of existing job titles for five members of staff.

When you look at the **StaffDetails** spreadsheet, note that job title appears in two columns, **Job Title** and **Supervisor Title**.

The way the list is presented means that you will have to make changes in two places. This increases the chance of introducing errors into the spreadsheet.

If a separate worksheet containing all job titles is created and then each person is **linked** to their job title and supervisor's job title from that worksheet, changes to job title will only have to be made in one area when staff or supervisors change departments.

Insert a new worksheet and **rename** it as **JobTitle**.

Task A – Creating the JobTitle worksheet

To create the **JobTitle** worksheet there are two possible methods. You can either import a text file, or enter the list via the keyboard. You decide which you want to use.

Method 1 – Import a text file

Method

1 Open a new workbook.

2 Import the text file **JobTitleList**.

3 Click the **Finish** button in Step 1 of the Text Import Wizard, to accept all default options.

4 Copy the **imported** data in cells A1:A20.

5 Paste the **imported** data in cell A2 of the **JobTitle** worksheet.

6 Enter the title **Job Title List** in cell A1.

7 Save the workbook.

8 **Close** the imported text file **JobTitleList** workbook without saving your changes.

Method 2 – Enter the list via the keyboard

1 **Select** the **JobTitle** worksheet.

2 Enter the title **Job Title List** in cell A1.

3 Enter the list of job titles below in cells A2:A21:

Job title list

General Manager (Administration)

Administration Assistant (Administration)

Manager Finance (Finance)

Administration Assistant (Finance)

Manager Public Relations (Marketing)

Manager Sales (Sales)

Administration Assistant (Sales)

Bookings Clerk

Clerical Assistant (Admin)

Clerical Assistant (Finance)

Clerical Assistant (Sales)

Courier

Finance Officer

General Assistant

Personal Assistant
Receptionist
Sales Officer
Senior Receptionist
Promotions Officer

4 **Save** the workbook.

Task 2 – Linking data to the JobTitle worksheet

1 Link individual job titles in **column F** of the **StaffDetails** worksheet to the **JobTitle** worksheet using an absolute reference in the formulas.

2 Link individual supervisor titles in **column G** of the **StaffDetails** worksheet to the **JobTitle** worksheet using an absolute reference in the formulas.

3 **Save** the workbook.

4 Scroll through the **StaffDetails** worksheet and check that all Job Titles and Supervisor Titles are now linked to the list on the **JobTitle** worksheet by a formula that uses an absolute reference.

The formula syntax should look like this example **=JobTitle!$A$2**

Who is the member of staff who has no supervisor?

What is their job title?

Task 3 – Updating links

Are all links working?

Edit the Job Title list as shown below with the **New Job Title**:

Old Job Title	New Job Title
Senior Receptionist (Administration)	**Office Manager**
Administration Assistant (Administration)	**Senior Administrator** (Admin)
Administration Assistant (Finance)	**Senior Administrator** (Finance)
Administration Assistant (Sales)	**Senior Administrator** (Sales)
Courier	**Driver Clerk**

Task 4 – Checking links

1 Select the **StaffDetails** worksheet.

2 Select cell A4 and apply AutoFilter.

3 Filter the list by the Supervisor Job Title **Office Manager**. This should display the new job title **Driver Clerk** in the job title column.

4 Filter the list by Supervisor Job Title **General Manager Administration**. This should display the new **Senior Administrator (Admin)**.

If you have data that is used in several areas consider storing the data separately and using formulas to access the data.

5 **Remove** all Filters.

6 Save and close the workbook.

Linking data between spreadsheets

As part of your training in a new department you have to learn how to link data between and within workbooks, worksheets, spreadsheets and word processing documents. These exercises your manager has designed are to help you practice the various linking skills.

People working for your company often use the same data in different ways. In this exercise you will link a number of spreadsheets to monitor a Division's training budget. The Division has three departments. The training budget for each department is recorded under two headings, Post Entry Qualification Training (**PEQT**) and Short and Internal Courses.

Each Department Manager in the Division needs a way of recording their training budget spending. It has been decided that each manager will record spending for PEQT and Short/Internal Courses on separate spreadsheets. These spreadsheets will be linked to a spreadsheet that will show the Division Head an overall picture of spending in their division.

This spreadsheet in turn will be linked to a master spreadsheet for the Finance Manager who controls the budget, to ensure that no overspends can occur.

This master spreadsheet will also include the budget for the year and show at any given time the current spending and current balance for the training budget. When it is completed, the spreadsheet linking structure will look like the diagram below.

Spreadsheet linking structure diagram

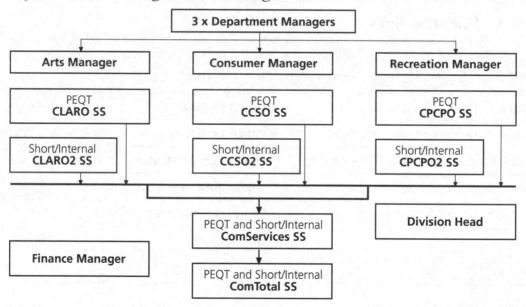

From the structure you can see that eight spreadsheets need to be included in the linking process you will create.

All Student files for the following exercises can be located on the accompanying CD-ROM.

The workbooks **CLARO, CCSO** and **CPCPO** each contain one worksheet that records **Post Entry Qualification Training (PEQT) Expenditure** for each department.

Workbooks **CLARO2, CCSO2 and CPCPO2** also each contain one worksheet that records Short Courses **Expenditure** for the departments.

Open the **CLARO** workbook.

Taking control of the view of your spreadsheet

The size of the monitor you are using will determine how much of the spreadsheet you can see when you scroll from left to right.

You need to be able to see the sub-division if you scroll to the right in your spreadsheet. At the moment if you scroll right you lose sight of the sub-division name labels.

Freeze column A, so that the sub-division name labels are always visible.

1 – Exploring the CLARO workbook

Method

1 Cell information:

   a Cell A2 contains the spreadsheet title e.g. **Arts Services**.
   b Cell A3 contains a description of the spreadsheet e.g. **PEQT Training Expenditure**.
   c Cell A4 contains the dates for the training budget period **01/01/2002 – 31/03/2003**.
   d Cell A7 contains the label **SUB DIVISION**.
   e The financial year in this company starts on the 1st April. The date **01/04/02** has been entered in cell B7.
   f **Cells C7:J7** contain the labels **May** through **December**.
   g The financial year in this company ends on the 1st January. The date **01/01/03** has been entered in cell K7.
   h Cells L7:M7 contain the labels **February** through **March**.
   i Cell N7 contains the label **Year Total**.
   j A **Medium Date Format** has been applied to the date labels in cells B7 and K7.
   k The cells B8:N13 have been **formatted** as **currency** two decimal places.

2 The **SUM** function:

   a A **SUM** function has been entered in cell B13 and copied to cells C13:N13 to total the contents of cells B8:B12. This will provide **Monthly Totals**. Example syntax: **=SUM(B8:B14)**.
   b A **SUM** function has been entered in cell N8 and copied to N9:N12 to produce a yearly total for each sub-division on the spreadsheet. Example syntax: **=SUM(N9:N12)**.
   C A **SUM** function has been entered in cell N13 to produce a yearly total for all sub-divisions on the spreadsheet. Example syntax: **=SUM(N8:N12)**.

This the basic outline for the spreadsheets you will be working with.

From the Linking Structure Diagram you can see that you need to link the Managers workbooks to the Division Head workbook.

3 The Division Head workbook needs to **Display** and **Link** as follows:

   a **Display** the **Current** spending for each Division by **PEQT** and **Short Courses**.
   b **Link** to each sub-division's Training Budget workbooks.

This view of the Manager's workbooks will enable the Division Head to monitor spending within each division.

2 – Update and format data

Method

1 Open the workbook **ComServices**. Select the **Community** worksheet.

2 Enter the title **COMMUNITY SERVICES** in cell C3, then change the title font size to **point 15** and font style to bold.

3 Enter the following labels in the cells indicated:

   a **Training Budget@** in cell C4.
   b **DIVISIONS@** in cell C5.

    c **PEQT@** in cell D5.

    d **SHORT COURSE@** in cell E5.

4 Change the label font sizes to **point 12** and font style to **bold**.

5 Date and time functions:

    a Enter a **Today** function in cells D4 and C6.

    b **Copy** the **Today** function from cell C6 to cells D6:E6.

    c **Format** the **Today** function as **Date** in a Medium Date Format.

    d Change the font style to **bold** for cells D4 and C6: E6.

    e Change the alignment of cells C6:E6 to Centre.

6 Enter the following labels in the cells indicated:

    a **Arts** in cell C7.

    b **Consumers** in cell C8.

    c **Recreation** in cell C9.

    d **TOTAL** in cell C10.

7 Save the **ComServices** workbook.

EXERCISE | ## 3 – Linking data between spreadsheets

The procedure is the same as for linking within a worksheet, but in addition the workbook name where the data is contained has to be included so that the link is established.

You want to **link** the Division Head workbook **ComServices,** worksheet **Community**, to the management workbook, **CLARO**, worksheet, **Sheet1**. The data to be linked is the overall year **Total** in cell N13 for the **Arts** sub-division.

Method

1 Open the workbook **CLARO**, which contains the **PEQT** figures for the **Arts** sub-division, then minimise the workbook.

2 Click cell D7 on the worksheet **Community** in the **ComServices** workbook.

3 Enter the **operator** for the system to use to process the data. You want cell D7 to be equal to another cell's contents, via the keyboard.

4 In the **CLARO** workbook, click on the **Sheet1** tab, then click cell N13.

5 Press the Enter key on the keyboard. You wil be returned to the **ComServices** workbook.

Info

Clicking the workbook sheet tab identifies the worksheet and linked cell. Pressing the Enter key tells the system that you have finished entering the formula.

6 Select cell D7, as this will no longer be the active cell. The action of pressing the Enter key moved the cursor to cell D8.

Info

The Formula Bar will display the following syntax when **cell D7** is the active cell and the linked workbook is **open**. This is the Short Link syntax reference address for the link: =[CLARO.xls]Sheet1!$N$13 and indicates that the **CLARO** spreadsheet is open.

7 The figure displayed in cell D7 should be **£124825**. Close the **CLARO** workbook.

Info

Look at the Formula Bar. The syntax for the link has now changed to the long link address. This is the fully qualified path to the linked file on the author's computer.

Your link address will point to where you have the files stored on **your** computer or network.

8 Using the above procedure open each workbook and link the stipulated cells to the **ComServices** workbook. Save and close each workbook after linking it with the **ComServices** workbook. Do not close the **ComServices** workbook.

a CLARO2 workbook:
   i **Freeze** column A, so that the **sub-division** name labels are always visible.
   ii Link cell E7 of the **Community** worksheet, **ComServices** workbook, to the **Sheet1** worksheet cell N13.

b CCSO workbook:
   i **Freeze** column A, so that the **sub-division** name labels are always visible.
   ii **Link** cell D8 of the **Community** worksheet, **ComServices** workbook, to **Sheet1** worksheet cell N15.

c CCSO2 workbook:
   i **Link** cell E8 of the **Community** worksheet, **ComServices** workbook, to the **Sheet1** worksheet cell N15.

d CPCPO workbook:
   i **Freeze** column A, so that the **sub-division** name labels are always visible.
   ii **Link** cell D9 of the **Community** worksheet, **ComServices** workbook, to the **Sheet1** worksheet cell N13.

e CPCPO2 workbook:
   i **Freeze** column A, so that the **sub-division name labels** are always **visible**.
   ii **Link** cell E9 of the **Community** worksheet, **ComServices** workbook, to the **Sheet1** worksheet cell N13.

9 Enter a **SUM** function in cell D10 **of the Community** worksheet, to **Total** the three sub-division figures, and copy the **SUM** function to cell E10.

10 Format cells D7:E10 as currency, two decimal places.

11 Format the **ComServices** spreadsheet.

a **Merge** and **centre** the title **Community Services** across cells C3:E3.
b **Change** the Title font size to Point 15, **embolden** the **title** Community Services.
c **Merge** cells D4:E4 and align Left.
d **Embolden** cells C4:D4.
e Cells C4:C10, D5:D10 and E5:E10 – **align** as **centre**.
f **Embolden** cells C5:E6 and C10:E10.
g Apply borders. Click the black arrow next to the **Borders** toolbar button [image] on the **Formatting toolbar** to display border style options:
   i Highlight cells C3:E10 and apply an **outline** border.
   ii Highlight cells C3 and apply a **bottom** border. This will place a line between row 3 and 4 within the spreadsheet.
   iii Highlight cells C4:D4 and apply a **bottom** border.
   iv Highlight cells C10:E10 and apply a **top** border.
   v Apply a Fill Colour of **Turquoise** to cell C3.
   vi Apply a Fill Colour of **Light Turquoise** to cell C5:E10.

12 Save your work!

4 – Testing links

Method

1 Close the **ComServices** workbook.

2 Open the **ComServices** workbook.

When you reopen the **ComServices** workbook, you should see the following system message:

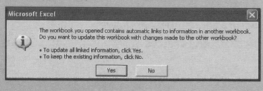

Figure 2.41 Links update system message

Info

Each time you open a linked workbook, all links to the workbook are refreshed by the system.

Click **Yes** to update changes. If you do not want to update a workbook at the time, click **No**. Each time you open a linked workbook you will be offered this option.

Method

The completed **ComServices** workbook, for the Division Head.

COMMUNITY SERVICES		
Training Budget@ 04:33:48 PM		
DIVISIONS@ 26-Sep-02	**PEQT@ 26-Sep-02**	**SHORT COURSE@ 26-Sep-02**
Arts	£112,450.00	£19,806.05
Consumers	£155,000.00	£51,471.00
Recreation	£240,500.00	£89,846.00
TOTAL	**£507,950.00**	**£161,123.05**

The final workbook that needs to be created is the Finance Manager workbook. This workbook will have access to all figures from each Division, and will include the budget figures for the financial year.

The Finance Manager workbook needs to **Display** and **Link** to the following:

1 **Display** the **Total** training budget for the financial year 01/04/02–31/03/03.

2 **Link** to the **Total** training budget commitments, within the Community Services Division, sub-divisions for:

   ○ PEQT
   ○ Short/Internal courses.

3 Show the Total of the Division commitments (**Total Spend**).

4 Show the Company's Total Balance at a given date (**Budget left@**).

Below is an example of the workbook you are aiming to create before any formatting is applied.

Completed **ComTotal** workbook example:

	D	E	F
1			
2	Local Services Training Budget 02/03		
3			
4	Total Budget		£268,820,000.00
5	Community Services PEQT		£520,325.00
6	Community Services Short/Internal Courses		£281,123.05
7	Total Spend		£801,448.05
8	Budget Left @	5-Dec-03	£268,018,551.95

The outline of the **ComTotal** workbook:

The Total Budget figures, cell F4.

This figure is entered at the start of the financial year as the budget for a company's training needs.

Community Services PEQT figures, cell F5.

Data in this cell is provided by the link to the ComServices workbook via cell F5 and represents the cost of a Professional Qualification Course, either started or due to start before the end of the financial year.

Community Services Short/Internal Courses figures, cell F6.

Data in this cell is provided by the link to the ComServices workbook via cell F6 and represents the cost of the general course, either started or due to start before the end of the financial year.

Total Spend figure, cell F7.

This figure is created via a **SUM** function that totals cells F5:F6. Function syntax example: **=SUM(F5:F6)**.

Budget Left @ figure, cell F8.

Subtracts the Total Spend from the Total Budget. Function syntax example: **=(F4-F7)**.

EXERCISE   5 – Practice

Using the information and formatting instructions below, create the **ComTotal** workbook.

Method

1 Open a new workbook and save this as **ComTotal**.

2 Rename **Sheet1** in the workbook as **TotalBudget**.

3 Enter the following labels in the cells indicated:

    a **Local Services Training Budget 02/03** in cell D2.
    b **Total Budget** in cell D4.
    c **Community Services PEQT** in cell D5.
    d **Community Services Short/Internal Courses** in cell D6.
    e **Total Spend** in cell D7.
    f **Budget Left @** in cell D8.

4 Enter a **Today( )** function in cell E8 and format this function to display the **date** in a **Medium Date Format**.

5 Data entry task: **enter** the **Total Budget** figure **268820000** for **Local Services** company in cell F4.

6 Linking Tasks:

   a Link cell F5 on the **TotalBudget** worksheet in the **ComTotal** workbook to the **ComServices** workbook, **Community** worksheet cell D10. This will provide the PEQT Figures.

   b Link cell F6 on the **TotalBudget** worksheet in the **ComTotal** workbook to the **ComServices** workbook, **Community** worksheet cell E10. This will provide the Community Services Short/Internal Courses figures.

7 Calculations tasks:

   a Enter a SUM function in cell F7 to total the figures in cells F5:F6: **=SUM(F5:F6)**.

   b Enter a formula to subtract **Total Budget** from **Total Spend** in cell F8: **=(F4-F7)**.

8 **Format** the spreadsheet:

   a Format cells F4:F8 as currency, two decimal places.

   b **Merge** and **centre** the title **Local Services Training Budget 02/03** across cells D2:F2.

   c **Embolden** the **title**, and all **labels** on the **TotalBudget** worksheet, including the **Date Label** in cell E8.

   d Apply an **outside** border to cells D1:F8 and D2:F2.

   e **Fill colour cells:**

   D1:F1 = **grey 40%**
   D2:F2 = **grey 25%**
   D3:F3 = **grey 40%**
   D4:D8 = **grey 25%**
   E4:E8 = **grey 40%**
   F4:F8 = **black**
   F4:F8 **Font colour = white**
   F4:F8 **Font style = bold**

Have you saved your work lately?

Updating a linked workbook

If you move a linked workbook you may need to update the link(s).

Method

1 Open the linked workbook.

2 Click **Links** from the **Edit** menu.

3 In the **Links** window, select the filename by clicking on this and then select the **Change Source** button.

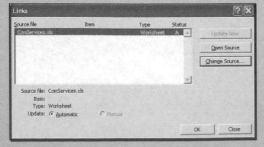

Figure 2.42 Change Source button

4 In the **Change Links** window locate the source file for the selected link.

Task 2.8 Linking data between spreadsheets

Figure 2.43 Change Links window

Select **OK** to change the link and **OK** again to close the **Change Links** window.

Watch points

The new cell link must have the same cell references, e.g. cell A1, as the original link, for this option to work without any other action.

Other action:
- Edit the cell reference in the Formula Bar once you have linked to the new worksheet.
- Reapply the worksheet linking procedure commands.

Note: when you create your links to other spreadsheets the system will automatically apply the automatic update option to the spreadsheet and the links. If you move your spreadsheet you will need to reconnect this.

The commands to create a linked spreadsheet are straightforward; the important point is to work out the structure of any linking to achieve your aim.

EXERCISE

6 – AutoFormat

Apply AutoFormats to the Management workbooks.

You created your own formatting for the **ComServices** and **ComTotal** spreadsheets. In this section you use AutoFormat to provide the formatting for the six Management workbooks.

Method

1   To Access **AutoFormat** click **AutoFormat** from the **Format** menu.

2   Open the **CCSO** workbook.

3   Select cell A2:N15.

4   Apply the **List 2 AutoFormat** to the spreadsheet.

Why did you have to select the cells to apply an **AutoFormat**?

If you have forgotten, review the **AutoFormat** Section.

5   Open the **CCS02** workbook.

6   Select cell A2:N15.

7   Apply the **List 2 AutoFormat** to the spreadsheet.

8   AutoFormat for **CLARO** and **CLARO2** workbooks cells A1:N13: **Classic 3** AutoFormat.

9   AutoFormat for **CPCPO** and **CPCPO2** workbooks cells A1:N13: **Colorful 2** AutoFormat.

Each group of workbooks now has its own formatting which will identify at a glance, that it is part of that group – helpful when working with several workbooks that perform the same function but apply to a different area.

In this worked example you have used one Division that has three sub-divisions. This is a system that can be built on for your own personal or professional needs.

Save and review your work before moving to the next section.

Close all open workbooks.

2.9 Linking data to a word processing file

Linking data via workbooks is one way to organise data to provide a different view of the same figures.

Another way to view data is to use a chart. When you use a chart to display figures, it is referred to as the **graphical representation of data**.

- In the following exercises two charts are created. One of the charts will be used in a word processing document.

Creating charts with the **Chart Wizard**.

To access the Chart Wizard click the **Chart Wizard** toolbar button ▥ on the standard toolbar.

Create a pie chart to display the actual and proposed spending for each sub-division's PEQT and short course.

The data to be displayed graphically is the company's current training budget commitments. The **ComServices** workbook has all the data needed to create the two charts.

EXERCISE 1 – Create a pie chart using Chart Wizard

Open the **ComServices** workbook you have just created. Close all other open workbooks.

Method

1 Select cell C3 and start the Chart Wizard.

2 Chart Wizard Step **1 of 4**:

   a **Standard tab**.
   b Chart Type = **Pie Chart**.
   c Chart sub-type = **Pie, display the contribution of each value to a total**. The default pie chart option when Pie Chart is selected.
   d Click the **Next** button.

3 Chart Wizard step **2 of 4**. Step 2 evaluates the data on the spreadsheet and estimates the **data range** and **series**, either **rows** or **columns**.

   The **range** suggested by the Wizard in Step 2 will be: **=Community!$C$3:$E$10**.

   a Amend the **range** reference to read as@: **=Community!$C$3:$E$9** (The original range reference included the **total** figures and these are not required for the chart).
   b Click the **Next** button.

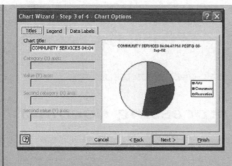

Figure 2.44 Chart Wizard window Step 3 of 4

4 Chart Wizard step **3 of 4**:

    a **Title tab**: amend the **title** to read **COMMUNITY SERVICES**.
    b **Data Labels tab**: click **Show percent** option button.
    c Click the **Next** button.

5 Chart Wizard step **4 of 4**:

    a Click **As new sheet**.
    b **Amend** the default name of Chart1 to **ChartBudget**.
    c Click the **Finish** button to create the chart.

The new worksheet **ChartBudget** will be inserted containing the pie chart.

EXERCISE ## 2 – 'Explode' all the segments in a pie chart

Click the **ChartBudget** worksheet to make this the active sheet within the workbook.

Method

Drag the pie shape outward so that a gap of approximately 6mm appears between the slices.

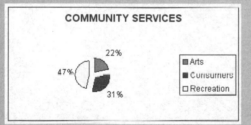

Figure 2.45 'Explode' pie chart example

EXERCISE ## 3 – Changing data in a linked document

If you change data in a spreadsheet that is linked to **ComServices**, will this be reflected in your chart?

The **Arts** figure should be **22%** in the pie chart you have just created.

Save and close the **ComServices** workbook.

Method

1 Open the **CLARO** workbook and add the **data** below to **Sheet1**, to test how changes made are reflected in a chart.

Data		
Department	**Month**	**Figure**
Archives	December	**4700**
Arts Monitoring Unit	December	**5500**
Events & Venues	December	**2175**

2 Save and close the **CLARO** workbook.

3 Open the **ComServices** workbook and select the worksheet **ChartBudget**. The figure of **22%** for **Arts** should now be **24%**.

4 – Linking a chart to a word processing document

In this exercise you will cover:

- How to create a chart as an object in the Community worksheet
- How to link worksheet data and charts to a word processing document.

Method

1 Select cell C3 of the **ComServices** workbook.

2 Start the Chart Wizard.

The instructions for the selections to apply are the same as for Exercise 2 for **ChartBudget,** except for the changes listed below.

3 Step 1 of 3:

  a Chart type = **Column**.
  b Chart sub-type = **Cluster column**, compares values across categories (usually the default option for column charts.

4 Step 2 of 3:

  a Data range tab.
  b **Series** in: = **Rows**.

5 Step 3 of 3: accept the default **As object in Community** worksheet.

6 Drag and drop the left corner of the new chart on to cell C13:E25.

7 Resize the chart so that it covers cells C13:E25.

8 Copy the chart to the **Clipboard**.

9 Open your word processing application.

All files for the following exercises can be located on the accompanying CD-ROM.

10 Open the standard letter **MemoChart**.

MemoChart is the document you will use each month to circulate the monthly Training Budget figures.

Ensure that the **Show/Hide** toolbar button ¶ is turned on, so that you can see all formatting marks in the document. The Show/Hide toolbar button is located on the standard toolbar.

11 Click in the document to place the cursor at the second **Enter key code** mark, after the title **Sub Division Chart**.

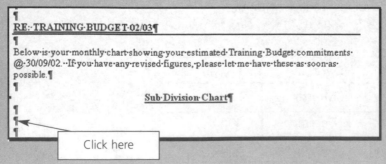

Figure 2.46 The MemoChart standard letter

12 Click **Paste Special** from the **Edit** menu to open the Paste Special window.

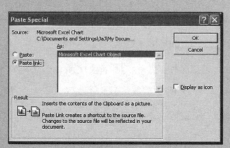

Figure 2.47 Paste Special window

The **Microsoft Excel Chart Object** option should be highlighted as the default choice as in Figure 2.47.

13 Select the **Paste Link** option. (When you select this option any changes you make to the Source file '**ComServices**' will be reflected in the chart contained in the memo).

14 Centre the chart under the sub-heading **Sub Division Chart**.

15 Save the file **MemoChart as today's date**: use a short date **Format** for the file name e.g. **010103**. Do not include hyphens or forward slashes in the file name.

16 Close the document.

5 – Linking data to another worksheet: practice

Method

1 Open and enter the following figures for the month shown in the workbook **CLARO2**:

Data				
Sub Division	**Month**	**Month**	**Figure**	**Figure**
Archives	February		**7000**	
Arts Monitoring Unit	February	March	**9000**	**15000**
Parks & Open Spaces	February	March	**8000**	**12000**
Events & Venues		March		**9000**
Cross Division Training	February	March	0	0

2 Save and close the workbook.

3 Open the **ComServices** workbook to update the data in it.

4 Save and close the workbook.

5 Open your word processing document containing the linked chart. When you open the document, a system message (Figure 2.48) should appear. Select **Yes** to update the linked data.

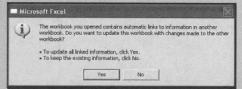

Figure 2.48

Are the changes in the **ComServices** workbook reflected in the chart contained in your word processing document, for example the **Archives** figures of **7000** for **February**?

6 After reviewing, save and close the file.

6 – Linking data to a word processing document: practice

● In this task you will link worksheet data to a word processing document.

You want to circulate the figures used to create the chart, as some managers prefer this view.

Method

1 Open the blank standard letter **MemoChart**. Save the document as **MemoFigures**.

2 Edit the word *chart* in the first sentence to **figures** and **title** to **Figures**. Save the document.

3 **Copy** the spreadsheet in the **ComServices** workbook, **Community** worksheet cells C3:E10. *Do not* copy the chart on the Community worksheet with the figures.

4 Switch to your word processing document **MemoFigures**.

5 Click **Paste Special** from the **Edit** menu to paste the contents of the clipboard into the word processing document as **worksheet object.** Select the **Paste link** option button if not already selected.

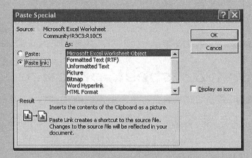

Figure 2.49 Paste Special window

6 Select **OK** to close the **Paste Special window** and insert the spreadsheet into the word processing document.

7 Centre the spreadsheet under the title **Sub Division Figures**.

8 Save and close the file.

9 Enter data to test the link between **ComServices** and **MemoFigures**. Open and enter the following data in the workbook **CCSO2**:

Data				
Sub Division	**Month**	**Month**	**Figure**	**Figure**
Rent Officers Services	February	March	**7000**	
Consumer Advice	February	March	**9000**	**15000**
Trading Standards	February	March	**8000**	**12000**
Health & Safety Section	February	March		**9000**
Registrars	February	March		
Consumer Monitoring Unit				
Cross Division Training				

10 Open the file **ComServices** to update the data in the workbook, then open your word processing document.

11 Select **Yes** when prompted to update the linked data and open the files.

Review your work.

Save and close the workbook when you are ready to move to the next section.

Task 2.9 Linking data to a word processing file

7 – Linking a chart to a word processing document

In this exercise you link the **RYCPlay** chart to the word processing document **News**.

The **chart** displays the progress of the team for this season. The word processing document is the club's newsletter.

All files for this exercise can be located on the accompanying CD-ROM.

Method

1 Open the workbook **RYCScore** and the word processing document **News**.

2 Carry out the following tasks:

   a **Copy** the chart on the **RYCPlay** worksheet.
   b Select the word processing document **News**.
   c Select and delete the following text in column 2: *(Delete this text and place chart here)*.
   d At the **insertion** point **Paste Special** the contents of the clipboard into the word processing document as **Microsoft Excel Chart Object**. Select the **Paste link** option button if not selected.

3 Adjust the chart as necessary.

   The following two lines of text should be displayed under the inserted chart:

   See you next season
   The RYC Team

   If necessary, insert line-spacing to move the text below the chart.

4 Save and review the contents of the word processing document **News**. How did the team do?

5 Close the **News** file when ready.

6 Close the **RYCScore** workbooks without saving any changes.

Save and review your work before moving to the next section.

In this section you have covered linked a data chart within a worksheet, between worksheets, between spreadsheets, into a word processing document.

In addition, the following skills were used to facilitate linking and presentation of data:

- Use paste special option Paste Link.
- Apply automatic formatting to a cell range.
- Freeze row and or column titles.
- 'Explode' all the segments in a pie chart.
- Filter data.

You have also had the opportunity to import a text file or create the data manually.

Using 3D referencing to calculate data between worksheets

All files for this section can be located on the accompanying CD-ROM.

Open the **StockOrderFruits** workbook. The data in the workbook was used in the custom number formats exercise.

At the moment if you want to see a **grand total** figure for all orders you would have to look at each individual worksheet and manually calculate the totals.

It would be useful to be able to see at a glance the grand total of all orders without having to look at each individual worksheet.

This is where a 3D reference would come in handy.

3D referencing consolidates data in adjacent worksheets using a 3D sum function.

The **3D** reference sum function syntax is similar to the sum function syntax.

You will have already used the sum function to calculate totals in spreadsheets, so the syntax should be familiar to you.

EXERCISE

1 – Create 3D references

Task A – File preparation

Method

1 **Insert** a new worksheet and ensure that it is the first worksheet in the workbook – in front of the **Ananas** worksheet. Carry out the following tasks:

   a **Rename** the new worksheet as **GrandTotal**.

   b In cell A1 enter the title **Stock Order**.

   c In cell A2 enter a label **Grand Total**.

Cell B2 will contain the **Grand Total** syntax and figure.

Task B – Creating the 3D references

Method

Cell F8 on each of the seven worksheets contains the formula that creates the **Total** figure on each individual worksheet.

You need to set a reference to cell F8 on each worksheet to sum all the totals together in cell B2 on the **GrandTotal** worksheet.

1 Select cell B2 of the **GrandTotal** worksheet.

2 Click in the formula bar and enter the **equal to** operator symbol.

3 Enter the word **Sum** in the formula bar. This tells the system the type of function you want to use in cell B2.

4 Key in an open round bracket: **(**

At this stage the formula bar should look like this: **=Sum(**.

5 Click the **Ananas** worksheet tab. (This is the first worksheet you want to create a reference to).

6 **Hold** down the **Shift** key on the keyboard.

7 Click the **Raisin** worksheet – the last worksheet in the set of seven.

8 Click cell F8 in the **Raisin** worksheet. (On all worksheets cell F8 contains the **Total figures**).

9 Key in a closing round bracket: **)**.

10 Press the **Enter** key to enter the data for processing.

11 Select cell B2 on the **GrandTotal** worksheet. The formula bar should display the following syntax: **=SUM(Ananas:Raisin!F8)**. The figure in cell B2 should be **2594.3**.

12 Format the **Grand Total** figure to Francs, two decimal places.

Have you saved your work lately?

What would you say the difference is between how a sum functions and the 3D sum functions used in the worksheets?

EXERCISE

2 – Working with data that is not logically organised

Method

1 **Unhide** the **Fraise** worksheet.

2 **Edit** the 3D reference syntax in cell A3 of the **GrandTotal** worksheet to include the new worksheet, which is now the last worksheet in the set. The edited 3D reference is **=SUM(Ananas:Fraise!F8)**, and the figure in cell B2 should now be **2,963. 10 F**.

3 Save and close the workbook.

The data in the **StockOrderFruits** workbook is arranged logically but this may not always be the case. Data you may want to calculate could be in rows on one sheet and columns on another. In the next exercise you will work with data that is not organised logically.

EXERCISE

3 – Working with data that is not logically organised

Method

1 **Open** the **3DDifferentLocation** workbook.

The data you want to total is located in *named ranges* in the following worksheets:

a Sheet1 *first* **cell A8**.
b Sheet2 *second* **cell F2**.
c Sheet4 *third* **cell G5**.

Each cell has been **named** to make the calculation syntax easier to understand. Use the **name box** to view each named range in the workbook.

2 Select cell D3 on the **Totals** worksheet.

3 In the **Formula Bar** enter the following syntax then press **Enter**: **=sum(first,second)**.

The **Grand Total** figure displayed in cell D3 on the Totals worksheet should be **5149**.

Info

If you have entered the syntax as shown the text sum will be converted to upper case if there is no error in the syntax.

4 Edit the syntax in cell D3 to include the calculation of the named range **Third**. The edited 3D reference: =SUM(First,Second,Third).

The **Grand Total** should now be **6565**.

As the data is in different locations on each worksheet the syntax for this calculation had to include the **named range** name.

The range operator **(:)** used in exercise one and two would not perform the necessary calculation.

5 Save and close the workbook.

4 – 3D sum function: practice

1 Open the workbook **3_3DLast**.

You use this workbook to record the expenditure from your bank and building society accounts.

All instructions to create the following 3D sum function are covered in the previous exercises.

The worksheets **Bank** and **BSociety** contain your estimated expenditure for the coming year.

2 Use a 3D sum function to calculate the named ranges **BankTotal** and **BSocietyTotal** in cell D1 of the **MyTotals** worksheet.

Worksheets **Jan** through **April** contain your actual expenditure for the first quarter of the year.

3 Use a 3D sum function to calculate the figures in cell B17 on worksheets **Jan** through **April** in cell D2 of the **MyTotals** worksheet.

Looks like you have overestimated your spending time for that holiday!

Save and review your work before moving to the next section.

In this section as well as using 3D referencing to calculate data between worksheets, you have also:

- Unhidden worksheets.
- Used a created custom number format.

Templates Tasks

2.11 Creating and working with templates

Spreadsheet templates are a basic document that you can use to create **new** spreadsheet **styles** from. Spreadsheet packages usually have some sample templates stored in the **default** template folder that you can use as a basis from which to create your own template.

If you are working on a college or business network, check with the Network Administrator that you can access and create **templates** from the system template folder.

To access an installed spreadsheet template

Click **New** on the **File** menu to open the **New** window.

The New window contains two tabs: **General** and **Spreadsheet Solutions**.

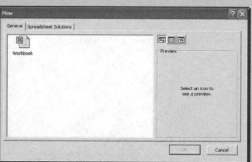

Figure 2.50 The New window General tab

The **General** tab contains the template for a basic blank new workbook.

Note: depending on your system configuration, your application may contain additional tabs in the **New** window.

The **Spreadsheet Solutions tab** contains sample templates. Your system may differ from the examples shown or you may not have any samples installed.

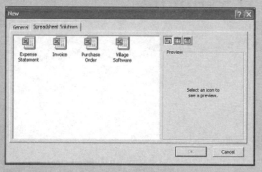

Figure 2.51 The New window Spreadsheet Solutions tab

If you have any templates installed, open one, and explore the contents or close the **New** window.

After you have explored the contents of any installed templates, close the file when you are ready to continue without saving any changes.

1 – Create and save a file as a template in a default template folder

After you have entered the data below you will save the workbook as a template.

1 **Open** a new workbook.

2 Using the example in Figure 2.52 create the **Workshop Invoice** data in cells A1:D13.

3 Formatting the **Workshop Invoice**:

    a Title

      i Merge and centre the title **Workshop Invoice** across cells A1:D1

      ii Bold = yes

      iii Font size = 12

Figure 2.52 Workshop invoice

	A	B	C	D
1	Workshop Invoice			
2				
3	Description	Quantity	Price	Total
4	CD Burning		1	
5	Faxing		1.5	
6	Faxing International		2.5	
7	Photocopying		0.2	
8	Printing B/W		0.4	
9	Printing Colour		1	
10	Scanning		1.5	
11				
12				
13	Total			

b Labels

   i Column heading labels

     ○ Cells A3:D3

     ○ Bold = yes

   ii Row labels

     ○ A4:A13

     ○ Font = Times New Roman

     ○ Bold = yes

   Ensure that all labels are clearly visible in cells.

c Cells

   Cells B13:C13, Fill colour = grey 25%.

4 Format cell C4:C12 and cell D4:D13 as currency, two decimal places.

5 Enter a **Multiplication** formula in cell D4 that will multiply the contents of cell B4 by cell C4, then copy the formula to cells D5:D12. The **multiplication** formula should look like this example: **=(B4*C4)**.

6 Enter a **SUM** function in cell D13 to total the contents of cells D4:D12. The **Function** should look like this example: **=SUM(D4:D12)**.

---

2 – Saving a workbook as a template

Method

1 Click **Save As** from the **File** menu to open the Save As window.

Figure 2.53 Save As window

Info

Templates have a specific file extension that informs the system of their function.

To ensure that the system saves your workbook as a template you need to change the Save as type: to **template**. The default is Microsoft Excel workbook. When this option is selected first your file is saved in a *default* template folder automatically.

2 Select the following options:

  a Save as type = **Template**

  b Enter the filename: **WksInvoice**

  c Save and close the file **WksInvoice.** Your workbook is now saved as a template.

Info

When you save a workbook in a *default* template folder, you access the template via the **New** command on the **File** menu; this forces the system to save the file with a new name and to close the original file.

The original file is therefore available for use later in its original state. Your copy of the file will contain your changes and or data if saved.

To access the **WksInvoice** template, select **New** on the **File** menu.

The **WksInvoice** should be available on the **General** tab. If not, check the **Spreadsheet Solutions** tab. If you are working on a network you may need to speak to the Network Administrator.

Figure 2.54 The New window General tab, displaying WksInvoice

3 – Opening several templates at once

Method

1 **Open** a copy of the **WksInvoice** template.

Info

Special features of a template

Look at the title bar of your spreadsheet application and note the name of the file you have just opened.

The system has automatically added a number as part of the file name. If you decide to save the file it already has a new filename.

New filename WksInvoice1

Figure 2.55 Filename

2 Add the following data to cell B4:B10 of the **WksInvoice1** file:

You have already created the calculation formulas for the Template. When the figures are entered, the **Total** column will display this.

3 **Save** the file with the default filename.

	4
	3
	7
	200
	50
	55
	18

	A	B	C	D
1	Workshop Invoice			
2				
3	Description	Quantity	Price	Total
4	CD Burning	4	£1.00	£4.00
5	Faxing	3	£1.50	£4.50
6	Faxing International	7	£2.50	£17.50
7	Photocopying	200	£0.20	£40.00
8	Printing B/W	50	£0.40	£20.00
9	Printing Colour	55	£1.00	£55.00
10	Scanning	18	£1.50	£27.00
11				£0.00
12				£0.00
13	Total			£168.00
14				

Figure 2.56 The completed workbook WksInvoice1

4 **Open** another copy of **WksInvoice** template. Note the file name in the title bar.

5 **Enter** some figures in the Quantity column.

6 **Close** the file *without* saving your changes when prompted by the system. The copy of the file you were using will automatically be deleted.

In the next set of exercises you will work with **Templates** files that have been saved outside of the *default* template folder, and therefore not available via the **New** command on the **File** menu.

Also, these templates files have not inherited the special feature of a template, which have a number automatically added as part of the filename, when opened. If you decide to **save** any changes to these **Templates** without overwriting the original contents of the file, you must use **Save As** on the **File** menu.

Task

Your manager is out at a business meeting. She has asked you to take personal responsibility for the following tasks being completed today:

- **Enter** and **Print** a stationery order for the department using the template **Stationery**.
- **Enter** and **Print** an expenses form using the template **ExpensesClaim**.
- **Enter** and **Print** the attendance of students on today's course, using the Template **Attendance**.

These **Templates** were created by your manager and have been saved in the **UseTemplates** section of the accompanying CD-ROM.

To see any files that have been saved as templates outside of a default template folder you may need to change the *Files of type* to **Template** in the **Open** window. The default is Microsoft Excel workbook.

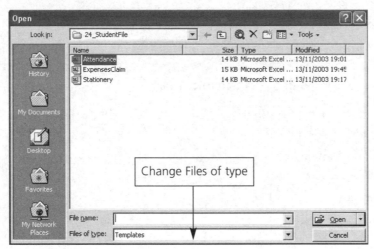

Figure 2.57 Open window with Templates selected as 'Files of type'

---

4 – Using templates in practice

Method

Open the **Stationery** template workbook.

Enter the following stationery order under the column labels **Goods** and **Quantity**, in cells B8:C20.

Goods	Quantity
Black Pens	100
Blue Pens	50
Headed Paper	2
Stapler	2
Envelopes A4	7
Plain Paper	4
Floppy Disks	100
Desk Tidy	2
Tape	6
Address Labels	3
Anti-static Screen Cleaner	3
Post-Its	20
Hole-Puncher	2

2 **Print** the **Stationery** spreadsheet if you have access to a printer.

3 Close the template **Stationery** without saving your changes.

4 Open the template **ExpensesClaim** and in cells A14:F20 enter the following data from your manager's handwritten expenses form below:

Date	Journey To/From	Fares	Entertainment	Subsistence	Hotel
05/05/03	Westfield Conference	75.00			
05/05/03	Westfield Conference				175.90
19/06/03	Sheffield/London	35.00			
30/06/03	Buyers Meeting		300		
03/07/03	Breakfast Meeting			40.00	
18/07/03	London/Leeds	45.00			
08/08/03	London/Birmingham	70.00			

5 **Print** the **ExpensesClaim** order if you have access to a printer.

6 **Close** the template **ExpensesClaim** without saving your changes.

7 **Open** the template **Attendance** and, from the table that follows; **Copy** and **Paste** the relevant following student attendance data from cells F2:F5 to cells B3:B25:

Cell	Attendance Type	Cell	Attendance Type
B3	Attended	B15	Attended
B4	Attended	B16	Attended
B5	Attended	B17	Attended
B6	Attended	B18	Sick
B7	Attended	B19	Authorised Absence
B8	Attended	B20	Sick
B9	Attended	B21	Attended
B10	Attended	B22	Attended
B11	Attended	B23	Attended
B12	Attended	B24	Attended
B13	Unauthorised Absence	B25	Attended
B14	Attended		

8 **Print** the **Attendance** order if you have access to a printer.

9 **Close** the template **Attendance** without saving your changes.

Save and review your work before moving to the next section.

In this task you have looked at how to access system templates, created and saved a template to a *default* template folder, and used templates created and saved outside of the **default** template folder.

In the next task you will **edit** the **templates** created by your manager and save these files in a *default* template folder.

2.12 Amending a template

After printing a **Stationery** order as in Exercise 4, you normally enter the price and total price for each item manually and calculate the grand total using a calculator.

After reviewing the three templates created by your manager you have decided to amend these to add functionality.

Figure 2.58 Stationery order

Support Services Stationery Order

Location	3rd Floor Internation House Surrey Mews	
Order Date	29/12/2003	

Goods	Quantity	
Black Pens	100	0.85
Blue Pens	50	0.85
Headed Paper	2	20
Stapler	2	7.5
Envelopes A4	1	29.96
Plain Paper	4	3.99
Floppy Disks	100	0.32
Desk Tidy	2	17.5
Tape	6	0.49
Address Labels	3	6.49
Anti-Static Screen Cleaner	3	2.45
Post-Its	20	0.99
Hole-Puncher	2	8.75

You have created copies of each workbook template with data and saved these under the following names:

- **EditStationery**
- **EditExpensesClaim**
- **EditAttendance**

1 – Editing the EditStationery workbook

To add real functionality to the spreadsheet you have decided that by adding **labels**, **currency formatting** and **sum functions** you will be able to complete your stationery order electronically.

Method

1 Open the **EditStationery** workbook.

2 Add the following labels to the workbook:

    a Cell D7 **Price**.
    b Cell E7 **Total**.
    c Cell A21 **Grand Total**.

3 Format cells D8:E20 as Currency, two decimal places

4 Formatting cell E21:

    a **Currency**: 2 decimal places.
    b **Fill Color** = grey 25%.
    c **Font Color** = red.

5 Enter a **Multiplication** formula in cell E8 that will multiply the contents of cell C8 by cell D8.

6 Copy the formula to cells E9:E20.

7 Enter a **SUM** function in cell E21 to total the contents of cells E8:E20.

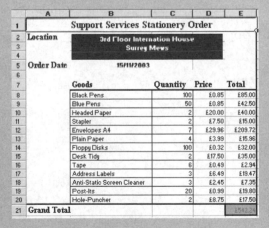

Figure 2.59 The completed Stationery order

To create the blank template

Method

1 **Delete** the data in cells C8:C20 and D8:D20.

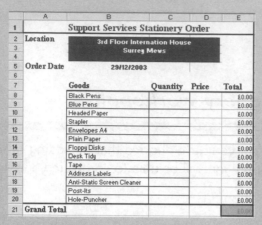

Figure 2.60 Blank template

2 Save the **EditStationery** workbook in a *default* template folder.

3 To access a *default* template folder change the *save as type:* to **Template** in the **Save As** window.

4 Enter a file with a name of your choice.

5 **Save** the file.

6 **Close** the workbook.

Is the template visible in the **New** window **General** tab?

7 Select **New** on the **File** menu to check.

EXERCISE

2 – Automatically calculating figures

The **EditExpensesClaim** workbook did not automatically calculate the figures entered.

If you add this feature you will reduce the opportunities for errors being entered and expenses claims being returned.

Method

1 Add the following labels to the **EditExpensesClaim** workbook:

   a In cell B24 enter the label **Totals**.
   b In cell B26 enter the label **Payable**.
   c Apply a **Thick Box Border** to cells B24:F27.
   d Format cells A14:A23 as **Date** using this format **01-Jan-03**.
   e Format cells C14:F24 as **Currency** two decimal places. Copy the formatting to cell C26.
   f Apply the **fill colour** grey 25% to cell C26. **Copy** the formatting to cells C24:F24.
   g Enter a **SUM** function in cell C24 to total the contents of cells C14:C23. **Copy** the **SUM** function to cells D24:F24.

While entering the figures for your manager's expenses you noted that she had entered the amount of her **Normal Return Fare to Work** in cell D11 of the spreadsheet.

Any travel expenses claimed are repaid minus Normal Return Fare to Work.

2 Enter a **SUM** Function in cell C26 to total the contents of cells C24:F24 and deduct any figure in cell D11. The function should look like the following example: **=SUM(C24:F24)-D11**.

3 Save the workbook.

4 Enter the following information in cell A2 to assist users of your template:

'Enter data only in the white cells. Amounts in gray-shaded cells will be calculated automatically.'

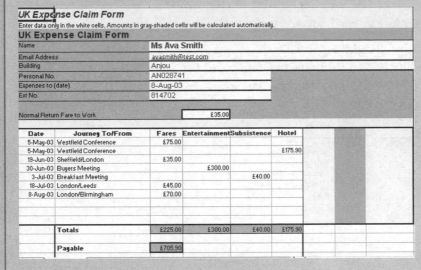

Figure 2.61 The completed EditExpensesClaim workbook

5 **Delete** any data in cells C14:F23, cells C4:C9 and cell D11.

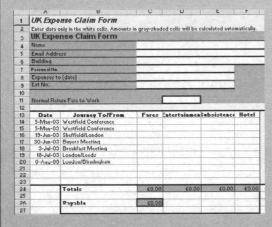

Figure 2.62 Blank template

6 Save the **EditExpensesClaim** workbook in a *default* template folder with a filename of your choice.

7 **Close** the workbook.

7 – Editing the EditAttendance workbook

To complete the attendance register for your manager you used **copy** and **paste** to place the relevant attendance type from the list in cells F2:F5 against student's names based on the list you were given by the facilitator.

	A	B	C	D	E	F
1	Course Attendance Register					Attendance Type
2	Name	Attendance Type				Attended
3	Fizal					Authorised Absence
4	Raymond					Unauthorised Absence
5	Hazel					Sick
6	Nisha					
7	Akida					
8	Samira					
9	Joanne					
10	Paul					
11	Steve					
12	Sonya					

Figure 2.63 The original Attendance spreadsheet

Editing the workbook

If you use a linking syntax in cells you will only have to edit the syntax for individual students attendance type before printing the list.

Method

1 **Open** the **EditAttendance** workbook and make the following changes:

   a **Link cells** B3:B25 to the **data** in cell F2.

   b **Edit** the **syntax** in cell B13 to display the data in cell F4.

   c **Edit** the **syntax** in cell B19 to display the data in cell F3.

   d **Edit** the **syntax** in cell B20 to display the data in cell F5.

	B20	▼	=	=$F$5		
	A	B	C	D	E	F
1	Course Attendance Register					Attendance Type
2	Name	Attendance Type				Attended
3	Fizal	Attended				Authorised Absence
4	Raymond	Attended				Unauthorised Absence
5	Hazel	Attended				Sick
6	Nisha	Attended				
7	Akida	Attended				
8	Samira	Attended				
9	Joanne	Attended				
10	Paul	Attended				
11	Steve	Attended				
12	Sonya	Attended				
13	Angie	Unauthorised Absence				
14	Fran	Attended				
15	Crystal	Attended				
16	Ernie	Attended				
17	Nellie	Attended				
18	Helen	Attended				
19	Kia	Authorised Absence				
20	Khurram	Sick				
21	Kaya	Attended				
22	Judith	Attended				
23	Christine	Attended				

Figure 2.64 The completed EditAttendance workbook

2 **Delete** the data in cells B3:B25.

3 Save the **EditAttendance** workbook in the *default* template folder with a filename of your choice.

4 **Close** the workbook.

Are the new templates visible in the **New** window **General** tab?

Save and review your work before moving to the next section.

In this section you have **edited** the **templates** created by your manager to include functionality, and saved these files in the *default* template folder.

By saving the **templates** in this folder you have protected your original design and made the templates available for all users of your system to use, or as a basis from which to create their own templates.

In this task you have amended a template and linked data within a worksheet.

The chart diagram shown below describes the various objects and areas that make up a chart.

Before you start the charts section take some time to study the diagram so that you are aware of the location of each area when you need to work with this.

Areas such as the **X and Y Axis** are not as visible as the chart **Title** or **Legend** when using a shortcut or double click to access the area.

Figure 2.64a The graph window

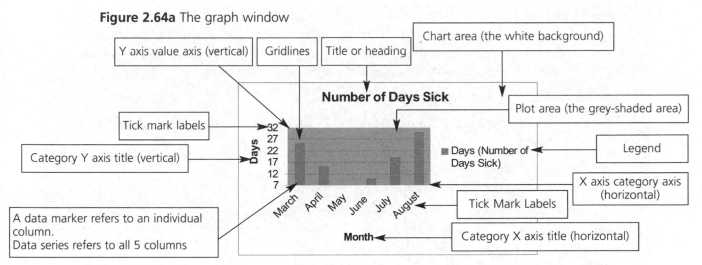

Y axis value axis (vertical)

Gridlines

Title or heading

Chart area (the white background)

Number of Days Sick

Plot area (the grey-shaded area)

Tick mark labels

Category Y axis title (vertical)

Days (Number of Days Sick)

Legend

X axis category axis (horizontal)

A data marker refers to an individual column.
Data series refers to all 5 columns

Tick Mark Labels

Month◄

Category X axis title (horizontal)

Figure 2.64a Data the chart example was created from

Month	Days (Number of Days Sick)
March	25
April	15
May	7
June	10
July	19
August	30

Charts and graphs Tasks

2.13 Task Changing the appearance of slices in a pie chart

The slices of a pie chart are **displayed** based on the order of the data on the worksheet when the chart is created.

If you need to change the way the data is displayed in a pie chart you will need to rotate the pie slices. The individual slices of a pie chart are called **data series.**

Open the workbook **Angle_1PieChart**. The file can be located on the accompanying CD-ROM.

The worksheet **Chart1** contains an exploded pie chart that records the total number of days sick leave for all employees in any month. As **March** is the first record on the worksheet that the chart was created from, it occupies the top **right** position in the chart when the chart is created.

Figure 2.65 Pie chart

EXERCISE 1 – How to change angle of pie chart slices

Method

1 **Double-click** the **March** slice of the pie chart to open the **Format Data Point** or **Format Data Series** window .

If the **Options tab** is not the default when the window opens, select the Options tab. In this window you can manipulate the angle of pie chart slices (**data series**).

The results of your changing the **Angle of first slice** should look like the example in Figure 2.66.

Figure 2.66 Format Data Point window

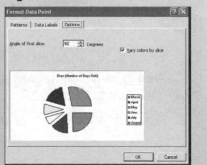

Exercise 1 Step 2

Enter the figure **92** in the **Angle of first slice** spin button text box. If you use the spin button, changes are immediately visible in the window. If you key in the figure you will need to press the Tab key on the keyboard to see the changes in the window you are using.

2   **Enter** the figure **92** in the **Angle of first slice**.

Changes are displayed in the **Format Data Point** window so you can decide if theses changes are appropriate.

3   Enter the figure **28** in the Angle of first slice text box.
Where is the August slice of the pie now located? Top left or bottom right?

4   Enter the figure **150** in the Angle of first slice text box.
Which pie slice is now bottom centre? March or July?

5   Select **OK** to close the window and apply the figure **150** to the Angle of first slice.

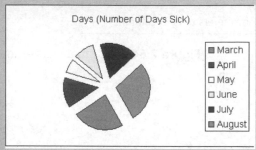
Figure 2.67 Example new chart view

EXERCISE ## 2 – How to spin pie chart slices

Method

Select the **Chart2** worksheet.

The **Chart2** worksheet displays Popular Toothpaste Flavours displayed by value in a pie chart. You would like the most popular flavour, **Cherry with 75%**, to occupy the top **right** position in the chart.

1   Open the **Format Data Point** window.

2   Use the **Angle of first slice** spin buttons to place the **Cherry** portion of the pie chart in the top **right** position in the chart.

Info

Spin buttons are the up and down arrows to the right of the text box.

Your changes should reflect the example below.

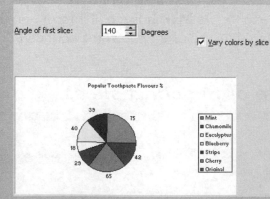

Figure 2.68 Popular Toothpaste Flavours pie chart

Note: You can also access the **Format Data Point** window by **clicking** a data series and clicking **Selected Data Series** from the **Format** menu.

Task 2.13 Changing the appearance of slices in a pie chart

3 – Practice

Method

Select the **Chart3** worksheet.

The **Chart3** worksheet displays percentages of book sales.

1   Use the **Angle of first slice** spin buttons to place the book **EEC Today** portion of the pie chart in the top **right** position in the chart.

2   What is the **Angle of first slice degree figure** needed to achieve this?

Save and review your work before moving to the next section.

2.14

Changing the appearance of axes in a chart

To format the **X** or **Y Chart Axes** you need to select this.

The **X Chart Axes** area is located at the bottom of the plot area. The **Y Chart Axes** area is located to the left of the plot area.

Review the chart diagram at the start of this section to identify these two areas.

How to select chart areas (**Objects**) and open the Formatting windows.

Technique 1 – Using the chart toolbar

Method

Chart objects have a specific toolbar that you can use to select areas of a chart.

The chart toolbar is automatically visible when you create or open a workbook that contains a chart.

If the chart toolbar is not visible when a chart is open, click any area of the chart to activate this. If the chart toolbar does not display, select Toolbars via the View Menu and click the Chart Option.

   **Figure 2.69** Chart toolbar

1   Rest the mouse pointer on each toolbar button to see a **screen tip** description of the function of the button.

2   To select a specific area of the **Chart** click the black arrow to the right of the **Chart Object List Box** to display a dropdown list of chart areas.

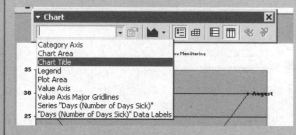   **Figure 2.70** Dropdown list of chart areas (object) names

Info

Clicking a chart area in the list will close the **Chart Object List Box** and place selection handles around the selected area in the chart.

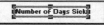   **Figure 2.71** Selected chart title

Once you have selected the chart area you want to format:

3 **Click** the **Format Object** toolbar button 🖼 on the chart toolbar to open the relevant window.

After using the **Chart Object** list box to select an area/object the **Format Object** button tool tip will display as **Format** and (**Object**) name.

Technique 2 – Using the menu bar

Method

1 Click the chart object.

2 Click the **Format** menu.

3 The menu will open with the selected object name as an option.

4 **Click** the **Object Name** from the menu to open the Format window.

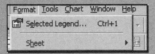

Figure 2.72 Menu bar

Technique 3 – Right click

Method

1 **Right click** the object.

2 **Click** the object name to open the Format window from the pop-up menu.

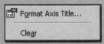

Figure 2.73 Pop-up menu

While most of the following exercises use the right mouse button, you should use the method of **selection** that you are most comfortable with.

EXERCISE ## 1 – Changing the chart title text

Open the workbook **FormatAxis**. The file can be located on the accompanying CD-ROM.

In this exercise you will format a line chart using the right mouse button to access pop-up menus, where appropriate. The chart was created from the data on the worksheet **DaysLost**.

Select the **SickLeave** worksheet.

Method

1 Click the chart title to select the title area [Number of Days Sick].

2 Use the left mouse button to click in the selected area, at the beginning of the text: 'Number'.

When you click in the selected title area the cursor will change shape to an **I beam** and start flashing, indicating that you can key in text.

3 Key in the new title **Sick Leave Monitoring**.

4 **Delete** the old title **Number of Days Sick**.

5 To remove the selection handles click outside the selected title area.

Remember to **save** your work regularly!

2 – Formatting the category axis

Method

In this exercise you will practice removing **tick mark labels** from the chart on the **SickLeave** worksheet.

1 **Right** Click the **X Axis** (Category Axis).

2 Select **Format Axis** from the **pop-up menu** to Open the **Format Axis** window.

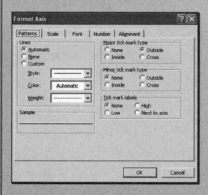

Figure 2.74 Format Axis window

3 Select the **Pattern** tab.

You want to remove the default **Tick mark labels** option.

Info

Tick mark labels are the labels that appear in the **Category Axis** at the bottom of a chart.

4 Click the **None** option button under the Tick mark labels section.

5 Click **OK** to apply your choice and close the Format Axis window.

The tick mark labels displaying the **months** of the year at the bottom of the chart will be removed.

3a – Format the data series

In this exercise you will practice adding **Data Labels** to the chart.

Method

1 Right click at any point the series "Number of Days Sick".

2 Select **Format Data Series** from the pop-up menu to open the window.

Figure 2.75 Select Format Data Series **Figure 2.76** The Format Data Series window

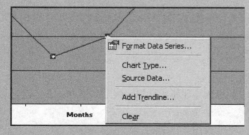

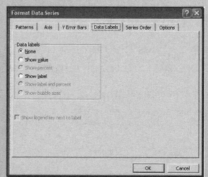

3 Select the **Data Label Tab**.

In the previous task you removed the **tick mark labels.** How do you identify the individual **Data Marker Point** of a **Series**?

Info

The two options available in this window are **Show value** and **Show label**.

The **Show value** option will display a percentage figure e.g. **25%**. The **Show label** option will display the labels that represent the data in cells A4:A9, the **months** of the year.

4 Select the **Show label** option.

5 Click **OK** to apply your choice and close the Format Data Series window.

Figure 2.77 Part of the line chart with Show label option added

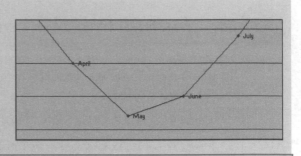

3b – Formatting the new data labels

Method

1 **Right** click a data label.

2 Select **Format Data Label** from the pop-up menu.

3 Select the following formatting from the **Font** tab:

   a Font style **bold**.

   b Font size **12**.

4 Click **OK** to apply your choice and close the Format Data Label window.

4 – Format the value axis

In this exercise you will practice formatting data in the **Value Axis** area of a chart.

These changes will format the figures on the left of the chart.

Method

1 **Right** click the **Y Axis** (value axis).

2 Select **Format Axis** from the pop-up menu.

3 On the **Font** tab select the font style **bold** and font size **12**.

4 Click **OK** to apply your choice and close the Format Data Series window.

5 – Changing the orientation of text

Select the **Hours** worksheet.

The chart displays the number of hours lost in a six-month period and was created from the data on the worksheet **HoursLost**.

Changing the orientation of the text in the **X Axis** (category axis).

Method

1 **Right** click the axis.

2 Select the **Alignment** tab.

3 Change the text **orientation** to '**–45**' degrees.

4 You can do this by:

   a Entering the figures **–45** in the degrees text box.
   b Drag the line marker to the appropriate degree marker.

Task 2.14 Changing the appearance of axes in a chart

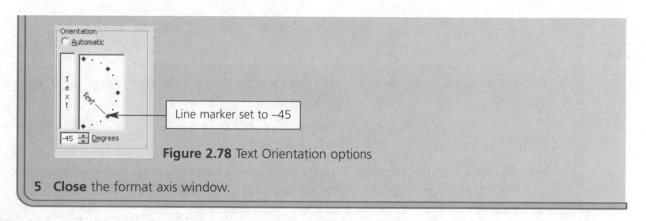

Figure 2.78 Text Orientation options

5 **Close** the format axis window.

6 – Displaying tick mark labels in a chart

Select the **DaysHours** worksheet. The chart displays the number of days and hours lost in a six-month period. The chart was created from the data on the worksheet **HoursLost**.

Method

1 Display high tick mark labels for the **X Axis** (category axis). Tick mark labels are available via the Pattern tab in the Format Axis window.

The tick mark labels for the chart should now be displayed at the top of the chart plot area as in Figure 2.79.

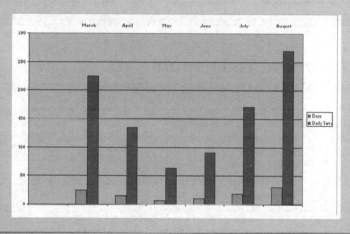

Figure 2.79 High tick mark labels

7 – Formatting chart objects and improving display

Select the **SubTotalChart** worksheet. The chart displays publication sales and was created from the data on the worksheet **PubSales**.

All tasks to be completed have been covered in previous exercises. Review these if you are unsure how to complete a task.

Fine-tune the chart using the right-click pop-up menus where appropriate.

Figure 2.80 The original SubTotalChart chart

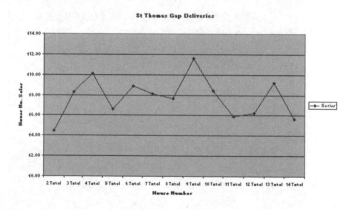

Method

1 **Remove** the tick mark labels displaying the **Total** for each figure on the **X Axis**.

2 **Delete** the Category Axis title.

3 Add **Data Labels** for the **Series 1** that represents the data in cells A9:A49 on the **PubSales** worksheet.

The chart, as it stands, looks acceptable, but there is a lot of empty space at the bottom of the chart plot area.

If the **Y Axis** (value axis) is adjusted to match the values in the sales figures will this have an impact on the view of the chart? The lowest sales figure in the chart is **£4**.

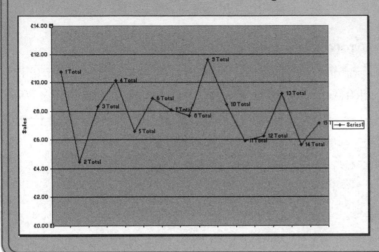

Figure 2.81 The SubTotalChart chart

8 – Formatting the value axis scale

Method

1 Open the **Format Axis** window and select the **Scale** tab.

Minimum 0 changes to 4

Figure 2.82 Format Axis window

In this example note that the **Value (Y) axis scale** minimum is set to **Zero (0)**, the default.

2 **Delete** the minimum figure zero (0) and replace this with the figure **4**.

3 Click **OK** to apply the changes and close the Format Axis window.

The chart's presentation now looks tidier and does not contain any unused areas.

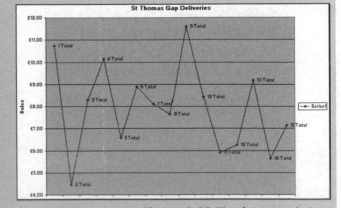

Figure 2.83 The formatted chart

If a data label is not aligned you will have to use the drag and drop technique to realign it.

Using drag and drop

Click the **chart object** with the left mouse button to select it. Selection handles will be placed around the object. **Drag** and **drop** the **object** in the new location.

Training Days   **Figure 2.84** Chart title with selection handles

To remove the selection handles surrounding the title click an area outside the handles.

Tip

If you drop an object in the wrong place use the **Undo** toolbar button.

The data used to create the chart was located in **columns A** and **G** and this will have contributed to the labels not being aligned accurately when the **Data Labels** were added.

EXERCISE

9 – Change number style and format X axis text

Select the **SalesPercentage** worksheet.

The chart was created from the data on the worksheet **Sales.** The figures should be displayed as percentages for each item. Unfortunately the figures are displayed as numbers.

In this exercise you will change the numbers to a percentage style and format the text in the **X Axis** (category axis).

Task A

Method

1   **Open** the **Format Axis** window for the **Y Axis** (Value Axis).

2   On the **Numbers** tab select **Percentage** from the category list box.

3   Click **OK** to apply your choice and close the Format Data Series window.

Task B

Method

1   Apply the following **formatting** to the **X Axis** (category axis).

    a   Font style **Bold**.
    b   Font size **12**.

The **SalesPercentage** worksheet should now appear as in Figure 2.85.

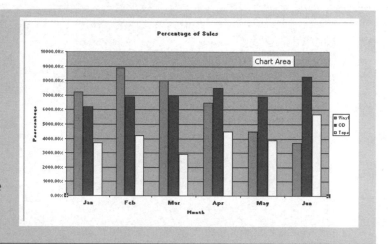

Figure 2.85 SalesPercentage worksheet

2   Save and close the file.

Formatting practice

The Expenditure workbook records all the outgoing cash for the Express'O Café.

Open the Expenditure workbook and make the following changes to enhance the presentation of the workbook.

The commands to carry out the various tasks were covered in the previous exercises in the **FormatAxis** workbook.

1 Make the following changes on the Finance worksheet, by opening the Format Axis window for the **Y Axis** (value axis):

  a **Format** the values as **Currency,** two decimal places.

  b Set the Minimum **Scale** to 600.

2 Make the following changes on the **TotalExpenditure** worksheet. **Open** the **Format Axis** window for the **X Axis** (Category Axis):

  a Select the **Tick Mark Labels** option **None**.

  b Add Data Labels to the Series Points of the chart.

  c Change the **Y Axis** (value axis) values to **percentages**.

Save and review your work before moving to the next section.

Close the workbook.

In this section, in addition to changing the appearance of axes in a chart, you have also changed a chart title text to facilitate selecting individual chart objects.

2.15 Moving labels in a chart

Info

When you use the Chart Wizard to create a new chart you can position chart objects such as **Legend**, and **Data Labels** in the Chart Options window in step 3 of the Wizard.

After a **Chart** has been created if you need to move chart objects around the **chart** or **plot areas** such as the **Title**, **Legend** or **Data Labels** you can use the **drag and drop** technique you used earlier to reposition data labels or the relevant Format windows tabs.

Move technique 1 – Drag and drop a title, legend or data label revision

Method

1 Click the **chart object** with the left mouse button to select this. Selection handles will be placed around the object.

2 **Drag** and **Drop** the **object** in the new location.

Move technique 2 – Move a legend

Method

1 Right click the legend.

2 Click Format Legend on the pop-up menu.

3 Select the placement tab.

4 Click a placement option button.

5 Close the window.

Move technique 3 – Move data labels

Method

1 Right click a **Data Label**.

2 Click format **Data Labels** on the pop-up menu.

3 Select the **Alignment** tab.

4 Select a **Label Position** from the dropdown list box.

5 Close the window.

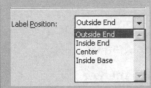

Label Position: Outside End
Outside End
Inside End
Center
Inside Base

Figure 2.86 Label Position selection in the Format Data Label window

Info

A chart title can only be repositioned via **drag and drop**.

EXERCISE

1 – Reposition chart elements using drag and drop

Method

Open the workbook **Move Chart Objects**. The file can be located on the accompanying CD-ROM. **Select** the worksheet **TrainingDays**.

In this task you will reposition the **Chart Title** and **Legend** within the chart area using **drag and drop**.

1 **Drag and drop** the **chart title** in a straight line on the left side of the chart area.

2 **Drag and drop** the legend under the chart title.

Info

If you drop an object in the wrong place use the **Undo** toolbar button.

The top of your worksheet should look like the chart in Figure 2.87 after you have repositioned the chart objects.

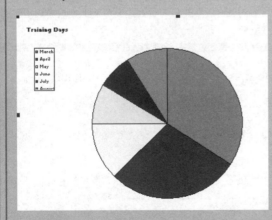

Training Days

□ March
■ April
□ May
□ June
■ July
■ August

Figure 2.87 The TrainingDays worksheet

2 – Move technique 2: practice

Select the worksheet **ChartFlavours**.

The data labels have been placed above the individual column data markers in error. This position is called **Outside End**.

You are not sure which position would best suit the data labels. Use move technique 2 to move **data labels**, to view the various positions.

Method

1 Reposition the data label in the position **inside end** of each **data marker**.

2 Reposition the data label in the position **inside base** of each **data marker**.

3 Reposition the data label in the position **outside end** of each **data marker**.

4 Reposition the data label in the **centre** position of each **data marker**.

The worksheet should now appears in Figure 2.88 after you have repositioned the **data labels** in the **centre** position.

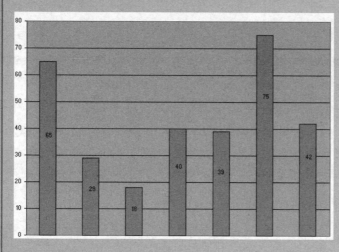

Figure 2.88 The ChartFlavours worksheet

5 Save your changes.

3 – Move technique: practice

Method

1 **Select** the worksheet **Days** and use **drag and drop** to make the following changes:

a **Drag and drop** the individual **data label** on the **data markers** below each label.

b **Drag and drop** the **chart title** in a straight line on the left side of the chart area.

c **Drag and drop** the **legend** in the top section of the **plot area**.

Figure 2.89 Repositioned chart objects

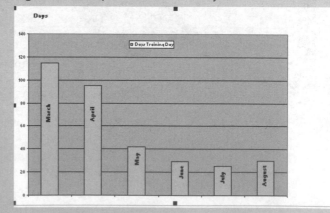

The worksheet should look like the chart in Figure 2.89 after you have repositioned the chart objects.

Repositioning the various chart objects has improved the appearance of the chart.

Save and review your work before moving to the next section.

Close the workbook.

Exploding pie chart slices

When you use the Chart Wizard to create a pie chart you have the opportunity to select an **Exploded Pie Chart** from the standard chart types via the Wizard in step 1.

You can also use the **drag and drop** technique to explode all segments of a pie chart.

In this set of exercises you will:

a **Explode** a pie chart using **Drag and drop**.

b Create an **Exploded** pie chart via the Chart Wizard.

c **Explode** two pie charts you have worked with in previous chart exercises.

EXERCISE

1 – Use drag and drop to exploded a pie chart

Open the workbook **MediaSales**.

Method

1 **Select** the worksheet **DaysExplode**.

2 Click the pie chart.

3 Use **drag and drop** to explode the pie chart.

Info

When you **drop** the pie chart the various pieces will separate to give an exploded appearance.

4 **Save** your work.

After it has been exploded, your chart should look like the chart in Figure 2.90.

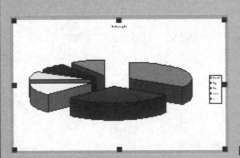

Figure 2.90 Exploded pie chart

2 – Create an exploded pie chart via the chart wizard

Select the worksheet Music.

The worksheet is used to record the percentage of sales of various music media such as vinyl and CDs.

Method

1 Use the data in cells B1:C6 to create an exploded pie chart **with 3D Visual Effect** via the chart wizard.

2 In **Step 4 of 4** within the chart wizard, select the option to place the chart on a new worksheet.

3 Change the **default** name of **Chart1** to **MusicExplode** for the new chart.

Your new chart should now appear as in Figure 2.91.

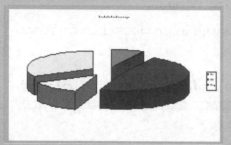

Figure 2.91 'Exploded' Music pie chart

4 Save and review your work before moving to the next section.

5 **Close** the workbook.

3 – Explode a pie chart: practice

In the following tasks you can explode the pie charts using drag and drop **or** the chart wizard.

If you decide to use the Chart Wizard to explode the existing charts, following the steps below:

Method

1 **Select** the chart.

2 **Click** the Chart Wizard Toolbar button.

3 In Step 1 of the Wizard:

  a **Select** the chart type.
  b **Click** the **Finish** button.

Task A

Method

1 **Open** the workbook **Angle_1PieChart**. You used the workbook in the Change angle of a pie chart slices exercises.

2 **Select** the **Chart3** worksheet.

3 **Explode** all segments in the pie chart.

Task B

Method

1 **Open** the workbook **MoveChartObjects**. You used this workbook in the Reposition title, legend or data labels in a chart exercises.

2 **Select** the **TrainingDays** worksheet.

3 **Explode** all segments in the pie chart.

Save and review your work before moving to the next section.

Close the workbook.

2.17 Removing data series from a chart

Open the workbook **SeriesDelete**. The file can be located on the accompanying CD-ROM.

EXERCISE 1 – Delete a data series via the keyboard

Select the **StudentNumbers** worksheet.

The worksheet was created to compare individual course take-up over the preceding six years.

You have discovered that the figures for the **Art** class have been recorded inaccurately and they need removing from the chart.

The **Art** class **Data Series** is displayed in yellow on the author's PC. Your system may represent the series in a different colour. Use the **legend** to identify each series you need to work with.

Info

Data series is the collective name for all columns of the same colour or pattern in a chart.

Data marker is an individual column.

Method

1 Click once with the left mouse button on any **data markers** representing the **Art** data series.

Info

When a data series has been clicked selection handles will be placed on each **data marker** in the series.

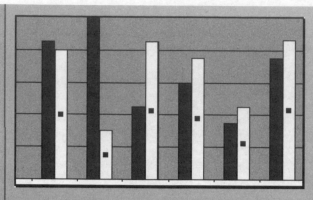

Figure 2.92 Selected data series

2   Press **Delete** to remove the **Art data series**.

    The Art data series is deleted from the **chart** but not from the source data on the worksheet **Students**.

3   Check the **Students** worksheet to verify the data is still available.

4   **Save** the workbook.

Other techniques for deleting a data series

Method

1   Using the **Edit** menu to delete a data series:

    a   Click any **data markers** representing the data series you want to delete.
    b   Point to **Clear** on the **Edit** menu.
    c   Click **Series** on the sub-menu to delete the data series.

2   **Shortcut** for deleting a data series.

    a   **Right** click a **data marker**.
    b   Select **Clear** from the pop-up menu.

If you **delete** a **data series** in error, use the **Undo** toolbar button to replace the **Series**.

2 – Deleting data series: practice

Task A

Method

Select the **LanguageStudents** worksheet.

This chart should contain the student figures for a language course. In error, other courses have been added to the source spreadsheet and now appear in the chart.

1   **Delete** the following **data series**. Use the **legend** to identify each **series**:

    a   Economics.
    b   Recreation.
    c   Media Studies.

The edited chart should look like the chart in Figure 2.93 and should only display **series** for the following:

○ French   ○ German
○ Spanish   ○ Italian

Figure 2.93 The LanguageStudents bar chart

Task 2.17 Removing data series from a chart

Method

Using one of the above techniques **delete** the following **data series**:

a On the **ChartBusiness** worksheet, delete the **Shorthand** data series.

b On the **ChartArts** worksheet, delete the **Jan** and **March** data series.

Save and review your work before moving to the next section.

Close the workbook.

2.18 Amending the chart type of a data series

Open the back-up copy of the workbook you used in the deleting a data series exercise.

The workbook is saved as **ModifyChartDataSeries** on the accompanying CD-ROM.

EXERCISE 1 – Changing the chart type

In the following exercises you will practice changing the **chart type** for a defined **data series** in a chart.

You want to change the **chart type** for the **data series** representing the **English** students figures to see how these compare with the inaccurate **Art** figures.

In order to clearly see this you have decided to use two chart types on the worksheet.

Method

1 **Select** the **StudentNumbers** worksheet.

2 Right click one of the columns representing the **data series** English.

3 Select **Chart Type** from the pop-up menu.

The **Chart Type** window will open for the selection of **a new chart type only**.

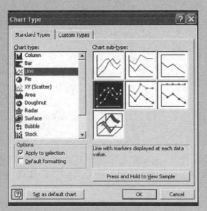

Figure 2.94 Chart Type window

4 Select chart type **Line**, sub-type 'Line with markers displayed at each data value', as you want this chart type to be applied to the selected series **English**.

5 In the **Options** section place a tick mark in the option **Apply to selection**, if this is not selected by default.

6 Click **OK** to apply your choice and to close the Chart Type window.

2 – Adding data labels

1 **Add** data labels to the new line chart **Data Series**.

2 Select the **Show Value** option button for the data labels.

Right click and use the pop-up menu to add data labels via the **Format Data Series** window.

Your worksheet should now look similar to the chart in Figure 2.95.

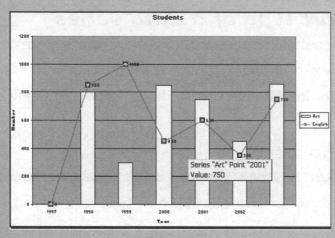

Figure 2.95 Bar chart with data labels showing value

3 **Save** the workbook.

3 – Modifying the chart type

The next set of exercises will help you to practice a sequence of commands to **modify** the **chart type** for a **defined data series**.

The basic commands to modify a chart data series are:

a Select the **data series**.
b Open the **Chart Type** window.
c Select the new **Chart Type** for the **data series**.
d Place a tick mark in the option **Apply to selection**.
e **Close** the window.
f **Save** your changes to the chart.

1 **Select** the **LanguageStudent** worksheet.

2 Create a pie chart from the data series **Media Studies**. Use the chart sub-type **Pie.** Displays the contribution of each value to a total.

The pie chart will be created behind the original chart, without data labels, and should appear as shown in Figure 2.96.

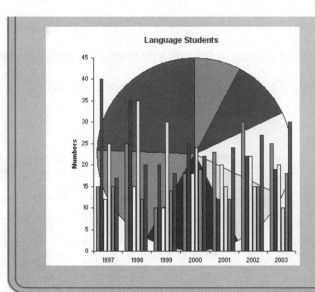

Figure 2.96 Pie chart and bar chart

4 – Practice

1 **Select** the **OtherCourses** worksheet.

2 Create a column chart from the data series **Economics**. Use the chart sub-type **Clustered Column** (Compares values across categories).

The completed worksheet should now look similar to the chart shown in Figure 2.97.

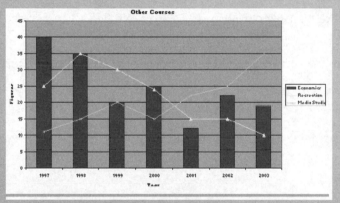

Figure 2.97 Formatted OtherCourses worksheet

Save and review your work before moving to the next section.

Close the workbook.

Making 2D charts clearer

In this exercise you will employ this technique in order to comply with a request from one of the managers in the department.

The manager has said that difficulties are sometimes encountered in identifying values in charts as the columns are close together.

1 – Clarifying charts

You will create a chart and then use this to practise widening the gaps between columns/bars in charts.

Task A – Creating the chart

Method

1 **Open** a new workbook.

2 **Save** the workbook as **ChartGapWidth**.

3 Rename **Sheet1** as **CarSalesData**.

4 **Enter** the data in the table, into cells A2:C9:

5 Create a **Comparative** chart from the **CarSalesData** worksheet data, choosing the following parameters:

   a Use the chart type **Column** and the chart sub-type **Clustered Column**.

   b The chart title is **Car Sales By Region**.

   c The category X axis title is **Month**.

   d The value Y axis title is **Figures**.

Month	North	South
	Car Sales	
March	25	15
April	6	10
May	8	15
June	11	14
July	20	18
August	9	12

6 Save the chart on a new worksheet, renamed as **CarSalesOne**.

7 **Save** your work!

The completed chart should look like the example in Figure 2.98 (system default chart colours will vary).

Info

The default **Overlap** of **0** (zero) has been applied to the chart via the Chart Wizard.

Data markers representing **North**, **South** and **East** sit next to each other in groups based on the category (month) that the sale took place in. The data markers do not overlap and can be clearly seen.

Figure 2.98 Gaps between groups of bars

In the example in Figure 2.99, the data markers sit on top of each other; this is described as overlapping.

Task 2.19 Making 2D charts clearer

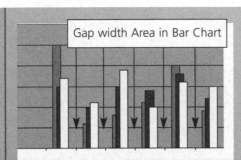

Gap width Area in Bar Chart

Figure 2.99 Data markers overlap

The default **Gap width** of **150** applies to the space between each category (months). These areas have been highlighted with arrows in the data marker overlap example (Figure 2.99).

Task B – Widening the gap between columns/bars in a 2D chart

1 **Right** click a data marker. Select **Format Data Series** from the pop-up menu.

2 Select the **Option** tab from the Format Data Series window.

An example of the chart you are working with will be visible in the window.

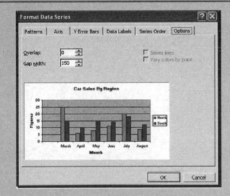

Figure 2.100 Format Data Series window

3 To display more space between the data markers in a category (month), **increase** the **overlap** figure by a *negative* figure and **increase** the **gap width** figure.

The default spacing for an **overlap** in a bar or column chart is **0** and the **gap width** is **150**.

The following restrictions apply to the values that can be entered via the keyboard or the spin buttons.

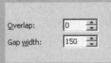

Figure 2.101 Overlap and Gap width spin buttons

You can only enter or use the spin buttons to increase or decrease a **gap width** value between **0** and **500**.

If you enter values outside of the range **0** and **500** for the **gap width** value, the following system error message will be displayed.

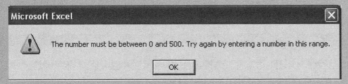

Figure 2.102 System error message – gap width

You can only enter or use the spin buttons to increase or decrease an **overlap** value between **-100** and **100**.

If you enter values outside the range **-100** and **100** for an **overlap** value, the following system error message will be displayed:

Figure 2.103 System error message – overlap

4   Once you have selected your **overlap** and **gap width** figures, close the Format Data Series window.

2 – Adding gaps between groups of columns

Method

1   Select the **North** data marker on the **CarSalesOne** worksheet.

2   Open the Format Data Series window and make the following changes.

   a   **Change** the default **overlap** figure to **–100** (minus 100).

   b   **Change** the default **gap width** figure to **300**.

   c   Click **OK** to apply your changes and to close the Format Data Series window.

Save your work!

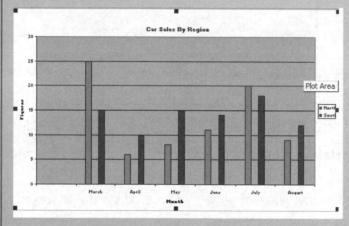

Figure 2.104 New overlap and gap width figures applied to chart

There is now increased space between the data markers in the same category (month). You could now show this to the manager to see if the new layout of the chart is what is needed to study the figures.

Save and review your work before moving to the next section.

Close the workbook.

3 – Increase the gap between columns in a 2D chart: practice

In the following short exercises you will practice adding and changing **overlap** and **gap width** values to consolidate your learning for this task item.

Open the workbook **GapWidthPractice**. The file can be located on the accompanying CD-ROM.

Task A

Method

1 Select the **SalesChart** worksheet.

2 Select any **data marker** on the worksheet.

3 Open the **Format Data Series** window and make the following changes:

   a **Change** the default **overlap** figure to **–50** (minus 50).
   b **Change** the default **gap width** figure to **350**.

4 Click **OK** to apply your changes and close the Format Data Series window.

5 Save your work!

Task B

Method

1 Select the **Students** worksheet.

2 Select any **data marker** on the worksheet.

3 Open the **Format Data Series** window and make the following changes:

   a **Change** the default **overlap** figure to **–95** (minus 95).
   b **Change** the default **gap width** figure to **400**.

4 Click **OK** to apply your changes and close the Format Data Series window.

Task C

Method

Adjust the **gap width** figure of **400** on the **Students** worksheet to **450**.

Task D

Method

1 On the **SalesChart** worksheet.

   a Adjust the **overlap** figure to **–100** (minus 100).
   b Adjust the **gap width** figure to **210**.

2 Save and review your work.

Close the workbook if you are moving to the next set of exercises.

The workbook now contains two charts that you can use for practising this task item at any time.

2.20 Adding an image to a chart

In this first exercise you will walk through the stages of inserting an image in a chart object. This will give you the opportunity to view the various windows you will be working with.

You can insert an image in the following chart objects:

- Plot area
- Data marker
- Chart area
- Legend

Open the workbook **1_ImagePlay**. All files for this section can be located on the accompanying CD-ROM.

Walking through the stages of inserting an image in a chart object

Method

1 Select the **Chart1** worksheet.

The chart was created from the data on Sheet1, and plots sales.

2 **Click** on the **plot area** of the **chart** to select it.

3 Click the **black** arrowhead next to the **Fill Color** toolbar button  to display the Fill Color window.

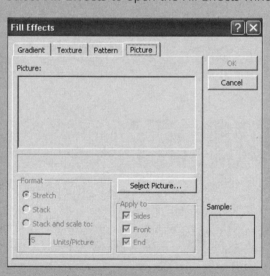

Figure 2.105 Fill Color

4 Select **Fill Effects** to open the Fill Effects window.

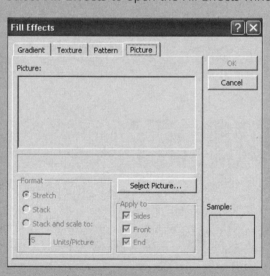

Figure 2.106 Empty Fill Effects window

5 Select the **Picture** tab.

6 In this instance, **clicking** the **Select Picture** command should open the **My Pictures** folder on your system. If the **My Pictures** folder is not opened by default, or the image is stored in a different location, navigate to the folders where the image is stored on your computer or network.

7 **Double-click** on the picture you wish to use. Double-click any image available on your computer for this exercise.

You will be returned to the **Fill Effects** window, where you can see a sample of the image you have selected.

Images can be manipulated by applying a display **format** for the image in the Fill Effects window.

8   When you have selected an image and applied any formatting necessary, click **OK** to insert the image into the selected object and to close the Fill Effects window.

Note: you must select a chart area before attempting to insert an image. If a chart area is not selected before clicking the black arrowhead next to the **Fill Color** toolbar button, the Fill Color window will display without giving you access to the **Fill Effects** button/window (see Figure 2.107).

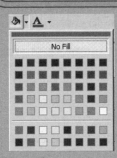

Figure 2.107 Fill Color window

Work through this section again if you are not ready to move to the next exercise.

8   Close the **1_ImagePlay** workbook without saving any changes.

2 – Inserting an image

All graphic files can be located on the accompanying CD-ROM.

1   **Open** the workbook **2 ChartImage**.

2   Select the **CarSale** worksheet.

3   Insert the Image **BCar** in the **plot area** of the **CarSales** chart.

Figure 2.108 Fill Effects window with image

When you select the **plot** or **chart areas** as the destination for an **image**, the **Format** and **Apply to** options are disabled and the default Stretch option is applied to the inserted image.

You will use the **Stack** Format option in the next exercise.

Your chart should now look similar to the one in Figure 2.109.

If your default system colours clash with the inserted image, change these. How?

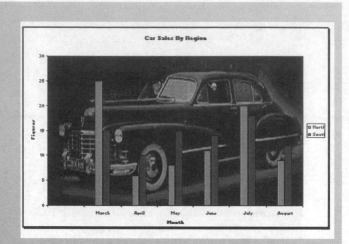

Figure 2.109 Chart with image inserted

3 – How to change data series pattern(s)

Method

1 Right click the **data series**.

2 Select **Format Data Series** from the pop-up menu.

3 Click the **Pattern tab**. In this window you can now select a new fill effect for the data series that complements the image you have inserted in the **plot area** section of the chart.

4 – Practice

Method

1 Select the **Hardware** worksheet:

    a Select a **Keyboard** data marker.
    b **Open** the Fill Effects window and select the image **keyboard-pc** from the images folder.
    c In the **Fill Effects** window, click the **Stack** format option button.
    d Click **OK** to insert the image **keyboard-pc** into the **Keyboard** data markers.

2 When you insert an image in a data marker you have the format option available to display the image multiple times if you choose the stack option:

    a **Insert** the Image **USB** in a **Stack** format in the **USB Connector** data markers on the **Hardware** worksheet.

3 You have found an image that you feel will brighten up the **Sales** worksheet:

    a **Select** the **chart** area of the **Sales** worksheet and **insert** the image **Background**.

4 The North team has achieved the highest sales in the final half of the year. You have created an image for the data marker that represents north on the spreadsheet:

    a **Insert** the image **North1st** in the **North** data markers on the **NorthSales** worksheet.

The workbook contains two charts that you can use to practice this task item at any time.

Save and review your work before moving to the next section. **Close** the workbook.

Section 3: Functions

Introduction

Function overview

Functions are pre-written and built into spreadsheet software packages to cover known types of what can be complex calculations, such as the **PMT Function.**

This section is an overview of the functions **Task Items** of the Syllabus.

Some functions, like formulas, you will use regularly. Others you many only come across in exercises for the course unless you happen to work or are training in that area e.g. mathematical functions.

In the test you will be asked to supply specific functions, to achieve a specific format or value.

Functions are inserted into formulas to assist with, or to work independently, to create calculations.

Function wizard

The function wizard gives you access to the predefined functions in your spreadsheet package, and lists the various arguments you need to provide for an answer to be returned that is accurate.

In the test, the function questions will ask you to add a named function to a specified cell of a particular worksheet.

Example test question: On **Sheet1** add a **round function** to cell B1.

The aim of the following function exercises is to help you understand arguments, and how and were to apply these.

Using functions – Part one

Accessing the function wizard

As with many computing tasks you can access functions in various ways, and in the end it is a personal choice. I will outline two methods that you can use as you work through the various exercises. As you gain more experience you will learn various other function shortcuts.

Method

1 Click **Function** on the **Insert** menu.

This will open the **Paste Function** window.

Figure 3.1 Insert menu

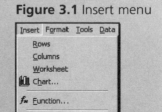

The Paste Function window can also be accessed via the Paste Function toolbar button f_x on the standard toolbar.

Getting information from the paste function window

You select the **Function Category** in the left window, and a list of **Function Names** appears in the right window.

A description of what a function will produce is available if you click the function name.

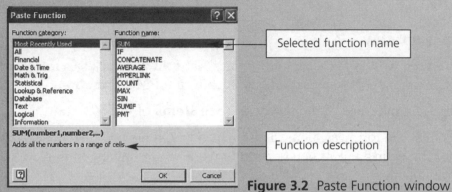

Figure 3.2 Paste Function window

The function category also has two useful categories that you can use. These are:

o **Most Recently Used**, which displays the names of functions that have recently been used on your computer in the right window.

o **All**, which displays all function names in alphabetical order.

2 When you have selected your function **category** and function **name,** click **OK** to close the Paste function window, and open the Selected Function window.

In the Selected Function window you set values for function arguments as appropriate.

Arguments

The **NOW** Function

This function inserts the **current date** and **time** in the active cell. The **NOW** function takes no arguments, which means there is no data for you to enter. If a function takes arguments you will need to enter these via the keyboard or select cells with the mouse pointer. Some functions can have as many as thirty arguments.

Function windows have their name displayed in the top left corner of the window, in upper case text (see Figure 3.3).

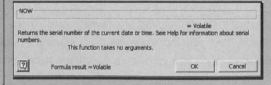

Figure 3.3 NOW Function window

3 To insert the current date and time into the active cell click **OK**. The date and time will be inserted and the **NOW** Function window will close.

When you have inserted the function your spreadsheet **formula bar** should display the function syntax. The **name box** will display the cell reference for the active cell.

The active cell will contain the results of the function.

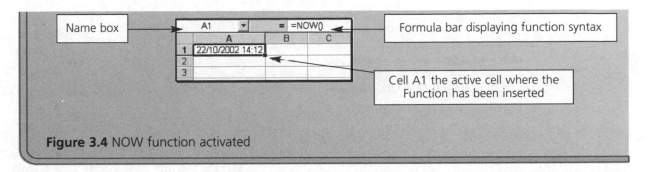

Figure 3.4 NOW function activated

1 – Setting values for function arguments practice

Open a new workbook.

The **ROUND** function will be used to demonstrate the setting of value arguments for functions.

Method

1 In cell A3 enter the value **15.7**.

   Round this figure to no decimal places and display the rounded figure in cell B3.

2 Click cell B3 and Start the function wizard. In the **Paste Function** window select:

   a Function Category: **Math & Trig**
   b Function Names: **Round**

3 Click **OK** to close the Paste Function window and to open the **ROUND** Function window.

Info

The **ROUND** function takes **two arguments**, **Number** and **Num_digits**.

The **Number** argument text box is currently the active object in the ROUND function window, and displays a description of the type of data you can enter for this argument.

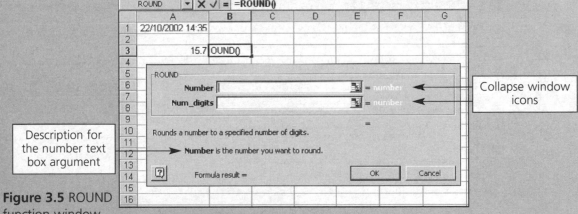

Description for the number text box argument

Collapse window icons

Figure 3.5 ROUND function window

The **figure** you want to **round** is in **cell A3**.

You could key in the cell reference via the keyboard, but using this option could introduce errors into your work.

Using the **collapse window** icon to **minimise** the window, and the mouse pointer to **select** the cell is more effective.

The collapse window icon

The collapse window icon is located to the right of an argument text box.

4 Minimise the **ROUND** function window by clicking the **collapse window** icon.

Figure 3.6 The ROUND function window minimised

After **minimising** the window if the window is covering cells, drag the window left or right to view cells.

5 Use the mouse pointer to select cell A3 by clicking the cell.

| A3 |

Figure 3.7 The ROUND window with selected cell reference

The graphics for the collapse dialog icon are different, to indicate that the window will be **restored** when clicked.

6 Click the **un-collapse dialog** icon.

If you are unable to access the **un-collapse dialog** icon press the **Esc** key to **restore** the function window.

7 Click the **Num_digits** argument text box.

The **Num_digits** argument relates to the number of decimal places you want your figure rounded to.

Note the description of the type of data you can enter in the description section.

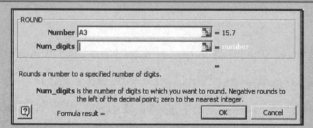

Figure 3.8 ROUND function window

8 The data needs displaying to zero decimal places. To achieve this enter 0 (zero) as the argument in the **Num_digits** text box.

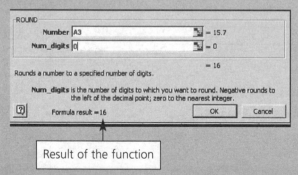

Result of the function

Figure 3.9 ROUND function window

The figure **15.7** should round to **16** as indicated by the **Formula result**.

How can I tell if I am entering arguments correctly?

Look at your screen: in the function window there are a number of indicators (see Figure 3.10).

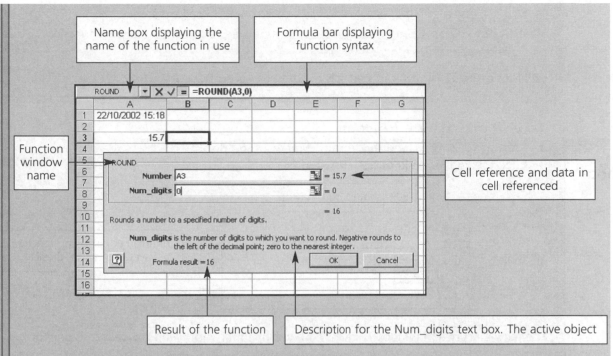

Name box displaying the name of the function in use

Formula bar displaying function syntax

Function window name

Cell reference and data in cell referenced

Result of the function

Description for the Num_digits text box. The active object

Figure 3.10 Spreadsheet and function window indicators

Info

9 To apply the function click the **OK** button.

The function window will close and the function will be applied to the data.

Cell B3 should display the figure **16**.

What if a function has more than two arguments?

Functions can have one or many different arguments; some arguments are optional, others are compulsory, *and if not used*, should be substituted by a **comma (,)** where the argument would normally appear.

The **RATE** function has a possible six arguments. Only five arguments are currently visible in the window figure.

Use the scroll bar on the right of the function window (Figure 3.11) to move up or down to enter arguments.

Figure 3.11 The RATE window with the first argument Nper visible

Figure 3.12 The RATE window with the last argument Guess visible after using the scroll bar

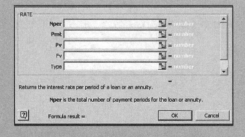

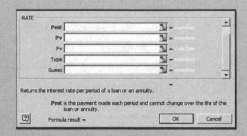

Summary of commands for creating a function

a Start the **Function Wizard**.
   i In the **Paste Function** window select:
   ii Function category: **Name of Category**.
b Function names: **Name of Function**.

c Click **OK** to close the Paste Function window and to open the relevant function window.

d **After** you have entered **arguments** as necessary, click **OK** to apply the function to your data and to close the function window.

10 Enter a **Today** function in **Cell A1:** function category: **Date & Time**.

To edit an existing function

Method

a **Click** the cell containing the function you want to **Edit**.

b **Click** the Edit Formula button (Figure 3.13).

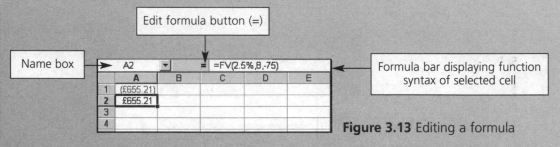

Figure 3.13 Editing a formula

The relevant function window (Figure 3.14) will open for you to edit the selected function

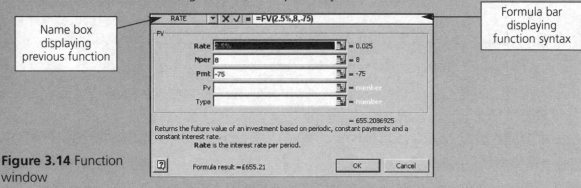

Figure 3.14 Function window

c Edit the function argument(s) and click **OK** to close and apply the function.

You can also use the Edit Formula button to access functions that have been used and stored in the name box or the Paste Function window.

To see a list of recently used functions

Method

a **Click** the **Edit Formula** button.

b Click the black arrowhead to the right of the name box to display the list.

c To use a function, click the function name.

d To access the Paste Function window, click the **More Functions** option in the dropdown list in the **name box.**

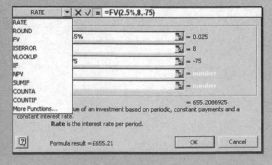

Figure 3.15 Name box displaying function names

Printing function and formula syntax

A simple way to protect specific data for future use is to have a hard copy of the data. It is useful to keep a catalogue of functions and formulas and their use, as you create them.

Some calculations you will use regularly and others only occasionally. A printed copy and/or worked copy of how the formula works, with comments, can save you a lot of time at a later stage.

Spreadsheet comments are covered in a later section.

To view functions and or formulas syntax on screen

Method

1 Select **Options** from the **Tools** menu.

2 **Select** the **View** tab.

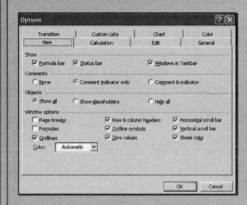

Figure 3.16 Options window – View tab

3 Under the **Window options** section, click the **Formulas tick box** to place a tick it.

4 Close the Options window.

Info

Keyboard shortcut to view/hide formulas

Ctrl key + this key

This key is located under the **Esc** key and to the left of the numeric key number 1, on the main keyboard.

EXERCISE

2 – Practice

All workbooks for the **Functions** section can be located on the accompanying CD-ROM.

Method

1 Open the workbook **1_ViewFormulas**.

2 **Display** and **print** all formulas on **Sheet1**.

Your printout should look like the example in Figure 3.17.

3 **Close** the workbook without saving your changes.

In the Functions Introduction section you have covered the steps for how to:

- Access the function wizard.
- Enter functions via the keyboard.
- Function syntax.
- Select function categories and names.
- Enter arguments.
- View additional arguments.
- Apply a function.
- Display all formulas or view location of all formulas in a worksheet.

Figure 3.17 1_ViewFormulas workbook printout showing formulas

In Part two you will work through the various **functions** task items (**method steps** are not included in all exercises).

If you are struggling at any time with the main functions section (Part two), return to the Introduction to refresh your memory, having first reviewed the exercise you are having difficulty with.

In this section you have:

- Used date and **time** function **DAY**.
- Used **mathematical** function **ROUND**.
- Displayed all formulas or viewed location of all formulas in a worksheet.

Using functions – Part two

3.1 Using text functions

These functions manipulate the copied contents of the cell they are equal to.

EXERCISE 1 – UPPER; LOWER; PROPER; CONCATENATE

The UPPER text function

This function converts selected text to upper case
Syntax: =UPPER(*text*)

Method

1 File preparation:

   a **Open** a **New** workbook. **Save** the workbook as **MyFunctions**.
   b **Rename** Sheet1 as **Text.**
   c In **cell A1** key in your first name.
   d In **cell B1** key in your surname.
   e In **cell A2** key in 'london is great'. You can substitute 'london' for the town you live in! Ensure that the text is entered in lowercase text as shown.

Your worksheet should look something like Figure 3.18.

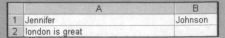

	A	B
1	Jennifer	Johnson
2	london is great	

Figure 3.18 Unformatted text

Task A

1 Select cell D1.

2 **Start** the Function Wizard.

3 In the **Past Function** window select:

    a **Function category**: Text.
    b **Function name:** UPPER.

Creating an **UPPER** text function from the data in cell B1.

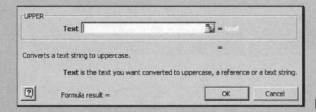

UPPER

Text [ ] = text

Converts a text string to uppercase.

    =

    Text is the text you want converted to uppercase, a reference or a text string.

Formula result =   OK   Cancel

Figure 3.19 UPPER Function window

The **UPPER** function takes one **argument**: a reference to where the data is that you want to convert to upper case. The argument is called **Text**.

4 Click the **collapse dialog** icon to minimize the **UPPER** window.

5 Select cell B1.

6 **Restore** the **UPPER** Function window.

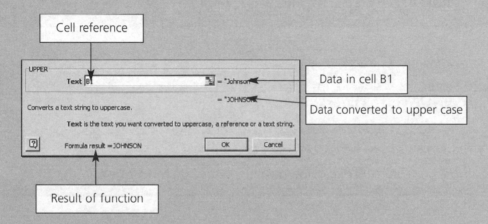

Cell reference

UPPER

Text B1   = "Johnson"   Data in cell B1

     = "JOHNSON"   Data converted to upper case

Converts a text string to uppercase.

    Text is the text you want converted to uppercase, a reference or a text string.

Formula result = JOHNSON   OK   Cancel

Result of function

Figure 3.20 Completed UPPER Function window

7 Click **OK** to apply the function and to close the UPPER Function window.

8 Reselect cell D1.

The **syntax** in the **formula bar** should be familiar to you if you have completed the linking sections. Syntax: **=UPPER(B1)**

Cell D1 is **equal** to the contents of cell B1 and is converted to **upper case text** by the function. The reference used to link the two cells is a **relative reference**.

Review the linking section if necessary, as many functions in this section use this type of syntax.

LOWER and **PROPER** text functions

The **LOWER** and **PROPER** functions take the same (one) **argument** (text) as the UPPER function: a reference to where the data is that you want to convert.

The LOWER text function

This function converts text to lower case. Syntax: **=LOWER**(text)

Task B

1 Select cell D2.

2 Create a **LOWER** text function from the data in cell A1.

The PROPER text function

The **PROPER** text function converts the first letter of each word, in text, to a capital letter. Syntax **=PROPER**(text)

Task C

1 Select cell D3.

2 Create a **PROPER** text function from the data in cell A2.

The Concatenate Function

The Concatenate text function joins text to create a continuous string or sentence of text. Syntax: **=CONCATENATE**(*text1,text2...*)

The Concatenate text function can take up to thirty arguments, as references to where the data is you want to join together as one text string.

The arguments are called **Text** followed immediately by a **number**.

Task D

1 Select **Cell D4**.

2 Start the Function Wizard.

3 In the **Paste Function** window select:

    a **Function category**: Text Functions.

    b **Function name**: CONCATENATE.

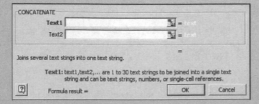

Figure 3.21 CONCATENATE Function window without any arguments entered

4 Click the **Text1** argument **collapse window** icon to minimize the **CONCATENATE** window.

5 Click cell B1.

6 Restore the **CONCATENATE** window using the un-collapse window icon.

7 Click the **Text2** argument **collapse** window icon to minimize the window.

8 Click cell A1.

9 Restore the window.

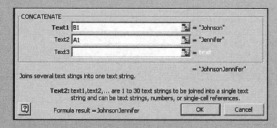

Figure 3.22 Completed CONCATENATE window

10 Click **OK** to apply the function and to close the CONCATENATE window.

If your results at any time are not as expected close the function window by clicking the **Cancel** button, then restart the Function Wizard.

When you concatenate text using the **CONCATENATE** syntax **text1**, **text2**, the text is returned as a continuous string of letters without any spaces, as in cell D4 (Figure 3.23).

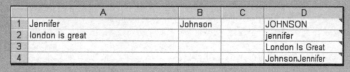

	A	B	C	D
1	Jennifer	Johnson		JOHNSON
2	london is great			jennifer
3				London Is Great
4				JohnsonJennifer

Figure 3.23 Cell D4

Task E

Method

Info

The returned string in **Cell D4** would look better with a space between the surname and first-name text.

When you want to concatenate strings and include spaces you need to make changes to the syntax and the number of arguments used. These changes are:

a Replace the word CONCATENATE with an ampersand operator (&).

b Enclose the space for insertion within the string in quotation marks (" ").

c Use one argument to create the string.

1 Select cell D5.

2 Open the **CONCATENATE** text function window, and create a **CONCATENATE** text function from the data in cell A1:B1, which includes a space between the strings in the **Text1** Argument.

3 Enter the following concatenate syntax below as the **Text1** argument: **=A1&" "&B1**

Info

Example concatenate syntax expressed verbally: **=A1&"*Press SPACEBAR*"&B1**

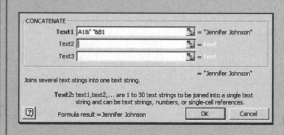

Figure 3.24 Completed CONCATENATE window

The returned data in cell D5 is now presented more appropriately if you need to separate text returned in a string (Figure 3.25).

	A	B	C	D
1	Jennifer	Johnson		JOHNSON
2	london is great			jennifer
3				London Is Great
4				JohnsonJennifer
5				Jennifer Johnson

Figure 3.25 Cell D5

The function syntax originally used in cell D4 should be used with text such as **Mon** and **day**, to create a continuous string like **Monday**.

EXERCISE 2 – Text functions practice

Enter data and apply text functions.

Task A

Method

1 Enter the title **UPPER FUNCTION** in cell A6.

2 Enter the data as shown in the table that follows, cells A7:A15:

3 Click cell D7.

4 Create an **UPPER** text function from the data in cell A7.

5 **Copy** the **UPPER** function to cells D8:D15.

userlist
unload
client
load
login
menu
lan
wan
net

Task B

Method

1 Enter the title **lower function** in **cell A16**.

2 Enter the data on the right in the table that follows in cells A17:A24.

3 Click cell D17.

4 Create a **LOWER** text function from the data in cell A17.

5 **Copy** the **LOWER** function to cells D18:D24.

TRAINING
WINDOWS
SYSTEM
GUIDE
SERVER
MONITOR
LABELS
FILE

Task C

Method

1 **Enter** the title **Proper Function** in cell A25.

2 **Enter** the data from the table on the right in cells A26:A32, exactly as shown.

3 Click cell D26.

4 Create a **PROPER** text function from the data in cell A26.

5 **Copy** the **PROPER** function to cells D27:D32.

| windows architecture |
| NETWORKING ESSENTIALS |
| virus scan |
| user account setup |
| FILE ALLOCATION TABLE |
| THE DREADED COMPUTER VIRUS |
| why yOU should bUy a tAPe dRIVE |

Task D

Method

1 Enter the title **CONCATENATE FUNCTION** in cell A33.

2 Enter the label **No space between words** in cell A34.

3 Enter the data in the table on the right in cells A35:A41.

4 **Enter** the text **day** in cell B35.

5 Click cell D35.

6 Create a **concatenate** text function from the data in cell A35:B35.

7 **Copy** the concatenate function to cells D35:D41.

| Mon |
| Tues |
| Wednes |
| Thurs |
| Fri |
| Satur |
| Sun |

Only the data in **cell D35** has picked up the second part of the string (Figure 3.26).

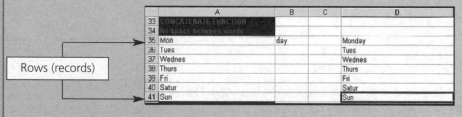

Rows (records)

Figure 3.26 Cell D35

Info

Text functions uses a relative reference in the syntax.

Editing the function syntax in cell D35.

What you need here is an absolute reference to refer to cell B35, the cell with the second part of the string.

8 Click the **Undo** toolbar button once.

9 Create an absolute reference, by clicking on cell D35. The **syntax** in the **formula bar** should be: **=CONCATENATE(A35,B35)**

10 Add the dollar sign **$** to the cell reference **B35** only (ensure that you do not delete the **comma** separating the two cell references).

The edited syntax should look as follows: **=CONCATENATE(A35,$B$35)**

11 Copy the **concatenate** function to cells D36:D41. The new string should now be created when copied.

Task E

Method

1 Enter the title **CONCATENATE FUNCTION** in cell A42.

2 Enter the label **Space between words** in cell A43.

3 Enter the data from the table on the right in cells A44:B51.

4 Click cell D44.

5 Create a **concatenate** text function from the data in cell A44:B44 with a space between the two text strings.

6 Copy the concatenate function to cells D45:D51.

Networking	Topology
Network	Security
Computer	Viruses
Floppy	Disk
Hard disk	Drive
Network Interface	Card
Print	Manager
Parallel	Port

3.2 Using date and time functions

EXERCISE 1 – TODAY; NOW

These functions are used to insert and/or manipulate the display of dates and time.

Info

The TODAY function

This function returns the current system date.

Syntax
=TODAY( )
The **TODAY** function takes **no arguments**.

Rename Sheet2 in the **MyFunctions** workbook as **Date**.

Inserting a function that returns today's date

Method

1 Select **cell A1** and start the Function Wizard.

2 In the **Paste Function** window select:

   a **Function category**: date & time.
   b **Function name**: today.
   c Select **OK** to apply the function and to close the **TODAY** window.

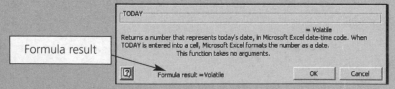

Figure 3.27 TODAY window

Today's date should now be visible in cell A1.

As a comparison to the **TODAY** function look at the **NOW** function, which also belongs to the Date & Time function category.

Info

The **NOW** function returns the **current** system date and time. Syntax: **=NOW( )**

The **NOW** function takes no arguments.

Insert a function that returns the date and time **NOW** in cell A2 on the **Date** worksheet.

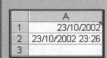

	A
1	23/10/2002
2	23/10/2002 23:26
3	

Figure 3.28 Data returned by TODAY and NOW functions

Note the difference between the data returned by the two functions.

The formula *results* for the **TODAY** or **NOW** functions in each window are **volatile**. The results depend on the date and time settings of a system's clock.

1 If a system's clock is inaccurately set, then an unreliable result may be returned.

2 The **date** and/or **time** displayed in the worksheet will depend on when you access the workbook containing these functions.

3 The **TODAY** function updates the date in the worksheet each day.

4 The **NOW** function updates the date each day. The time portion of the function updates with the system clock by the **hours**, **minutes** and **seconds**.

5 To update the time displayed in a workbook containing a **NOW** function, close and reopen the workbook.

If you need to keep an absolute record of a **specific** date within a spreadsheet enter the date via the keyboard.

How are date and time stored internally in your computer?

Info

1 On the **Date** worksheet format cell A1 as **number**: **General**.

Cell A1 should display the **date** as a **serial number** in the **cell** and the **today function syntax** in the formula bar.

Your spreadsheet package generally stores data such as dates and time internally, in these formats:

a Dates as serial numbers

b Time as decimal fractions.

2 Format cell A2 as **number**: **General**.

Cell A2 should display the **date** portion of the **NOW** function as a **serial number** and the **time** portion as a **decimal fraction**.

Figure 3.29 shows an example of the serial numbers and decimal fractions returned by formatting the cells containing the **TODAY** and **NOW** functions, as general types.

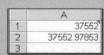

	A
1	37552
2	37552.97853
3	

Figure 3.29 Formatted cell

Note: ensure that you do not need to record a specific date. If you do, these functions are not for you! These functions are better used in templates etc.

2 – Date and time function – practice

Comparing **dates** and **serial numbers** – preparation.

On the date worksheet

1 Enter the label **Date** in cell E1, and **Serial No** in cell F1.

2 Enter the **dates** from the table that follows, in cells E2:E11, and copy these to cells F2:F11.

03/11/58
11/11/58
21/11/58
04/05/59
12/11/58
11/11/77
11/11/02
08/08/66
24/12/75
10/08/02

3 Format the **dates** in cells F2:F11 as **General**, to display serial numbers.

E	F
Date	Serial No
03/11/1958	21492
11/11/1958	21500
21/11/1958	21510
04/05/1959	21674
12/11/1958	21501
11/11/1977	28440
11/11/2002	37510
08/08/1966	24327
24/12/1975	27752
10/08/2002	37478

Figure 3.30 Worksheet with serial number displayed and corresponding dates

Windows date and time shortcut

1 To enter the current date in a cell via the keyboard, press the **Ctrl+;** (semi colon) keys on the keyboard.

2 To enter the current time in a cell via the keyboard, press the **Ctrl+Shift+:** (colon) keys on the keyboard.

3 – DAY; MONTH; YEAR

Use date and time functions **DAY; MONTH; YEAR**

The functions **DAY; MONTH; YEAR** can be used to extract **information** to:

a Analyse a specific DAY in a period e.g. 11th DAY.

b Analyse a specific MONTH in a period e.g. March.

c Analyse a specific YEAR in a period e.g. 1999.

These functions takes one **argument**, called *serial_number*.

The **DAY** function syntax: **=DAY**(*serial_number*)

This function is used to extract the **DAY** portion of a date.

01 would be extracted from the date **01/01/04** using the **DAY** function as long as the system **Regional and Language Options** are set as **English (United Kingdom)**.

Task A – File preparation

Method

1 **Rename** Sheet3 as **DateTime** in the **MyFunctions** workbook.

2 **Enter** the **labels** and **data** in the following table, in cells A1:D1:

DATE	DAY	MONTH	YEAR
01-Mar-02			
15/05/01			
06-Oct-99			

3 **Enter** the **labels** and **data** in the table below, in cells A7:D10:

TIME	HOUR	MINUTE	SECONDS
13:30:22			
17:33:58			
22:17:10			

Task B – Extracting the individual portions of a date

Method

Create a **DAY** Function using the data in cell A2 as the (Serial_number) argument.

1 Click cell B2.

2 **Start** the function wizard.

3 **Select** function category: **Date & Time**.

4 **Select** function name: **DAY**.

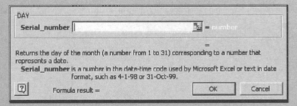

Figure 3.31 DAY function window

5 Click cell A2.

6 Select **OK** to apply the function, and to close the **DAY** window.

Result: The **DAY** portion of the date (**1**) should be extracted and placed in cell B2.

7 **Copy** the **DAY** function in cell B2 to cells B3:B4.

Info

The **MONTH** function syntax: **=MONTH**(*serial_number*).

Task C – Create and copy a month function

Method

1 Select cell C2.

2 **Start** the Function Wizard.

3 Using the **month** function in the **date** and **time** category, extract the **MONTH** portion of the **Date** in cell A2.

4 **Copy** the **MONTH** function in cell C2 to cells C3:C4.

Task D – Create and copy a year function

Info The YEAR function syntax: **=YEAR**(*serial_number*).

1 Select cell D2 and extract the **YEAR** portion of the **date** in cell A2 to cell D2.

2 **Copy** the **YEAR** function to cells D3:D4.

Info As a comparison to the date and time functions **DAY**; **MONTH**; **YEAR** look at the **HOUR**, **MINUTE** and **SECOND** functions which also belong to the Date & Time function category, and share the same one argument (**serial_number**).

EXERCISE 4 – Date and time function – practice

Extracting portions of time.

Info Function syntax for **HOUR**, **MINUTE** and **SECOND**: **=FunctionName**(*serial_number*)

Task A

Method

1 **Extract** the **HOUR** portions of the **time** from cell A8 to cell B8 using the appropriate function.

2 **Copy** the function to cells B9:B10.

Task B

Method

1 **Extract** the **MINUTE** portions of the time from cell A8 to cells C8:C10.

2 **Extract** the **SECONDS** portions of the time from cell A8 to cells D8:D10.

Your spreadsheet data should look like the example in Figure 3.32.

D8		=	=SECOND(A8)	
	A	B	C	D
1	DATE	DAY	MONTH	YEAR
2	01-Mar-02	1	3	2002
3	15/05/2001	15	5	2001
4	06-Oct-99	6	10	1999
5				
6				
7	TIME	HOUR	MINUTE	SECONDS
8	13:30:22	13	30	22
9	17:33:58	17	33	58
10	22:17:10	22	17	10

Figure 3.32 Spreadsheet with extracted data

The extracted data is now ready for any processing you may want to undertake with date or time data.

3 **Save** and close the workbook.

In an earlier exercise you created the workbook **ImportDates** by importing a text file containing dates and saving this in a spreadsheet format.

You will now use a copy of the original file with the following **date** and **time** functions: **DAY**, **MONTH** and **YEAR**.

All student workbooks associated with this section can be located on the accompanying CD-ROM.

5 – Date and time function – practice

Extracting portions of dates

Open the workbook **MyImportDates**.

Task A

1 Select cell B10 and use the **DAY** function to extract the **day** from the **date** in cell A10.

2 **Copy** the **DAY** function to cells B11:B1024.

Task B

1 Select cell C10 and use the **MONTH** function to extract the **month** from the **date** in cell A10.

2 **Copy** the **MONTH** function to cells C11:C1024.

Task C

1 Select cell D10 and use the **YEAR** function to extract the **year** from the **date** in cell A10.

2 **Copy** the **YEAR** function to cells D11:D1024.

3 Save the **MyImportDates** workbook.

	A	B	C	D
9	Data April - Nov	DAY	MONTH	YEAR
10	01/04/2000	1	4	2000
11	01/04/2000	1	4	2000
12	01/04/2000	1	4	2000
13	01/04/2000	1	4	2000
14	01/04/2000	1	4	2000
15	01/04/2000	1	4	2000
16	01/04/2000	1	4	2000
17	01/04/2000	1	4	2000
18	02/04/2000	2	4	2000
19	02/04/2000	2	4	2000
20	02/04/2000	2	4	2000

Figure 3.33 The Extracted data using the date and time functions DAY, MONTH and YEAR

Using statistical functions

1 – COUNTIF

The COUNTIF function

This function counts the criteria argument that exists in a range argument. Or put another way, if this number (11) is in the column called DAY, count it and tell me how many times it appears.

Syntax: **COUNTIF**(range,criteria)

The **COUNTIF** function has two arguments, **range** and **criteria**.

1 The **range** argument is the range of cells where all the **data** you want to **count** is **stored**.

2 The **criteria** argument is the **specific data** to be **counted**. In this instance it is the number **17** in the **Day** column.

Task A

You need to know **how many times** the figure **17** appears in the range **B10:B1024**.

Method

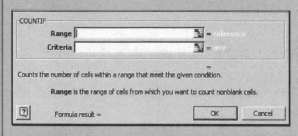

Figure 3.34 COUNTIF function window

Open the **MyImportDates** workbook.

1 Select **cell B1025** and start the Function Wizard.

2 In the **COUNTIF** function window.

3 Enter **B10:B1024** as the **range argument**.

4 Enter **17** as the **criteria** argument.

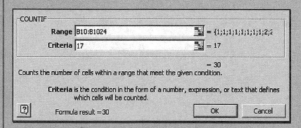

Figure 3.35 The completed COUNTIF window

5 Select **OK** to apply the function and to close the **COUNTIF** window. The formula result is **30**.

The number **17** appears **30** times in the range B10:B1024.

Task B

To count another day, **Edit** the **COUNTIF** function in the formula bar.

Method

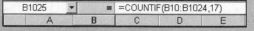

Figure 3.36 Edit the COUNTIF function

1 Change the number 17 to **14** and then press **Enter**, to enter the new data for processing as part of the COUNTIF function.

Note: Ensure that you do not delete the comma separating the cell reference from the criteria or the closing Parentheses of the argument '**)**'.

The new **COUNTIF** function argument when cell B1025 is selected in the **formula bar** should be as follows: **=COUNTIF**(B10:B1024,14).

The **result** should be **25** in the function window and cell B1025.

Task C

Method

- Count how may times the month **7** appears in the **range C10:C1024**.
- Count how many times the year **2000** appears in the **range D10:D1024**.

Expected results:

a   The number **7** should appear **418** times in the **range C10:C1024**.
b   The year **2000** should appear **379** times in the **range D10:D1024**.

You may like to experiment with alternative dates in cells B1025:D1025 using the **COUNTIF** function.

When you are ready to start the next exercise save and close the workbook.

EXERCISE   *2 – COUNTA*

Info

The COUNTA function
This function **counts** how many **values** are in the list of arguments.

Values are **cells that are not empty** when using the **COUNTA** function.

Syntax: **COUNTA**(value1,value2, ...)

The **COUNTA** function takes up to 30 arguments.

You are receiving a lot of data electronically from a recent audit of software. You need to ensure that the data being returned is completed. You do not want to check each spreadsheet physically.

In this exercise you will use the **COUNTA** function to check the contents of the spreadsheet data values being returned, to verify how many rows of data on the sheet are completed.

- **Column A** of the spreadsheet you will create will contain a list of software.

- **Column B** will contain the corresponding version number.

- When the workbooks are returned you need to know if all version numbers have been entered. If not you need to return the workbook.

Task A – Preparing the workbook

Method

1   **Open** a new workbook.

2   **Save** the workbook as **MyCount** and **rename** Sheet1 as **CountA**.

3   **Enter** the data from the table that follows on worksheet **CountA** in cells A1:B18.

SOFTWARE	VERSION
windows 98 Second Edition	4.1
Internet Explorer	
Access	
Excel	5
Excel	8
Exchange Client	4
Office Professional 97	8.0 SR-1
Outlook 97	
Outlook Express	5
PowerPoint	8
Schedule + 95	
Word	6
Word 97	8.0 SR-1
Works	
WinZip	7
Nuts and Bolts	2
McAfee Virus Scan	

Task B – Creating the function

Method

1 Click cell B19 and **start** the **Function Wizard**.

2 In the **Paste Function** window select the **Statistical** function category.

3 The function name is **COUNTA**.

You want to enter a COUNTA function in cell B19 to **count** the number of cells that are not empty on a returned spreadsheet. The argument for **Value1** is the cell range of the data you want to evaluate.

4 Enter or select cells B2:B18 if your system has not detected this.

5 Click **OK** to apply the **COUNTA** function to cell B19 and to **close** the function window.

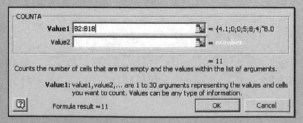

Figure 3.37 Completed COUNTA function window

The function syntax in the formula bar should be: **=COUNTA(B2:B18)**.

The return in this workbook is **11**.

Do you need to return the sheet for completion?

You are looking for a return of **17**. Anything else and the workbook will need to be returned.

3 – COUNT

The COUNT function

This function counts any cell that contains a numeric value.

Syntax: **COUNT**(value1,value2, ...).

The **COUNT** function takes up to 30 arguments.

1 Enter the following data on Sheet2 of the **MyCount** workbook, in cells A1:E22:

EXAM PASSED BY AREA				
LOCATION	Grade A	Grade B	Grade C	Grade D
BEXLEY	120	200	27	0
BIRMINGHAM CENTRAL	100	75	16	2
BIRMINGHAM CENTRE	600		33	
BRACKNELL	824	941	45	
BRISTOL	759		12	
FELTHAM		357	11	1
IPSWICH	147	159	11	
LONDON CENTRAL	987	751		
LONDON EAST	210	258	35	6
LONDON NORTH	987	400	37	
LONDON SOUTH	741	365	48	
LONDON WEST	159	710	22	
MANCHESTER CITY	753	862	65	
MANCHESTER WEST	841	175	42	
NORWICH	125		44	1
READING	874	50	20	
SLOUGH	159	22	2	
STEVENAGE	547	17	1	
WATFORD		10	15	
WINDSOR	543	8	29	

2 File preparation:

a Rename Sheet2 as **Count** in the **MyCount** workbook.

b **Merge** and **centre** the title **EXAM PASSED BY AREA** across cells A1:E1.

Task A

1 Select **cell D23** and start the Function Wizard.

2 In the **Paste Function** window select the **Statistical** function category. The function name is **COUNT**.

3 Enter **D3:D22** as the **Value1** argument to find the number of cells in the range **D3:D22** that contain numeric values.

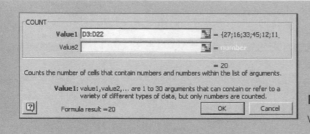

Figure 3.38 Completed COUNT function window

The result should be **20**. All cells in the range contain numeric value.

Task B – Copying the function

Method

1 **Copy** the COUNT function to cell A23.

The result should be **0**. The data in column A is text (the **COUNT** function will only process numeric values).

2 **Copy** the COUNT function to cells B23, C23 and E23.

The result should be **18**, **16** and **5**.

3 Save and close the workbook.

4 – COUNTA function practice

Method

1 Open the workbook **CountAPractice**.

2 On the **Leave** worksheet enter a COUNTA function in cell E39 to *count* the number of cells that are not empty on the **Leave** worksheet in cells E3:E3.

What is the font colour of the figure in cell F39 after entering the COUNTA Function?

a If the colour is red then you will need to return the sheet as this is incomplete.
b If the colour is teal all the requested data has been entered for you to process the completed sheet.

3 Save and close the workbook.

5 – COUNT function practice

Method

1 Open the **COUNTPractice** workbook.

2 Enter a **COUNT** function in cell C19 to count the numeric values in cells C2:C18.

The cells contain the version number of software.

Do you think the data in cells C2, C8 and C14 will be included in the count?

If the result is **9** then cell C2 has rightly been included. Cells C8 and C14 contain alphanumeric data and are therefore not included in the result.

3 Save and close the workbook.

Using mathematical functions

1 – SUMIF

Info

The SUMIF function

This function calculates figures based on criteria. The criteria can be a number or numbers using operators to analyse data.

Syntax: **=SUMIF**(range,criteria,sum_range).

The **SUMIF** function has 3 arguments.

Arguments explained:

a The **range** argument is where the data is located that you want to evaluate.

b The **criteria** argument is the criterion you want to evaluate the **range** by.

c The **sum_range** argument is the criterion you want to **evaluate by**.

Open the workbook **MySumIf**.

The workbook contains the weekly savings for three individuals. You will evaluate the data to test out the various arguments of the **SUMIF** function.

As you will be using **calculation operators** in this section, you may need to review these first. Open your application help system and search for **operator**.

When you are ready, continue with the exercise.

Task A

Method

1 Select cell G2 and start the Function Wizard.

2 In the **Paste Function** window select the **Math & Trig** function category. The function name is **SUMIF**.

While this function takes up to three arguments, in this task you will only use two of the available arguments, **range** and **criteria**.

3 For the **range** argument enter **C3:C13**.

4 The system will automatically add the quotation marks, as shown in Figure 3.39: you *do not* need to enter these. To see the quotation marks in the SUMIF function window, click on the Range or Sum_range text box or press the Tab key.

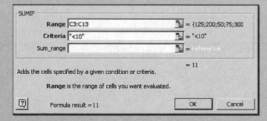

Figure 3.39 Completed SUMIF function window

5 Select **OK** to apply the function and to close the **SUMIF** window.

You have asked the function to **total** all figures in the cell range **C3:C13** that are **less than 10**.

You should have a response of **11** in **cell H2**.

How was the calculation performed?

Cell C10 contains the figure **5** and cell C13 the figure **6**: a **total** of **11**.

Task B

1 In cell G3 enter a function that will total all figures **greater than** or **equal to 200**.

Function arguments

a Enter **C3:C13** for the **range** argument.
b Enter **>=200** for the **criteria** argument.

The function syntax when cell H3 is the active cell in the formula bar is:
=SUMIF(C3:C13,">=200")

Task C

Method

In **cell G4** you want to calculate the total savings for **Annetta.**

In order to perform this type of calculation you will now need to use the **third argument** of the **SUMIF** function, **sum_range**.

1 Click cell G4 and start the Function Wizard.

2 Select the **SUMIF** function.

Column **B** contains the **names** that correspond to a figure in column C. Each name has more than one entry in column B.

3 Enter **B3:B13** as the **range** argument (the system will search all names in the **range B3:B13** in **Column B**).

4 Enter **=Annetta** as the **criteria** argument, the individual you are searching for (the system will find each occurrence of this name in the **range B3:B13**).

5 Enter **C3:C13** as the **sum_range** argument. The system will sum together any figures that correspond to the name **Annetta** in the range **C3:C13** and produce a **total** figure from all occurrences.

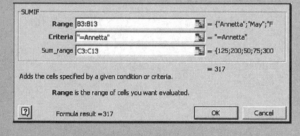

Figure 3.40 Completed SUMIF function window

6 Close the **SUMIF** window.

---

2 – Practice

In the previous SUMIF tasks **a to c** you covered how to access and apply the function using **calculation operators** and **text** as **criteria** arguments. Review these as necessary to complete tasks 2a to 2d below. A new operator is used in task 2e and the syntax is shown.

2a – In **cell G5** apply a **SUMIF** function to show a total for **Fay**.
2b – In **cell G6** apply a **SUMIF** function to show a total for **May**.
2c – In **cell G7** apply a **SUMIF** function to total all figures greater than or equal to 100.
2d – In **cell G8** apply a **SUMIF** function to total all figures between week 1 and 11. The criteria argument for this task is **=SUMIF(A3:A13,">Week2<Week10",C3:C13)**
2e – In **cell G9** apply a **SUMIF** function to total all figures between week 3 and 9.

Expected results:

2a – 132
2b – 511
2c – 625
2d – 534
2e – 960

Save and close the workbook.

3 – Practice

Open the workbook **SUMIFPractice**.

In the Analysis area create the following **SUMIF** functions using the figures in **cells D3:D34**:

3a – In **cell G3** apply a **SUMIF** function to show a total for North.
3b – In **cell G4** apply a **SUMIF** function to show a total for South.
3c – In **cell G5** apply a **SUMIF** function to show a total for East.
3d – In **cell G6** apply a **SUMIF** function to show a total for West.
3e – In **cell G7** apply a **SUMIF** function to sum all figures greater than or equal to 90.
3f – In **cell G8** apply a **SUMIF** function to total all figures less than or equal to 35.
3g – In **cell G9** apply a **SUMIF** function to sum all figures between cells D3:D34 greater than 1.

Expected results:

3A – 1360
3B – 519
3C – 498
3D – 1128
3E – 2440
3F – 158
3G – 3505

Save and review your work before you move to the next section.

4 – ROUND

Info

This function rounds a figure up or down based on the number of digits specified by you.

Syntax: **=ROUND**(*number, num_digits*)

The **ROUND** function has two arguments as discussed in the Part 1 introduction.

In this exercise you will look at the ROUND function and the Format Cells formatting options, to get a view of their similarities.

1 **Open** a new workbook. Save the workbook by the name **MyRound**.

2 File preparation.

   a Enter the **label** and **data** from the table below in the cells B1:B10:

RAW DATA
97.8
15.3
11.8
16.9
12.11
82.89
7.5
16.3
16.9

   b   **Copy** and **paste** cells **B2:B10** in cell A2.

   c Enter the label **Format** in cell A1.

   d Enter the **label** and **data** from the table below in cells E1:E10:

RAW DATA
6.1
6.2
6.3
6.4
6.5
6.6
6.7
6.8
6.9

   e   **Copy** and **paste** cells E2:E10 in cell D2.

   f Enter the label **Format** in cell D1.

   g **Enter** the label **ROUND** in cells C1 and F1.

Task A – Entering a ROUND function to display a specified figure to zero decimal places

The **ROUND** function takes two arguments: **number** and **num_digits**.

1 Select cell C2 and start the Function Wizard.

2 For the **number** argument enter or select cell B2.

3 For the **num_digits** argument key in **0** (zero) (this will round the figure to the nearest integer, with no trailing zeros).

4 Select **OK** to apply the function and to close the ROUND window.

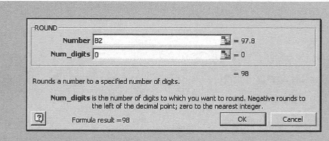

Figure 3.41 Completed ROUND function window

5 **Copy** the **ROUND** function to cells C3:C10.

Task B

Method

1 Apply a **ROUND** function to cells F2 to ROUND the figure in cell E2 to zero decimal places.

2 Copy the **ROUND** function to cells F3:F10.

Task C

Method

1 **Highlight** cells **A2:A10**.

2 **Format** the **cells** as **number** zero decimal places.

3 **Format** cells D2:D10 as **number** zero decimal places.

   The columns **Format** and **ROUND** should display whole numbers no trailing zeros.

   The figures displayed in the **Format** column are not necessary the actual figure in the cell.

4 Click cell A2, then compare the figure in the **formula bar** with the figures displayed in the cell.

	A	B	C	D	E	F
	Format	RAW DATA	ROUND	Format	RAW DATA	ROUND
1						
2	98	97.8	98	6	6.1	6
3	15	15.3	15	6	6.2	6
4	12	11.8	12	6	6.3	6
5	17	16.9	17	6	6.4	6
6	12	12.11	12	7	6.5	7
7	83	82.89	83	7	6.6	7
8	8	7.5	8	7	6.7	7
9	16	16.3	16	7	6.8	7
10	17	16.9	17	7	6.9	7

A2 = 97.8 ← Formula bar

Figure 3.42 Formula bar syntax

Info

The *stored values*, the figures *entered by you*, are the figures that will be used in calculations.

Be aware of what you need to achieve when deciding between the **ROUND** function and **formatting** numbers, in relation to display purposes.

5 Save and close the workbook.

EXERCISE ## 5 – Practice

Open the workbook **RoundPractice**.

Task A

Method

1 Select the **Donations** worksheet.

2 On the **Donations** worksheet enter a **ROUND** function in cell D3 to round the figure of **Contributions** in cell C3 to 0 (zero) decimal places.

3 Copy the **ROUND** function in cell D3 to cells D4:D34.

Task B

Method

1 Select the **FREvents** worksheet.

2 On the **FREvents** worksheet enter a **ROUND** function in cell C3 to round the figure of **Funds** in cell B3 to **two** decimal places.

3 Copy the **ROUND** function in cell C3 to cells C4:C35.

Save and review your work before moving to the next section.

3.5 Using financial functions

EXERCISE 1 – FV

Info

The FV function

FV is an abbreviation for the term **future value**.

This function returns the future value of an investment based on **periodic**, **constant payments** and a **constant interest** rate.

Syntax: **=FV**(*rate,nper,pmt,pv,type*).

The **FV** function has five arguments. Two of these arguments, *pv* and *type*, have system default values that will be applied if you do not add values to the arguments.

o The **pv** default is 0 (zero). No lump-sum included in the calculation.
o The **type** default is 0 (zero). Paid at the end of the period.
o **Rate** is the interest rate for that period.
o **Nper** is the total number of payment periods in an **annuity**, e.g. 12, 6, 3, 1.
o **Annuity** is a fixed annual allowance, especially one provided by a form of investment.
o **Pmt** is the payment made each period. This payment will not change over the life of the annuity, e.g. 24 payments of £20 over 24 months.
o **Pv** represents the **present value** of the future value of a series of payments of say, £100.
o **Type** – when the payment is made, i.e. at the **End (0)** or the **Start (1)** of the period.

For these financial functions:

a When you pay any sum in, it must be represented by a negative figure e.g. **–25**.

b If you receive any interest on your savings it should be represented by a positive figure e.g. **25**.

When entering figures do not using any formatting, such as commas (,) or full stops (.). Always format your figures using **cells** on the **Format** menu, and apply a format **category**.

Open the **MyFunctions** workbook you created earlier and **Insert** a new worksheet. **Rename** this as **FV1**.

Task A

In this exercise you will enter a basic **FV function** in the **formula bar** without using the function wizard. You will not use all **FV function** arguments in this exercise; and the system defaults will therefore apply.

You have decided to save **£75** (**pmt**) for 8 years (**Nper**) at a 2.5% interest (**rate**).

1 Select **cell A1** and enter the following **FV function** syntax. Ensure that you enter the syntax as shown including the two commas: **=FV(2.5%,8,75)**

2 **Press** the **Enter** key to enter the data for calculation.

3 Enter the following syntax in cell A2 and press **Enter**: **=FV(2.5%,8,-75)**

The system should returns the same **value** result in cells A1:A2.

The figures in cell A1 should have the font colour **red** and be surrounded by round brackets. Depending on your system defaults, the formatting may show negative numbers as red with a minus sign in front and no brackets, or other variations. Cell A2 should have standard **black** text, if black is your default font colour.

Why is the value in cell A1 Red?

Result cell A1: **(£655.21)**   **Result** cell A2: **£655.21**

Understanding cell A1

If you have not spotted it yet, the **pmt** figure in the syntax is a positive figure.

When you pay any sum into the savings account this must be represented by a negative figure e.g. **−25**.

If you receive any interest on your savings account it should be represented by a positive figure e.g. **25**.

Task B

In this task you will calculate the possible **FV** of a **figure** based on various payment periods (**Nper**). All arguments of the FV function will be used in this task.

File preparation:

1 **Insert** a new worksheet. **Rename** the worksheet as **FValue**.

2 Enter the **labels** and **data** as shown in the table that follows, in cells B2:H8:

	B	C	D	E	F	G	H
2	Annual Interest	RATE	Nper	Pmt	Pv	Type	FV
3	6%		12	-250	-5000	1	
4	6%		4	-250	-5000	1	
5	6%		12	-250	-5000	1	
6	12%		12	-250	-5000	1	
7	12%		48	-250	-5000	1	
8	12%		12	-250	-5000	1	

3 **Format** cells C3:C8 as **percentages**, one decimal place.

4 **Format** cells E3:F8 as **currency**, two decimal places.

Creating the Figures to perform the **FV** function calculation:

Info

The **RATE** argument

Cell B3 displays an **annual** interest rate of 6%.

This percentage figure must be divided by the **Nper** to find the **RATE** for 12 months.

Enter a division formula that divides The **annual interest** by **Nper**.

5 Enter the following formula syntax, in **cell C3**: **=(B3/D3)**

Info

The result of the division formula should be **0.5%** in cell C3.

The **6%** figure shown in Cell B3 represents the interest rate for a year.

You will save a fixed sum once a month for 12 months and interest will be applied each time a payment is made.

The new **percentage** figure in cell C3 is the **RATE** that will be added to each payment you make.

Cell H3 will contain the function to find the **FV** of your initial investment of **-£5,000.00** and monthly payments of **-£250** based on the contents of cell C3.

Info

Example **FV** function syntax entered via the **keyboard** with default options applied for the pv and type arguments:
=FV(2.5%,8,75)
=FV(2.5%,8,-75)

Example **FV** function syntax used via the function wizard with all arguments entered:
=FV(C3,D3,E3,F3,G3)

Note: Commas (,) separate the arguments in syntax examples.

6 Click cell H3 and start the Function Wizard.

7 In the **Paste Function** window select the **Financial** function **category**. The function name is **FV**.

8 **Enter** or **select** the following **cell** references as **arguments** in the **FV** function window.

   a **Rate** argument cell C3
   b **Nper** argument cell D3
   c **Pmt** argument cell E3
   d **Pv** argument cell F3
   e **Type** argument cell G3

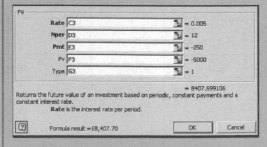

Figure 3.43 Completed FV function window

9 Close the **FV** function window.

10 **Copy** the division formula in cell C3 to cell C4.

11 Copy the **FV** function in cell H3 to cell H4.

In the above examples the **FV** function is being applied consistently.

What happens if the **FV** function is not applied consistently?

Task C

1 Click cell H5 and start the Function Wizard.

2 **Enter** or **select** the following **cell** references as **arguments** in the **FV** function window:

    a **Rate** argument cell B5.
    b **Nper** argument cell D5.
    c **Pmt** argument cell E5.
    d **Pv** argument cell F5.
    e **Type** argument cell G5.

Results:
You should get a return value of **£14,531.52** in cell H5. Compare this with the value in cell H3.

While the values in Row 3 and 5 look similar two different types of calculations have been used.

In cell H3 the **6%** rate is **divided** by **12** (Nper) and applied as a percentage each month.

In cell H5 the **6%** annual interest is applied each month for 12 (Nper) months.

The FV calculation in cell H5 is inaccurate for this calculation as the **annual interest** figure has been used and not a percentage of this as in cell H3.

The Nper 12 could refer to 12 years.

To display 12 years as the Nper calculation: multiply **years** by **payments** e.g. 12 *12 = 144, and display the figure separately as in cell C3.

Note: Do not mix your calculations when applying any of the financial functions.

If the **annual rate is 6%** on your savings and you decide to make a (pmt) of **–2500** and a single **Nper payment** your calculation should look like the following example, as used in the calculation for cell H5:

Rate argument 6%
Nper argument 12
Pmt argument –2500
Pv argument –5000
Type argument 1

If the annual rate is 6% on your savings and you decide to make a (pmt) of **–2500** and 12 separate Nper payments, your calculation should **divide** the annual rate of 6% by 12 to reflect the fact that you will make 12 separate Nper payments, as used in the calculation for cell H3.

Task D

1 **Copy** the **Division** formula from cell C4 to cells C6:C8.

2 **Copy** the **FV** function from cell H4 to cells H6:H8.

    AutoFormat the **FValue** worksheet. (Review the **AutoFormat** section if you need help with this task.)

3 Select cell B2 and apply the **Colourful 2 table format** to the **FV function** worksheet.

2 – NVP

The NPV function

NPV is an abbreviation for the term **net present value**.

This function calculates the *current* *net* value of an *investment* by using a *fixed rate* and a series of *future* **payments**.

The value arguments in the function syntax **Net** refers to **Net Profit**, after tax etc. has been deducted from the gross profit.

Syntax: **=NPV**(rate,value1,value2, ..).

The **NPV** function can take up to 29 arguments as values.

The **rate** argument is the *fixed rate* for that period.

The **value** *arguments* is an expected payment.

Insert a new worksheet. **Rename** the worksheet **NPValue**.

Task A

Can I make a profit on what I put in?

You are considering buying a share of **£4500** in an investment syndicate. The investment estimates a return of **£1500** in year 1, **£2000** in year 2 and **£3500** in year 3. The **rate** is **3.15%**.

1 File preparation:

   a Enter the title **Net Future value of £4500** in cell B1.
   b Merge and centre the title through cells B1:G1.

2 Enter labels in cells B2:G2 as follows:

   a Rate
   b End of Period Investment (Value1)
   c Year1 (Value2)
   d Year2 (Value3)
   e Year3 (Value4)
   f Current Net Value

3 Enter data in cells B3:F3 as follows:

   a 3.15%
   b −4500
   c 1500
   d 2000
   e 3500
   f Format cells C3:F3 as currency, 2 decimal places.

4 Select cell G3 and start the Function Wizard.

5 In the **Paste Function** window select the **Financial** function. Category and the function name **NPV**.

6 Use the function window example (Figure 3.44) to complete your function window.

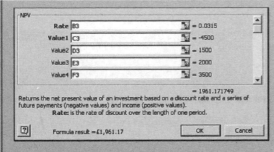

Figure 3.44 Completed NPV function window.

Results:

After applying the **NPV** function you should have a **current net value** answer of **£1961.17**.

Info

The current net value answer of **£1961.17** will only be accurate if the *investment seller has been accurate* about the estimated return values in **Value2**, **Value3** and **Value4** arguments.

The important issue here is to understand *how to apply the function* while the software provides the built in calculations based on the function name.

Task B

Method

In this task you will use the same figures as in cells B3:F3 to test a **beginning** of year investment. In the previous exercise an **end** of year investment is used.

1 **Copy** and **paste** the contents of cells B2:G2 in cell B6.

2 **Amend** the **label** in cell C6 to read as **Beginning of Period Investment**.

3 **Copy** and **paste** the contents of cells B3:F3 into cell B7.

4 The function for the **Beginning of Period Investment** is constructed differently.

    a Click cell G7 and start the Function Wizard.
    b Select the **NPV** function.
    c Cell B7 is the **rate** argument.
    d Cells D7:F7 contain the **Value1** argument.
    e Select **OK** to apply the function and to close the NPV window.

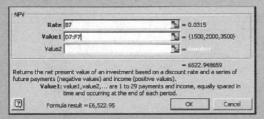

Figure 3.45 Completed NPV function window

5 Click cell G7 in the **formula bar** and add the following to the end of the **NPV** function syntax: **+C7**.

6 Press **Enter** to ensure that the additional information is added to the function and calculated by the system.

Amended function syntax: **=NPV(B7,D7:F7)+C7**.

Info

When a payment is made at the beginning of the period, as in **Task A**, this is not included as a value in the **NPV** function.

Will you make a profit on your investment?

3 – PMT

Info

The PMT function

The **PMT** function **calculates** a loan **payment** based on **constant payments** and a **constant interest rate**.

Syntax: **=PMT**(*rate,nper,pv,fv,type*)

The **PMT** function can take up to five arguments as values.

The *fv* and *type* are optional arguments. If you do not add data to these arguments the system defaults of 0 (zero) will apply to both arguments.

The PMT function arguments can also read as:
=PMT(Interest Rate, Number of Payment Periods, Principal)

Principal is equal to a *capital sum*, as distinguished from the interest or income on it.

Capital equals wealth or property, which is used or invested to produce more wealth.

Insert a new worksheet and **rename** the worksheet **PMT**.

Task A

How much will a **loan** of **£20000** cost you to repay over 10 years?

You have been to three banks and received the following figures for the loan. Each bank has quoted a different interest rate per month.

Method

File Preparation:

1 Enter the title **Loan £20000** in cell B1.

2 Create the spreadsheet based on the layout below, on the **PMT** worksheet in cells B3:E6.

Bank	Interest Rate	Repayment Period (Years)	Loan Figure
BBA International	4.05%	10	20000
South Local	3.44%	10	20000
United Shares	3.06%	10	20000

3 Before you apply the **PMT** function, fine-tune the spreadsheet. The data in the column **Repayment Period (Years)** need to be displayed in months for the calculation to work correctly.

   a **Cut** the **label** and **data** from cells E3:E6 **paste** these in cell G3:G6.
   b Enter the label **Number Per Year** in cell E3. This column will contain the number of repayments you will make in a year.
   c Enter the figure **12** in cell E4:E6. You will make a repayment once a month for each month in the year.
   d **Format** cells G4:G6 as **currency**, two decimal places.

4 You now need to multiply the **Repayment Period** (Years) by **Number Per Year**, to convert years to months:

   a Enter the label **Repayment Period (Months)** in cell F3.
   b Enter a multiplication formula in cell F4 that will **multiply** the **Repayment Period (Years)** by **Number Per Year**. Syntax: **=(D4*E4)**.

The formula used should return a value of 120 cell F4.

5 Copy the formula to cells F5:F6.

6 Enter the label **Repayment Per Month** in cell H3.

7 **Wrap the text** in cells D3:F3 and H3.

8 **Adjust** the columns and rows so that the label text in these cells is wrapped and fully displayed.

9 So you can quickly see the data to include in the PMT function, highlight specified columns with a fill colour. Format the following cells:

   a Turquoise in cells C4:C6.
   b Light Green in cells F4:F6.
   c Grey-25% in cells G4:G6.
   d **Merge** and **centre** the title **Loan £20000** through cells B1:H1.
   e **Change** the **title font size** to **point 12**.

Task B – Applying the PMT function

Method

1 Click cell H4 and apply the PMT function via the Function Wizard.

2 The arguments are:

   a The rate argument is **C4/12**.
   b The Nper argument is **F4**.
   c The Pv argument is **-G4**.

Do not enter any values for the **fv** or **type** arguments.

3 Select **OK** to apply the **PMT** function and to close the PMT window.

Info

PMT function syntax in cell **H4 =PMT(C4/12,F4,-G4)**

The PMT function explained

Rate divided by **12**, which represents the 12 payments you will make each year; length of loan 120 months minus the loan of **£20000**.

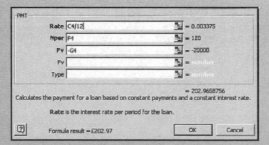

Figure 3.46 Completed PMT function window

Result: a value of **£202.97** should be returned in cell H4.

4 **Copy** the PMT function to cells H5:H6.

Info

The PV function

PV is an abbreviation for the term **present value** and returns the present value of an investment.

Syntax: **=PV**(rate,nper,pmt,fv,type).

The **PV** function can take up to five arguments as values.

The **rate** argument:
When you make monthly payments the interest rate needs to be divided by 12 to represent each month of the year.

For example **4.00%/12** will display as **0.3%** if the cell is formatted to one decimal place, and will display as **0.33%** if the cell is formatted to two decimal places.

The **Nper** argument:
The Nper argument represents the total number of payments you will make in the life of the plan, displayed in months. If your saving plan is for **5 years** you need to **multiply** the **5 years** by **12** to display the 5 years as months e.g. **5 * 12 = 60 months**.

The **PMT** argument:
The pmt argument represents the payment made each month. This payment cannot change and remains static if you start with £25 in year 1 it will still be £25 in year 5.

Note: The *fv* and *type* arguments are optional for the PV function. If you do not enter a value for these two arguments they will contain the system default values of 0 (zero).

Task A

You have recently seen a saving plan that would require an initial £1000 investment. The plan promises to pay you £25 every month for 5 years. The annual interest rate is 4%. Is this a good investment for you?

Use the PV function to check the present value of the plan before you decide to invest or not.

Method

Insert a new worksheet in the **MyFunctions** workbook. **Rename** the worksheet as **PV**.

1   File preparation:

   a   Enter the title **Present Value** in cell B1.
   b   Merge and centre the **title** through cells B1:E1.
   c   Change the title's **font size** to **point 12**.
   d   Enter the following labels in cells B3:E3:
      i   **Rate** (interest)
      ii   **Payments Number** (Nper)
      iii   **Monthly Payments** (PMT)
      iv   **Present Value**

2   Enter the following data in cells B4:D4.

   a   4%
   b   60
   c   25

3   Format the **rate** figure as **percentage**, two decimal places.

4   Format the **PMT** figure as **currency**, two decimal places.

Task B

Method

1 Click cell E4 and open the **PV** function window.

2 Collapse the **PV** function window and use the mouse to select cell B4.

3 After selecting cell B4 as the rate argument to complete the function syntax **enter** the **division sign /** and the **figure 12**, to **divide** the **contents** of cell B4 by the figure **12**.

4 Select cell C4 as the **Nper** argument.

5 Select cell D4 as the **PMT** argument.

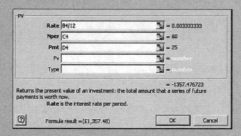

Figure 3.47 Completed PV function window

6 Click **OK** to apply the **PV** function and to close the PV window.

Select cell E4 and note the function syntax in the **formula bar**, and shown as follows:
=PV(4/12, 60, 1000)

Info

Result: the result of the formula displayed in cell E4 should be **–£1,357.48**

Your initial investment was £1000. The return is £357.48p from the initial investment @ £25 per month.

The PV function used in **Task B** could also be written as: **=PV(B5/12,C5*12,D5)**.

Task C – Use an alternative PV function syntax

Method

1 Enter the data below in cells B5:D5:

    a 4%

    b 5

    c 25

2 **Format** the percentage and **currency** cells as in **Task A**.

3 In cell E5, use the example shown (Figure 3.48) to apply the PV function syntax.

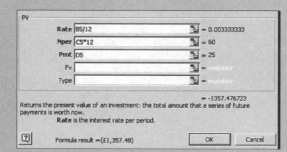

Figure 3.48 Completed PV function window (alternative arguments)

Info

The function should return exactly the same answer as the first exercise. Why? Re-read or research the explanation on **Nper** if you are unsure why the calculation works.

5 – RATE

The RATE function

This function returns the interest rate per period of an annuity.

Syntax: **=RATE**(*nper,pmt,pv,fv,type,guess*).

The arguments *fv*, *type* and *guess* are optional. The guess argument represents the rate a percentage if you do not enter a **value** the system default option of 10% will be applied. The *fv* and *type* arguments are as discussed before.

Task A

1 **Insert** a new worksheet in the **Myfunctions** workbook. **Rename** the worksheet as **RATE**.

You have **£5000**. If you loaned this sum to a bank you would want to make a profit over the period of the loan. Use the **RATE** function to look at the various rate options to assist you in choosing the best rate to lend you money at for the best return.

2 In cell B1 enter the title **Rate Value**.

3 Enter the following labels in cells B3:F3:

   a **Payments Number (Nper)**
   b **Monthly Payments (PMT)**
   c **Value (pv)**
   d **Rate (Guess)**
   e **Result**

Calculate the **rate** of a five-year **£5000** loan with **monthly** payments of **£125** at a **rate** of **12.9%**.

RATE function syntax: =RATE(60, -125, 5000, , ,12.9) equals 1.4%

Commas (,) separate or represent an argument not used in the syntax example.

4 Enter the following figures in cell B4:E4:

   a 60
   b −125
   c 5000
   d 12.9%

5 **Format** cells C4:D4 as **currency**, two decimal places.

6 Click cell F4.

7 Start the function wizard and use the mouse to select the contents of each cell as shown in Figure 3.49. Do not enter any arguments for the Fv or Type argument.

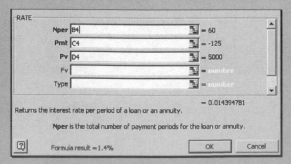

Figure 3.49 RATE function

8 Select cell E4 as the **Guess** argument.

Task 3.5 Using financial functions

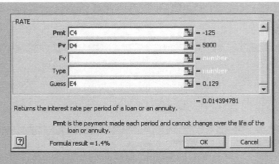

Figure 3.50 RATE function window with Guess argument displayed

Info

Result:

Cell F4 should contain the percentage figure **1.4%** which is the monthly rate.

If you receive an answer of 1% or 1.44% in cell F4 the cell is formatted to 0 (zero) decimal places or two decimal places. Adjust the cell formatting to one decimal place.

Task B

Method

1 Enter the following figures in cell B5:D5.

 a 60

 b −200

 c 5000

 Leave cell E5 blank. The default of 10% will be applied by the system.

2 Click cell F5 and apply the **rate** function. Do not copy the function from cell F4.

 The function syntax construction should like this example: **=RATE(B5,C5,D5)**.

 Is this the same as the syntax construction in cell F4?

 If you copy the function from cell F4 you will reference an empty cell in the new row of data in cell E5.

Info

Result:

The result in cell F5 should be **3.5%**. If you get a value of 3.49%, adjust your percentage formatting to one decimal place.

Task C

Method

1 Enter the following data in cells B6:E7:

120	-250	8000	2.5%
120	-150	8000	5%

2 Enter a **rate** function in cells F6 using the system defaults for the **Fv** and **Type arguments** as in Task A.

3 **Copy** the function to cell F7.

Info

Results:

Cell F6 should be 3.0%.

Cell F7 should be 1.6%.

1 – IF

Info

The IF function

This function evaluates values entered and will return one value if **true** and another value if **false** as specified by you.

Syntax: **=IF**(*logical_test,value_if_true,value_if_false*).

Method

The spreadsheet example in Figure 3.51 will display a figure for profit in **Column F**, whatever the amount as a formula has been entered to produce this.

	B	C	D	E	F	G
			Music Formats			
	Product	Wholesale Price	Retail Price	Quantity Sold	Profit	Watch
	CD	15	22.5	250	=(D4-C4)*E4	
	MiniDisc	17.5	25	150	=(D5-C5)*E5	
	Tapes	6.5	11.5	30	=(D6-C6)*E6	
	Vinyl	12.5	15	162	=(D7-C7)*E7	
	DVD	19.5	29.5	300	=(D8-C8)*E8	

Figure 3.51 Music Formats spreadsheet

Using an **IF** function you can obtain visual display at a glance, of sales that are meeting targets.

You want the message **"OK"** to display in **column G** (**watch**) if the Profit figure in **column F** is above £1000.00, or display the message "**NO**" if profit is less than £1000.00 for a product.

You can translate the above sentence so that your system will understand and act upon this.

In **column G, row 4** you could enter the following **IF** function syntax: **=If**(*F4>1000,"OK","NO"*).

This **IF** function uses the **operator symbol Greater Than (>)**

Info

We need to look at the function to see a) how it is applied and b) how it returns the responses requested.

The IF function syntax: **=If(F4>1000,"OK","NO")**

Different font tones have been used to display the function syntax so you can see how each argument operates.

IF (Logical Test, value if true, value if false)

Logical test
Any condition you wish to test. e.g. **=IF(A1=B1 or A1<>B1)**.

Value if true
What you want to see displayed in the cell.

Value if false
What you want to see displayed in the cell.

For text to be displayed it must be enclosed in double quotation marks, e.g. "No", "Yes".

Value if **true** or **value** if **false** could refer to a **number (23)** a **cell** reference (**L7**) or another **function and/or formula** (L4*M4, G2+82).

Task A – Creating an IF function without the Function Wizard

Method

1 File preparation:

   a Open a new workbook and save this as **MyIffunction**.
   b **Enter** the figure **75** in cell F4 on **Sheet1**.

2 Select cell G4 and enter the syntax below in the **formula bar**, exactly as shown.

IF function syntax: **=If(F4>1000,"OK","NO")**

Info

The **logical test** is **IF F4>1000**
The **value if true** is **OK**
The **value if false** is **NO**

Result: cell G4 should display the message **NO**.

3 **Enter** the following figures in cell F5:F10.

   a 150
   b 2500
   c 3000
   d 650
   e 900
   f 4005

4 **Copy** the **IF** function in cell G4 to cells G5:G10.

5 **Rename** Sheet1 as **IFOne**.

You now know how to enter a basic **IF** function syntax without using the Function Wizard.

In the following tasks you will enter the **IF** function syntax via the Function Wizard.

Task B – Creating the music formats spreadsheet shown above.

Method

1 File preparation:

   a **Rename** Sheet2 as **IFTwo**.
   b Enter the title **Music Formats** in cell B1.
   c Key the six labels in the table that follows in cells B3:G3:

Product
Wholesale Price
Retail Price
Quantity Sold
Profit
Watch

2 Key in the following in five labels in cells B4:B8:

CD
MiniDisc
Tapes
Vinyl
DVD

3 Widen columns as necessary to ensure that all text in labels can be seen.

4 Key in the following figures in cells C4:E8:

15	22.5	250
17.5	25	150
6.5	11.5	30
12.5	15	162
19.5	29.5	300

5 Format cells C4:D8 as currency, two decimal places.

Task C

Method

1 Enter a formula In cell F4 that *subtracts* the **Retail Price** from the **Wholesale Price** and then *multiplies* the result by the **Quantity Sold**, to display the **Profit** figure from the sale.

The formula should be constructed in the following way:

Info

The subtraction calculation must be performed first. Instruct the system to do this by placing this part of the formula in parentheses as shown in the example below.

=(D4-C4)*E4

The **result** of your first calculation should equal **£1,875.00**

2 **Copy** the formula to cells F5:F8.

Task D

Method

1 Enter a formula in cell G4 that will display the message **OK** if profit in cell F4 is **greater than** £1000 or **NO** if profit is **less than** £1000.

2 Applying an **IF** function to evaluate the figure(s) in cell F4.

   a Select cell G4 and start the Function Wizard.
   b In the **paste function** window select the **logical function** category and the function name **IF**.
   c Collapse the **IF** function window and select cell F4 as the **Logical_Test** argument.
   d Maximise the **IF** function window.
   e Add the following after F4 in the Logical_Test argument box via the keyboard **>1000**.

3 Using the keyboard, enter:

   a **OK** for the *value_if_true* argument.
   b **NO** for the *value_if_false* argument.

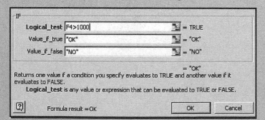

Figure 3.52 Completed IF function window

The system will add the quotation marks to the **value arguments** entered.

4 Select **OK** to apply the **IF** function and to close the function window.

Result: cell G4 should display the **OK** message.

5 **Copy** the IF function to cells G5:G8.

The **final result** should be **three OK** messages and **two NO** messages in cells G5:G8.

Task E – Formatting the spreadsheet

1 **Merge** and **centre** the title **Music Formats** across cells B1:G1.

2 **Embolden** the **title**.

3 Change the title **font size** to **point 14**.

4 **Embolden** all labels in cells B3:G3 and B4:B8.

5 Select **B3:G8** and **centre** all labels and values contained in cells.

Have you been saving your work regularly?

What do you think? The IF function is not hard to apply and can be used in many circumstances as a reminder or trigger for other events.

6 **Save** and close the workbook **MyIffunction**.

7 **Close** all open workbooks.

Task F

In the next exercise you will create a spreadsheet to record current stationery supplies, which will alert you, via the use of an IF function, when you need to reorder stock.

Import a text file

1 **Import** the text file **Stationery**. The file can be located on the accompanying CD-ROM.

2 Accept all the defaults offered by the Text Import Wizard, by clicking the **Finish** button in **Step 1 of 3**.

3 Save the **imported** text file as **IFStationery** in a spreadsheet format.

The imported text file data should all be located in **column A**.

4 **Cut** and **paste** the data in cell A1 in cell B1, to create a **title**.

5 **Cut** and **paste** the data in the cells A2:A21 to cell B4, to create a new **column** location.

6 Select cell B3 and enter the label **Stationery**.

7 In cells C3:E3 enter the following labels.

   a **Stock Level**
   b **Order Level**
   c **Order**

The data on the **Stationery** worksheet should now be in cells B4:B23.

Task G

1 File preparation:

   a Select cell B3.
   b Click **Sort** on the **Data** menu.

The labels and data in the **Stationery Spreadsheet** should be highlighted and the Sort window visible.

Figure 3.53 Sort window

Info

The system should have detected that you only have data in column B and offer the suggestion of Sort by **Ascending**. No other data options may be detected.

The list has a header row which you have just created.

2 Make sure the **Header row** option button is selected.

3 Close the **Sort** window.

The First item in your newly **sorted** list should be **A4 Dividers** in cell B4, and the last item, **Tape** in cell B23.

4 **Enter** the data from the following table in the Stock Level and Order Level Columns:

Stationery	Stock Level	Order Level
A4 Dividers	3	5
A4 Files	7	5
A4 Pads	9	5
A4 Paper Headed	20	5
A4 Paper White	15	5
A5 Pads	4	5
Box Files	9	5
Fax Paper	2	5
Flip Chart Pad	1	5
Floppy Disks	7	5
Highlighters	5	5
Markers Black	4	5
Paper Clips	8	5
Pencils	1	5
Pens Ink Black	4	5
Pens Ink Blue	8	5
Pocket Files	2	5
Printer Cartridges	3	5
Staples	1	5
Tape	3	5

Task H – Applying an IF function to evaluate the figures in cell F4

Method

1 Enter an **IF** function in cell E4 that **looks** in cell C4: If the contents of cell C4 are **less** than the **contents** of cell D4 display the message **Order Now** in cell E4.

Info

Stationery order **IF** function syntax: **=IF(C4<D4,"Order Now","OK")**

2 Apply the IF function to cell E4. You can use the Function Wizard or enter the function syntax directly in the formula bar.

Cell E4 should display **Order Now**, if all has gone well. If not, **undo** your changes, check the data entered and apply the function again.

3 **Copy** the function to the cells E5:E23.

Save and review your work before moving to the next section.

Close the workbook.

EXERCISE

2 – AND

Info

The AND function

This function will only return **True** if all arguments presented are **True**.

Syntax: **=AND**(logical1,logical2, ...)

The **AND** function takes up to 30 logical arguments in the function.

Method

File preparation:

a **Open** a new workbook and save this as **MyAndfunction**.
b **Rename** Sheet1 in the workbook as **ANDfunction**.
c **Enter** the title **Desktops** in cell B1 of the **ANDfunction** worksheet.

Task A

You are going to look at the desktop specifications of a number of computers to see which need to be upgraded to the new 2000 Specification.

What must be upgraded?

All computers that do not have a:

a 2000 specification for operating system and Office suite for bought applications.

b Email and voice software Version 5.

c Phone and location guide software Version 6.

1 Create the spreadsheet shown in the table below, within the cells B3:H9:

	B	C	D	E	F	G	H
3	Name	Operating System Version	Office Suite Version	E-mail Version	Voice Software Version	Phone and Location Guide Version	Upgrade? Y/N
4	Lyn	95	95	2.4	2.1	4	
5	Mick	95	95	2.4	2.1	4	
6	Glen	98	95	2.4	2.1	4	
7	Roy	95	95	2.4	2.1	4	
8	Roxanne	2000	2000	5	5	6	

2 Wrap the text of the **labels** in cells C3:G3.

3 Adjust the column width as appropriate.

Task B

You are going to ask the system to use the **AND** function to look in the individual cells and test the contents of these against specified criteria.

The specified criteria:

If the contents of cell C4 are less than **2000**, D4 less than **2000**, E4 less than **5**, F4 less than **5** and G4 less than **6**. If all these conditions evaluate to **True** then display **True** in cell H4.

1 **Select** cell H4 and start the Function Wizard.

2 In the **Paste function** window select the logical function category and the function name **AND**.

Function construction

3 Use the mouse to collapse the **AND** function window, then select **individual** cells.

4 Use the keyboard to enter relevant operators for the cell reference in the individual AND arguments as follows:

a **Logical1** argument cell C4<2000   d **Logical4** argument cell F4<5
b **Logical2** argument cell D4<2000   e **Logical5** argument cell G4<6
c **Logical3** argument cell E4<5

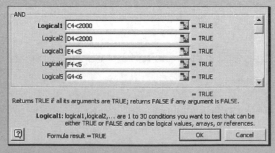

Figure 3.54 Completed AND function window

The **result** should equal **TRUE** in cell H4 after you have closed the Function Wizard.

AND function syntax in the formula bar when cell H4 is selected:

=AND(C4<2000,D4<2000,E4<5,F4<5,G4<6)

5 **Copy** the **AND** function to cells H5:H8.

The **results** should show that all staff, with the exception of **Roxanne** must be upgraded.

Task C

1 Add the details from the table below, in Row **9** for **Jamial**:

Name	Operating System Version	Office Suite Version	E-mail Version	Voice Software Version	Phone and Location Guide Version	Upgrade? Y/N
Jamial	2000	95	5	5	6	

2 **Copy** the **AND** function in cell H8 to cell H9.

The **result** should be **False**. Can you see why? Look again at the role of the **AND** function. The **AND** function will only return true if all **arguments** are true.

Despite the fact that the **Office suite version** for **Jamial** was below the specification the function did not return a **True result**, as all arguments did not evaluate as being **true**.

Note: Before you use this function work though what you want returned, to ensure that you get the right result.

3 **Format** the **ANDfunction** spreadsheet with the **Classic 2 Auto Format**.

If you need to review how to apply an **AutoFormat**, revisit section 1.2, page 6.

Save and review your work before moving to the next section.

Close the workbook.

3 – OR

The OR function

This function will return **True** if any argument is true, or **False** if all arguments are false.

Syntax: **=OR**(logical1,logical2,...)

The **OR** function takes up to 30 logical arguments.

File preparation:

a Open a new workbook and save this as **MyORfunction**.
b In cell B1 enter the Title **Days Worked**.
c **Rename** Sheet1 in the workbook as **ORfunction**.

Task A

The specified criteria:
In this exercise you want to see which member/s of staff **did not** work every day last week e.g. Monday to Friday. 0 (zero) represents a non-working day.

Function construction

If the contents of cell C4 are greater than (0) zero, it is a **True** statement. All arguments do not have to evaluate as **True** in the OR function, only **one** argument need meet this criteria for the system to return a True evaluation, which is what you are looking for in this exercise.

For this argument to evaluate as **False** all arguments must evaluate as False.

1   Create the spreadsheet shown in the table that follows within cells B3:H10 on the **ORfunction** worksheet:

Name	Monday	Tuesday	Wednesday	Thursday	Friday	Worked?
Pauline	7	7	7	7	0	
Ishmael	0	0	0	5	7	
Sharma	0	0	0	0	0	
Lil-Li	0	5	3	7	0	
Aniel	0	0	0	0	7	
Shabaz	0	0	0	0	0	
Cosria	0	0	7	5	7	

2   Select cell H4 and start the Function Wizard.

3   In the **Paste** function window select the **logical** function category and the function name **OR**.

4   Use the mouse to collapse the **OR** function window and to select the individual cells.

5   Use the keyboard to add the operator to the cell reference in the individual arguments as follows:

   a   **Logical1** argument **C4>0**
   b   **Logical2** argument **D4>0**
   c   **Logical3** argument **E4>0**
   d   **Logical4** argument **F4>0**
   e   **Logical5** argument **G4>0**

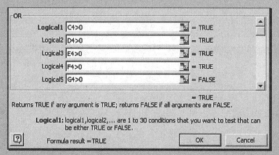

Figure 3.55 The completed OR function window

Example **OR** function syntax in cell H4: **=OR(C4>0,D4>0,E4>0,F4>0,G4>0)**

The **result** should equal **True** in cell H4.

6   **Copy** the **OR** function to cells H5:H10.

The **result** should display False for *Sharma* and *Shabaz* only; all others should evaluate as True.

7   Spreadsheet formatting.

   a   **Format** the **ORfunction** worksheet with the **List 1 AutoFormat**. Ensure that you select a cell within the spreadsheet before applying the AutoFormat.
   b   **Merge and centre** the title **Days Worked** across cells B1:H1.

   Save and review your work before you move on.

4 – ISERROR

The ISERROR function

The **ISERROR** function is now part of nine worksheet functions, used for testing value or reference on a worksheet. The **functions category** will now be **Information**.

The group is collectively known as **IS functions**.

The **ISERROR** function is used for testing the value of an error.
Syntax: **=ISERROR**(*value*)

The **ISERROR** function returns **True** if a cell contains one of the following errors as a value:

Error Value	General Description or error type
#N/A	Value not available for a function/formula
#VALUE!	The wrong type of argument or operator is used
#REF!	A cell reference is not valid
#DIV/0!	Formula divided by 0 (zero), or reference to a blank cell
#NUM!	A function requires a numeric argument and you have used another type of argument
#NAME?	Text in a formula is not recognised
#NULL!	Cell reference or Range operator inaccurate

Note: Use the **ISERR** information function if you want to test for the **#N/A** error only. This is a function that you can insert yourself as a placeholder while creating a spreadsheet.

Task A

In the following tasks you will practice inserting the **ISERROR** function to test the value of cell contents.

Open the workbook **IsError**. The file can be located on the accompanying CD-ROM.

Select the **Error** worksheet.

Cells A4:F23 are the area of the worksheet where you will enter a function to test for an error value in a specified cell and where the responses to the function will be displayed.

The data you will test is located in a range of cells starting in cell H26.

1 Click cell A4 and start the Function Wizard.

2 In the **Paste function** window select the **information** function category. The function name is **ISERROR**.

3 Enter **B43** as the value argument.

The **ISERROR** window (Figure 3.56) gives you an immediate response as to the contents of the cell and a value of True or False.

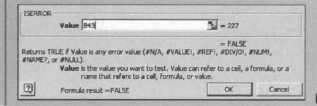

Figure 3.56 The ISERROR function window

4 Close the function window.

Using the fill handles, copy the **ISERROR** function to cell A5:A18, to test the range for any errors in these cells.

The **results** should be 6 True and 9 False.

Task B

1 Click cell C4.

2 Test cell K36 to see if this contains an error using the **ISERROR** function window. The **result** should be False.

3 Go to cell K36.

o Press the **F5** function key

o Enter the cell address in the GoTo **Reference** text box at the bottom of the window.

The cell contains the **error value #NAME?** Why has the system returned **False**?

This error value indicates that a name used in the formula syntax does not exist, e.g. a **named range**, therefore the system is unable to tell if this is a genuine error or a syntax error.

Task C

1 In cell C5 use the **ISERROR** function to test cell I28.

2 In cell C6 use the **ISERROR** function to test cell I29.

3 In cell C7 use the **ISERROR** function to test cell K45.

Your **results** should be **True**, **False** and **True** respectively. If you did not use the **ISERROR function window** to test the cells, the expected results will not be achieved.

4 Use **Go To** and check the cell contents values of cells **I28**, **I29** and **K45**, to confirm the expected results.

Are your results accurate?

Save and review your work before moving to the next section.

Do not close the workbook; you will use this in the next exercise.

| 3.7 | *Using nested functions* |

Nested function can best be described as functions and/or functions/formulas, contained within one calculation.

Task A

ROUND the contents of cell K37 on the **Error** worksheet and display the rounded figure in cell L37 if it does not contain an error.

If cell L37 contains an error you want to display a message in cell L37.

To create this nested function will require the use of three functions to achieve the outcome.

Example of the nested function syntax you will be creating:

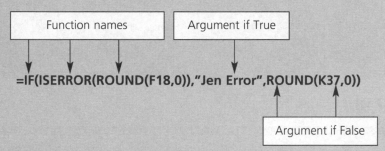

```
=IF(ISERROR(ROUND(F18,0)),"Jen Error",ROUND(K37,0))
```

The function syntax shown above uses the following functions:

o **IF** logical function
o **ISERROR** information function
o **ROUND** math & trig function

This nested function is created via the **IF** function window. The **IF** function as you are aware, will perform a logical_test on the contents of cell K37 and return one **Value_if_true** and another **Value_if_false**.

1 Select cell K37 and start the Function Wizard.

2 In the **Paste function** window select the **Logical** function category and the **IF** function name.

3 Using the example in Figure 3.57, enter the various arguments in the IF function window.

In the **Value_if_true** argument use **your name** or a **message** of your choice.

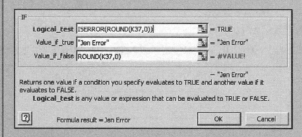

Figure 3.57 The IF function window

4 When you have entered the three function arguments, click **OK** to apply the function and close the IF function window.

The **result** should display the **Value_if_true** error message, as the cell contains an error value.

5 To ensure that the function is working correctly use the fill handles to **Copy** the function to cell L38.

This **result** should produce a **ROUND** figure of **27**.

Select cell K37 and click on the Paste Function toolbar button to open the SUM function window. The **Number1** argument produces the **#VALUE!** error on screen in the open function window but displays the correct formula result in cell K37. Close the function window.

Select cell L37 and click the Paste Function toolbar button to open the **IF** function window.

The **Value_if_false** argument produces the **#VALUE!** error on screen in the open function but displays the correct formula result in cell L37. Close the function window. Can you see why this error is returned to the function windows? Is the argument supplied to the **Number1** and **Value_if_false** arguments the right type of argument?

Reread the descriptions for the **#VALUE!** error at the start of the **ISERROR** function section.

In a later exercise you will add comments to these cells to remind you why particular results were produced.

Save and review your work before moving to the next section.

Close the workbook.

1 – ABS and PMT

In the following tasks you will use the **ABS** and **PMT** functions to create a nested function.

The **ABS** function will **return** the **absolute** (positive) **value** of **X**.

Example: **ABS** nested function syntax: **=ABS(PMT(B5/36,C5,D5))**

When you use the **ABS** function you do not need to display negative numbers as in the PMT function. The **ABS** function **returns** the **absolute** (positive) **value** of **X**. In the above example, **X** is the value of the contents of **cell D5**.

Task A

In this task you will use the **ABS** and **PMT** functions to create a nested function and compare the **ABS** and **PMT** function syntaxes.

1 File preparation:

   a Open a new workbook and save this as **NestedFun**.
   b Rename **Sheet1** in the workbook as **Nestedfunction**.
   c Create the spreadsheet example below in **cells B1:E5** on the **Nestedfunction** worksheet:

	A	B	C	D	E
1		Nested Functions			
2		RATE	MONTHS	LOAN	REPAYMENT PER MONTH
3					
4		0.08	36	10000	
5		0.08	36	10000	

2 Creating the spreadsheet:

   a In cell B1 enter the title **Nested Functions**. Merge and centre the title across cells B1:E1.
   b Enter the labels **RATE, MONTHS, LOAN** and **REPAYMENT PER MONTH**, in cells B3:E3.
   c Enter the data shown below in cells B4:D5.

	B	C	D
4	8.00%	36	10000
5	8.00%	36	10000

Task 3.7 Using nested functions

Task B – Creating the PMT function

Info

The **PMT** function **calculates** the **payment** for a loan based on **constant payments** and a **constant interest rate** as discussed in the financial functions section.

Method

1   Click cell E4 and enter the following PMT function syntax via the formula bar: **=PMT(B4/36,C4,-D4)**

The **result** should be £289.35 in cell E4.

Task C – Creating and entering the nested ABS/PMT function

Method

This nested function will be created in the **ABS** function window.

1   Click cell E5 and start the function wizard.

2   In the **Paste function** window select the **Math & Trig** function category, and the function name **ABS**.

3   Enter **PMT(B5/36,C5,D5)** as the ABS **Number** argument.

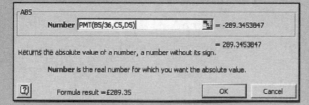

Figure 3.58 Completed ABS function window

4   Select **OK** to apply the function and to close the ABS window.

The **result** should be £289.35 in cell E5.

The **ABS** and **PMT** functions should return the same answers.

Compare the syntax used in cells E4:E5.

Info

If you do not want to use negative values in your calculations you can use the ABS function as part of a nested function to get around this.

Save and review your work before moving to the next section.

Close the workbook.

EXERCISE

2 – Practice

In this task you will add a nested function to calculate commission up or down for the sales of two products, bulbs and seeds, in a gardening store.

Open the workbook **NestedFunTwo**. The file can be located on the accompanying CD-ROM.

Method

Select **Sheet1**.

Sheet1 contains sales figures which are processed using the **IF** function to evaluate the figures and then carry out an instruction, from a choice of two options.

IF function options:

a   If the **total** figure is **greater** than **250**, an **average** figure from cells D17:D21 is added, plus the contents of cell B17.

b If the **total** figure is **less** than **250**, an **average** figure from cells E17:E21 is added, plus the contents of cell C17.

Sheet1 IF function construction

Cells F2:F3 contain an **IF** function that looks at cells B7:C7. If the figure in these cells is **greater** than **400**, the cell will display **25 Up**; if **less** than **400**, the cell displays **2 Down**.

Task A

Add a **nested function** to test the **total** Figure in cell B7 and **copy** this to cell C7 to produce the commission type results in cells F2:F3.

The nested function construction required if typed in English might look something like this:

IF the figures in cells B2:B6 when totalled are greater than 250.

Then

Find the average figure in cells D17:D21 plus sum cells B2:B6 plus cell B17

Or else

Find the average figure in cells E17:E21 plus sum cells B2:B6 plus cell C17.

1 Click cell B7 and start the Function Wizard.

2 In the **Paste function** window select the **Logical** function category, and the function name **IF**.

3 Enter the following as the various arguments to the IF function:

   a The **Logical_test** argument is: **SUM(B2:B6)>250**.
   b The **Value_if_true** argument is: **AVERAGE(D17:D21)+SUM(B2:B6)+B17**.
   c **Value_if_false** argument is: **AVERAGE(E17:E21)+SUM(B2:B6)+C17**.
   d Select **OK** to apply the function and to close the **IF** function window.

The nested function syntax construction in cell B7:

=IF(SUM(B2:B6)>250,AVERAGE(D17:D21)+SUM(B2:B6)+B17,AVERAGE(E17 :E21)+SUM(B2:B6)+C17).

4 Using the Fill Handle, **copy** the Nested function to cell C7.

Result:
Copying the function to a new location has produced the **#DIV/0!** error. In the ISERROR section this error was described as; formula divided by 0 (zero) or reference to a blank cell.

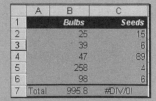

Figure 3.59 #DIV/0! error

Where in the syntax is the function trying to divide by zero or references a blank cell?

5 Click cell C7 and look at the function syntax in the formula bar.

Example function syntax in cell C7.

=IF(SUM(C2:C6)>250,**AVERAGE(E17:E21)**+SUM(C2:C6)+C17,**AVERAGE(F17:F21)+SUM(C2:C6)+D17)**

The function has shifted all cell references once to the right, and is now pointing at invalid references.

What you need to do here is add an absolute reference to the parts of the calculations that should be applied if the condition is **True** or **False**.

Click the **Undo** toolbar button to remove the function copied to cell C7.

Task B

Method

1 **Edit** the function syntax in cell B7, by adding the dollar sign to create absolute references for total up, total down, average up, and average down cell ranges. These are shown in bold in the following formula:

=IF(SUM(B2:B6)>250,AVERAGE(**$D$17:$D$21**)+SUM(B2:B6)+**$B$17**,AVERAGE(**$E$17:$E$21**)+SUM(B2:B6)+**$C$17**)

2 Select cell B7 and click the **edit formula** button to open the completed IF function window.

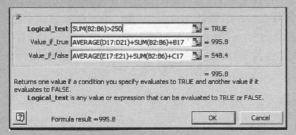

Figure 3.60 Completed IF function window

3 In the **IF** function window, **edit** the **Value_if_true** and **Value_if_false** arguments as shown below (Figure 3.61).

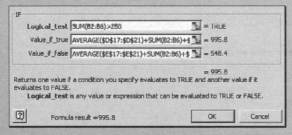

Figure 3.61 Completed IF function window – Edited

4 Close the function window.

Task C

Method

1 **Copy** the function to cell C7.

What is the result this time?

If you have a figure of **201.4** your nested function is working.

Cell F2 should display **25 up** and cell F3 **2 down**.

Save and review your work before moving to the next section.

Close the workbook.

1 – VLOOKUP

Info

VLOOKUP function syntax

=VLOOKUP(*lookup_value,table_array,col_index_num,range_lookup*)

HLOOKUP function syntax

=HLOOKUP(*lookup_value,table_array,col_index_num,range_lookup*)

These functions look up reference information for specified data. HLOOKUP looks at reference information horizontally VLOOKUP looks at reference information vertically.

Arguments explained:
The HLOOKUP and VLOOKUP functions have four arguments:

a The **lookup_value** *argument* is the information you want to find.
b The **table_array** *argument* is how the data is stored, such as in a named range.
c The **col_index_num** *argument* is where in a named range the data you want to use is stored. The named range may have more than one column or row.
d The **range_lookup** *argument* decides if you find an exact match False, or use the closest match for the data you are looking up, True – the default.

This function works well with spreadsheets where data can be stored in **rows** or **columns**.

Note: The technical description for a row is **record**, and for a column, **field**.

A **field** (column) contains a single piece of information that contributes to all the details that create a record.

	A	B	C	D	E	F	G
1	Expenses						
2	Name	Travel	Comms	Lunch	Entertaining	Total	Over
3	Developers	£800.00	£600.00	£250.00	£0.00	£1,650.00	OK
4	Engineers	£2,500.00	£8,500.00	£700.00	£0.00	£11,700.00	OK
5	Project Managers	£7,000.00	£4,500.00	£0.00	£10,000.00	£21,500.00	What!
6	Testers	£0.00	£0.00	£1,500.00	£0.00	£1,500.00	OK
7	DB Administrators	£350.00	£150.00	£100.00	£600.00	£1,200.00	OK
8	Support Staff	£0.00	£0.00	£0.00	£16,000.00	£16,000.00	OK
9	Total					£53,550.00	

Figure 3.62 Example of spreadsheet field and record

A **record** (row) contains all the pieces of a single record when you read from left to right.

In the spreadsheet field and record example in Figure 3.62 above, **Rows 3** to **8** contain seven pieces of information for each of the six individual records.

Row 9 has two pieces of information that create the **Total** record in the row.

Method

1 Open the workbook **LookupFunOne**. The file can be located on the accompanying CD-ROM.

Spreadsheet construction

2 Select the **Vlookup** worksheet for this exercise.

The worksheet contains the daily code that represents the price of a publication on a given day. You need to produce a daily price list for wholesalers to calculate bulk sales prices for retailers.

The lookup data (**table_array** argument) is stored in two columns, cells AA101:AB108 that you can view by selecting **DailyPrice** from the name box, as a named range has been created for the lookup data.

3 Select **DailyPrice** from the name box and view the named range.

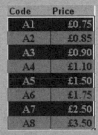

Code	Price
A1	£0.75
A2	£0.85
A3	£0.90
A4	£1.10
A5	£1.50
A6	£1.75
A7	£2.50
A8	£3.50

Figure 3.63 Example of the named range DailyPrice

As the data is stored **in columns**, to use these as look up data you must use the VLOOKUP function.

On the **HLookup** worksheet the lookup data (**table_array** argument) is stored in two rows, in the named range **SecondPrice**.

4 Select **SecondPrice** from the name box and view the named range.

Task A

Use the VLOOKUP function to **look up** the **publication cost** that *matches* the **code** in cell C4 and *place* this in cell D4.

Method

1 Select cell D4 on worksheet **VLookUp** and start the function wizard.

2 In the **paste function** window select the function category **lookup & reference**.

3 Function name **VLOOKUP**.

4 **Close** the paste function window.

Applying the function arguments

5 Enter the following syntax as the **lookup_value** argument: **$C$4:$C$8**. Absolute cell references are necessary.

6 The **table_array** argument is **DailyPrice**, the named range.

7 The **col_index_num** argument is **2**. The named range **DailyPrice** has 2 columns. The data to be used is in the second column.

8 The **range_lookup** argument is **False**. False is not the default argument for the **range_lookup** argument. You must find an **exact match** for the data in cell A1 in the named range **DailyPrice** column **2** that matches the **lookup_value** data contained in **cells $C$4:$C$8**.

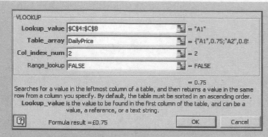

Figure 3.64 Completed VLOOKUP function window

9 Close the **VLOOKUP** window.

Result: The **result** should be **£0.75** in cell D4.

Info

You can now use the fill handle to copy the VLOOKUP function in cell D4 to cells D5:D8 as the **lookup_value argument** is an **absolute cell reference**, to the data in cells C4:C8, which contain the daily code that represents the price of a publication on a given day.

10 Copy the **VLOOKUP** function in cell D4 to cells D5:D8.

The **Cost** column for **Mon** should look like the example in Figure 3.65 after copying the **VLOOKUP** function to cells D4:D8.

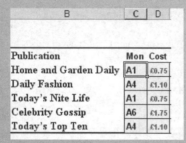

Publication	Mon	Cost
Home and Garden Daily	A1	£0.75
Daily Fashion	A4	£1.10
Today's Nite Life	A1	£0.75
Celebrity Gossip	A6	£1.75
Today's Top Ten	A4	£1.10

Figure 3.65 Spreadsheet contents

Task B

Method

Create the following **VLOOKUP** function:

1   Select cell F4, start the function wizard and **select** the function name **VLOOKUP**.

2   For the **lookup_value** argument enter **$E$4:$E$8**.

3   For the **table_array** argument enter **DailyPrice**.

4   For the **col_index_num** argument enter **2**.

5   For the **range_lookup** argument enter **False**.

6   **Close** the Paste function window.

Result: The **result** should be **£0.75** in cell F4.

7   **Copy** the **VLOOKUP** function in cell F4 to cells F5:F8.

Task C

Method

To **enter** and **copy** the **VLOOKUP** functions to complete the spreadsheet, only the following new information will be provided:

   a   Cell to be selected to enter the new function.

   b   Syntax for **lookup_value** argument to be entered.

   c   Where to **copy** the function.

   d   Arguments 2 through 4 are the same as in **Task B** above.

1 Select cell **H4** and create the following **VLOOKUP** function.

   a For the **lookup_value** argument enter **$G$4:$G$8**.
   Result: The **result** should be **£0.75** in cell H4.

2 Copy the **VLOOKUP** function in cell H4 to cells H5:H8.

   a Select cell J4.
   b **lookup_value** argument enter **$I$4:$I$8**.
   Result: The **result** should be **£1.10** in cell J4.

3 Copy the **VLOOKUP** function in cell **J4 to** cells J5:J8.

   a Select cell L4.
   b **lookup_value** argument **$K$4:$K$8**.
   Result: The **result** should be **£1.75** in cell L4.

4 Copy the function in cell J4 to cells L5:L8.

   a Cell N4.
   b **lookup_value** argument **$M$4:$M$8**.
   Result: The **result** should be **£2.50** in cell N4.

5 Copy cell J4 to cells N5:N8.

   a Cell P4.
   b **lookup_value** **$O$4:$O$8**.
   Result: The **result** should be **£0.75** in cell P4.

6 Copy cell P4 to cells P5:P8.

	B	C	D	E	F	G	H	I	J	K	L	M	N	O	P
1	Publication Costs														
2															
3	Publication	Mon	Cost	Tue	Cost	Wed	Cost	Thu	Cost	Fri	Cost	Sat	Cost	Sun	Cost
4	Home and Garden Daily	A1	£0.75	A1	£0.75	A1	£0.75	A4	£1.10	A6	£1.75	A7	£2.50	A1	£0.75
5	Daily Fashion	A4	£1.10	A4	£1.10	A5	£1.50	A6	£1.75	A7	£2.50	A8	£3.50	A2	£0.85
6	Today's Nite Life	A1	£0.75	A1	£0.75	A3	£0.90	A3	£0.90	A1	£0.75	A5	£1.50	A1	£0.75
7	Celebrity Gossip	A6	£1.75	A1	£0.75	A1	£0.75	A6	£1.75	A8	£3.50	A1	£0.75	A1	£0.75
8	Today's Top Ten	A4	£1.10	A4	£1.10	A1	£0.75	A6	£1.75	A2	£0.85	A2	£0.85	A8	£3.50

Figure 3.66 Completed worksheet

Do your **Cost** figures look like the completed worksheet in Figure 3.66?

If not, review all tasks in Exercise 8 – Lookup and reference functions.

EXERCISE 2 – HVLOOKUP

HVLOOKUP function

In this task you will use the same data as the VLOOKUP function to see why the choice of which function you use depends on **where** the lookup data is stored in the **table_array** argument for these functions.

Select the **Vlookup** worksheet.

The lookup data (**table_array** argument) is stored in two rows, on the **HLookup** worksheet in the named range **SecondPrice**.

Select **SecondPrice** from the name box and view the named range cells AA95:AH96.

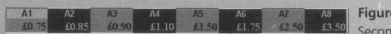

A1	A2	A3	A4	A5	A6	A7	A8
£0.75	£0.85	£0.90	£1.10	£1.50	£1.75	£2.50	£3.50

Figure 3.67 The named range SecondPrice

As the data is stored **in rows** to look these up you must use the **HLOOKUP** function.

Task A

Use the HLOOKUP function to **look up** the **publication cost** that *matches* the **code** in a specified **cell** and *place* this in a specified cell.

Method

1 Select cell D4 on worksheet **HLookUp** and start the Function Wizard.

2 In the **Paste function** window select the function category **Lookup & Reference**.

3 Function name **HLOOKUP**.

4 **Close** the paste function window.

5 Enter the following function arguments.

    a For the **lookup_value** argument enter **$C$4:$C$8**.
    b For the **table_array** argument enter **SecondPrice**.
    c For the **col_index_num** argument enter **2**.
    d For the **range_lookup** argument enter **False**.

6 **Close** the function window.
    Result: The **result** should be **£0.75** in cell D4.

7 Copy the **HLOOKUP** function in cell D4 to cells D5:D8.

Task B

Method

To **enter** and **copy** the **HLOOKUP** function to complete the spreadsheet, only the following new information is necessary: the **table_array** argument is **SecondPrice**. All other arguments remain the same as the **Vlookup** worksheet.

Example **HLOOKUP** function: **=HLOOKUP($C$4:$C$8,SecondPrice,2,FALSE)**

How you complete the spreadsheet is your decision. You can use the Function Wizard or copy and paste the relevant function from the **VLookup** worksheet and edit it.

Save and review your work before moving to the next section.

When deciding between **VLOOKUP** and **HLOOKUP**, the layout of the **lookup** date should determine which one you use.

VLOOKUP data list (vertical):

Code	Cost
A1	0.75
A2	0.85
A3	0.90
A4	1.10
A5	1.50
A6	1.75
A7	2.50
A8	3.50

A1	A2	A3	A4	A5	A6	A7	A8
0.75	0.85	0.90	1.10	1.50	1.75	2.50	3.50

EXERCISE | *3 – Practice*

In this exercise you will create a timesheet that uses **VLOOKUP** to establish the meaning of codes entered by staff to record working hours.

Task A – Creating the spreadsheet

Method

Cell	Label	Formatting
B3	Surname:	Font Bold
E3	First Name:	Font Bold
B4	Week Ending Sunday:	Font Bold and Word Wrap Text
B5	Day:	Font Bold
I5	Duration:	Font Bold
C6	PECodes	
D6	ProgrammeEvent	
E6	ActivityCode	
F6	Activity	
G6	RoleCode	
H6	Role	
I6	Start Time	
J6	Finish Time	
K6	Hours	
B6:K6		Fill Color = Grey 40% Font Color = White and Bold
B7:B13	Days of the Week, starting with Monday	Font Bold
B14	Total	Font Bold
B14:K14		Fill Color = Light Turquoise
K7:K13		Fill Color = Light Turquoise
B16	Balance of Hours Brought forward from Previous Period	Font Bold and Word Wrap Text as shown. This will ensure the right shape for the cells in this area if the font size is 10
B17	Total Hours in current period	Font Bold and Word Wrap Text
B18	Total	Font Bold
B19	Contracted Hours for Period	Font Bold and Word Wrap Text
B20	Balance of Hours Carried forward to Next Period	Font Bold and Word Wrap Text
B21	Signed:	Font Bold
H21	Date:	Font Bold
C16:20		Fill Color = Light Turquoise

Task B – Entering the lookup data

1 Key in the **data** below in the cells as indicated:

Cell	Labels/Data	Cell	Labels/Data
R26	EventsCode	S26	EventsProg
R27	EASTOne	S27	East Junction
R28	HEADQ	S28	London
R29	NAW	S29	Leave
R30	SC	S30	Sick
R31	TOIL	S31	Time-Off in Lieu
T26	ActivityCode	U26	Activity
T27	DE	U27	Development Events
T28	CurDev	U28	Curriculum Development
T29	FTA	U29	Follow-Through Activities
T30	FTT	U30	Follow-Through Training
T31	GBA	U31	General Business Administration
T32	PCT	U32	Pre-Course Training
T33	PFR	U33	Programme Fund Raising
T34	PPA	U34	Programme Planning Activity
T35	PRES	U35	Presentations
T36	RIT	U36	Residential Training
T37	N/AL	U37	Leave
T38	N/AS	U38	Sick
T39	N/AT	U39	Time-off in Lieu
V26	CodeRole	W26	Role
V27	OffAdm	W27	Office Administration
V28	PAR	W28	Participant
V29	PPM	W29	Project Manager
V30	SBUp	W30	Support/Back-Up
V31	TRA	W31	Trainer
V32	OOO	W32	Out Of Office

2 Formatting cells. Format the following cells as indicated below:

Cells	Formatting
R26:W26	Fill Color = Grey 25% Font = Arial Font Size = 8
R27:W39	Font = Times New Roman Font Size = 10

Task C – Creating named ranges

Method

1 Create the following Named Ranges.

   a Highlight **cells R26:S31** and enter the name **PCode** in the name box.

   b Highlight **cells T26:U39** and enter the name **ACode** in the name box.

   c Highlight **cells V26:W32** and enter the name **CCode** in the name box.

2 Test the named ranges by selecting a name from the name box. The entire range, e.g. **cells R26:S31** should be highlighted by the system if these have been created accurately.

Task D – Entering data

Enter the following data to use with the VLOOKUP function:

Cell	Data	Cell	Data	Cell	Data
C7	EastOne	E7	DE	G7	PPM
C8	HeadQ	E8	CurDev	G8	OffAdm
C9	EastOne	E9	DE	G9	PPM
C10	HeadQ	E10	GBA	G10	OffAdm
C11	NAW	E11	N/AL	G11	OOO
C12	EastOne	E12	PRES	G12	TRA
C13	Toil	E13	PRES	G13	TRA

Note: If you enter the data as specified, you will not need to sort the list. When using **VLOOKUP,** by default, the data must be sorted in ascending order.

Task E – Create the functions

1 Look up the **Programme Event** in the named ranges **PCode** that matches the **PECode** in cell **C7** and place this in cell **D7**.

In the Wizard you will complete all four arguments.

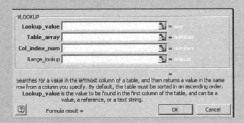

Figure 3.68 VLOOKUP window

VLOOKUP arguments

The **Lookup_value** argument is **C6:C13**.

Entering the **PECodes** cell range as the argument tells the system to look for the **Programme Event** that matches the **PECodes** in these cells.

The **Table_Array** argument is **PCode**.

The **Table_Array** argument looks for the area where your lookup data is stored. In this instance you have used a named range, called PCode. But this argument could also be an individual cell.

The **Co_Index_No** argument is **2**.

This argument represents the data you want to copy to cell D7. The named range PCode is made up of two columns, EventsCode and EventsProg. The data you want copied is in column 2 **EventsProg**, as you already have the EventsCode in cell C7.

Figure 3.69 Named range PCode

The **Range_lookup** argument is False.

This argument determines how the cells are searched by the system. You need an absolute match of data. To ensure this, enter **False** as the argument.

2 Click cell D7 and start the Function Wizard.

3 In the **Paste function** window select the **lookup & reference** function category, and the function name **VLOOKUP**.

4 Enter C6:C13 as the **Lookup_value** argument.

5 **Enter PCode** as the **Table_Array** argument.

6 **Enter** 2 as the **Co_Index_No** argument.

7 **Enter** False as the **Range_lookup** argument.

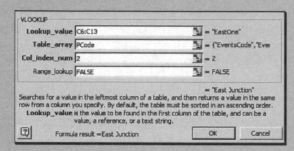

Figure 3.70 Completed VLOOKUP function window

8 Click **OK** to apply the function and close the function window.

The completed VLOOKUP function syntax in the formula bar when cell D7 is selected should look like the following: **=VLOOKUP(C6:C13,PCode,2,FALSE)**.

Result: The **result** should be **East Junction** in cell D7.

9 **Copy** the function to cells D8:D13.

10 Select cell F7 and start the Function Wizard.

11 Enter the following values as the various arguments in the VLOOKUP function window:

   a **E6:E13**
   b **ACode**
   c **2**
   d **False**

Result: The **result** should be **Development Events** in cell F7.

12 Copy the function to cells F8:F13.

13 Select cell H7 and start the function wizard.

14 Enter the following values as the various arguments.

   a **G6:G13**
   b **CCode**
   c **2**
   d **False**

Result: The **result** should be **Project Manager** in cell H7.

15 Copy the function to **cells H8:H13**.

Task F – Fine-tune the timesheet

Method

1 Add **formatting** to cells as indicated in the table:

Cell	Formatting
C3:D3	Merge Cells
C4:D4	Merge Cells
F3:G3	Merge Cells
I5:J5	Merge Cells
I6:J6	Wrap Text

Task G – Check the timesheet

You will now add the hours of work to the timesheet to ensure that it is functioning.

Method

1 Add the data in the following table to the cells indicated, **exactly** as shown:

Cell	Data
I7	9
J7	17.50
I8	9
J8	16
I9	8
J9	14
I10	10
J10	19
I11	9.5
J11	17.5
I12	9
J12	17
I13	13
J13	16

The data and formula below is reference data that you need to include to test the timesheet function. Add the data below to the cells indicated:

Cell	Data
C16	35
C19	37

Enter the following **Equal to** formula in cell C17: **=(K14)**

Task H – Calculating time entered in the timesheet

In this task you enter a formula to calculate the hours worked.

To calculate the number of hours worked per day you must **subtract** the **Finish Time** from the **Start Time**. The figures for the start and finish times have been entered using the 24-hour clock model to facilitate the calculation.

1 Select cell K7 and enter the following formula syntax: **=(J7-I7)**

Result: The **result** should be **8** in cell K7.

2 **Copy** the formula to cells K8:K13.

Task I

To calculate the number of hours worked per week you must **sum** together all the figures in cells **K7:K13**.

Adding a function to cell K14 to **sum** cells K7:K13. **Enter** the following **sum** function syntax in cell K14: **=SUM(K7:K13)**

Result: The **result** should be **49** in cell K14.

Task J

Add a **sum** function to cell C18 to total the **hours brought forward** plus **hours in current period**.

1 Enter the following **sum** function syntax in cell C18: **=SUM(C16+C17)**.

Result: The **result** should be **84** in cell C18.

Task K

Add a formula to cell C20 to calculate **total** current hours worked including any hours **brought forward** from cell C16, and **subtract** contracted **hours** from cell C19.

1 Enter the following formula syntax in cell C20: **=(C18-C19)**.

Result: The **result** should be **47** in cell C20.

Task L – Apply conditional formatting

As the Manager receiving and authorising timesheets you need to know at a glance if anybody is more than six hours in debit.

1 Select cell C20 and apply a conditional format to do the following:

If cell C20's calculated value is **less than or equal to – 6**, then apply these changes to the cell via the **format** button:

a Change cell **font colour** to **red**.
b **Double underline** cell contents.
c **Strikethrough** cell contents.

Figure 3.71 Completed conditional formatting window.

Task M – Testing the applied conditional formatting

Alter the existing data to test that the set conditions are working.

1 Select cell C16 and enter the following **symbol** and **figure**: **-20**

Result: The **result** should be **8** in cell C18.

2 Save the workbook.

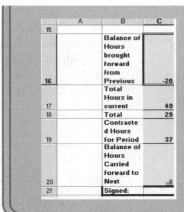

Figure 3.72 Result from the applied conditional formatting

Task N – Protect designated cells with a password

You have created a spreadsheet that can be edited and used in many ways. If you protect the cells that you **do not** want **altered** or **used**, and leave cells open for *data entry* only, it could be a spreadsheet used by many.

1 **Unlock** the following cell/cell **ranges**:

2 **Protect** the worksheet contents with the password **globe**.

3 Save your work.

Cell/Cell Ranges
C3
F3
C4
C7:C13
E7:E13
G7:G13
I7:J13
C16

Task O – Testing locked cells

1 Select cell B7 and press **Delete** on the keyboard.

Result: You should receive the following error message (Figure 3.73).

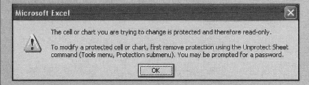

Figure 3.73 Sample system error message

If you delete a cell that should be locked click the **Undo** toolbar button and repeat the unlock cells and protecting contents procedure.

2 Save the workbook.

Task P

Method

1 **Enter** a **today function** in cell C4 to display today's date.

2 **Delete** the contents of the following cells:

Deleting the contents of these cells will give you another opportunity to test locked cells and protection of contents options, and should produce the following error message: **#N/A**

Cell/Cell Ranges
C3
F3
C4
C7:C13
C16
E7:E13
G7:G13
I7:J13

Info

When you have deleted the data in the workbook, the cells that contain a VLOOKUP function will display the **#N/A** error message.

	PECodes	ProgrammeEvent	ActivityCode	Activity
Monday		#N/A		#N/A
Tuesday		#N/A		#N/A
Wednesday		#N/A		#N/A
Thursday		#N/A		#N/A
Friday		#N/A		#N/A
Saturday		#N/A		#N/A
Sunday		#N/A		#N/A
Total				

Figure 3.74 #N/A error in spreadsheet

What does the error message #N/A mean?

The #N/A error value occurs when a value is not available to a function or a formula.

If you create a spreadsheet with function or formulas and the data will be added at a later stage you could enter the #N/A error yourself to the relevant cells.

You now have a blank workbook with all the relevant functions and formulas in place for use at any time as long as you use **Save As**…, to ensure that you always have a blank copy of the workbook.

Task Q – Saving the workbook as a template

If the workbook is saved as a template, it will then have advantage of the special features of templates.

Method

1 Lock cell C19.

This cell contains the contracted hours. If contracted hours change you can unprotect the sheet, unlock the cell, change the hours figure, and then re-lock the cell and re-protect the sheet.

2 **Save** the timesheet workbook as **SheetPlate** in a **default** template folder.

3 Close the template.

In this section, you have revisited the following skills:

- Name cell range(s) in a worksheet for use with a function.
- Use conditional formatting to display deficits in a hours of work.

- Use date and time function Today to display today's date.

- Protect designated cells in a worksheet with a password.

To facilitate using the timesheet, you have saved this in a template format by the new name **SheetPlate**.

Using functions – Part three

Using available database functions

In this section you will cover the following database function topic:

- Use the various database functions to manipulate the database.

Question: What is a database?

Answer: A database is a logical way to organise data.

In the address book of a mobile phone, all the people you have entered in the address book section under **name recall**, (regardless of when you entered the name), are listed alphabetically by the name you have entered.

If you look up the same person in the address book section under **position recall**, the position **number** will depend on when the **entry** was made. This gives you the opportunity to find an individual, based on the *criteria* **name** or **position number** in the phone's address book.

Open the workbook **MyDatabase**.

All student workbooks for this section can be located on the accompanying CD-ROM.

The **MyDatabase** workbook records course bookings information and has been sorted by the **course title** column in **ascending** order.

To identify each course booking, the course has a unique booking number.

File preparation

Before you work with the database, enter a formula in cell E3 on the **DSum** worksheet to calculate the total cost of a **booking**. The formula syntax is *places booked****Course Cost**, which translates as: **=D3*C3**.

1 **Copy** the formula to cells E4:E22 on the **DSum** worksheet.

2 **Copy** the formula to cells E3:E22 on the **DMin**, **DMax** and **DCount** worksheets.

3 **Delete** any totals that show as errors, e.g. **#VALUE!** on the worksheets **DSum**, **DMin** and **DMax** only, do not delete these on the worksheet **DCount**.

As the spreadsheet is quite small at this stage all records can be seen, but should it grow, this could become a problem if a unique identification number for each course booking had not been included in the spreadsheet makeup.

At any stage you can do a sort by **booking number** to place the list in the original order the bookings were taken.

Each of the database functions **DSUM**; **DMIN**; **DMAX**; **DCOUNT** is used to manipulate data in a spreadsheet in specific ways.

The DSUM function adds together the figure specified by you in the criteria argument.

Method

File preparation:

1 Insert seven new rows at the top of the **DSum** worksheet.

2 Create a **named range** called **DSumFigure** from cells A9:E29.

3 Copy the labels in cells A9:E9 and paste these in cell A1.

You should now have a **copy** of the **labels** in cells A9:E9 in cells A1:E1 and should have created the **named range** called **DSumFigure**.

Creating a results area:

4 Enter **total course cost > £80.00** as a **label** in cell B4.

5 Cell C4 is where your results will appear.

6 Place a **thick box border** around cells A1:E2 and cells B4:C4.

Info

Database arguments

All the database functions have the same three arguments as described below.

Database function name(*database,field,criteria*)

The **database** argument is the named range that makes up the list of data in your database; in the **DSUM** exercise you have called the range ***DSumFigure***.

The *field* argument represents the data you want to work with. The data in the **DSUM** exercise is in the **total** column. You can enter the column label as the argument or select the cell containing the label with the mouse via the collapse window icon.

The **criteria** argument represents the conditions that you want to apply to the data values you are working with. In this exercise the criteria range is made up of the label in **cell E1** and the entry in **cell E2** below.

7 Enter the condition **>80.00** in cell E2.

Info

When setting this argument the specific label(s), value(s) and or condition(s) must be included in the **criteria** function argument.

In this exercise you will work through the steps to create the database function **DSum**, to view the function window arguments and how these can be entered.

EXERCISE

1 – Create the database function DSum

On the **DSum** worksheet you want to create a function in cell C4 to **total** cost of all course that cost **more than** £80.00.

Method

1 Select cell C4 and start the Function Wizard.

2 In the **paste function** window select the **database** function category, and the function name **DSUM**.

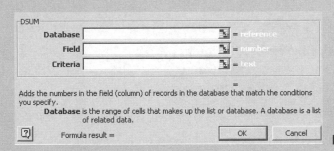

Figure 3.75 The DSUM function window

3 For the **database** argument enter **DSumFigure**.

This is the named range of the **data** and **labels** in your database cells **A9:E29**.

4 The **field** argument is the **total** label. Enter the text **Total** as the **field** argument; the system will add quotation marks (**""**) to the text.

The **criteria** argument is located in cells E1:E2.

5 Use the collapse window icon to minimise the DSUM function window.

6 Use the mouse pointer to select cells E1:E2.

Info

Cell E1 contains the label **total**.

Cell E2 contains the conditions the data must meet to be included in the calculation, **Sum** any **figure** in the **Total column greater than £80.00**.

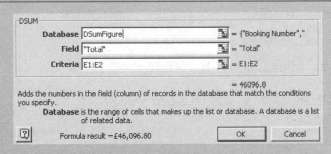

Figure 3.76 The completed DSUM function window

7 Select **OK** to apply the function and close the DSUM window.

8 **Format** the resulting figure **4609680** in cell C4 as currency, two decimal places.

The DSum argument **syntax** in Cell C4 should be as follows:

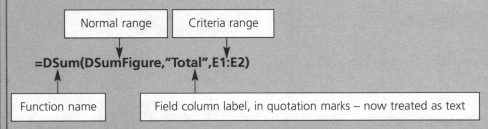

Commas are used to separate the various arguments.

Note: You used the **cell label text** 'Total' in this exercise as the **field** argument value. In the following exercises you will use the cell reference address as the argument value.

10 Save the workbook.

2 – Edit the worksheets DMin, DMax and DCount

Method

1 Insert seven new rows at the top of each of the three worksheets.

2 Create **named range** from cells A9:E29 on each worksheet:

   a   On the **DMin** worksheet name the range **MinFigure**.
   b   On the **DMax** worksheet name the range **MaxFigure**.
   c   On the **DCount** worksheet name the range **DcountFigure**.

3 Copy the labels in cells A9:E9 and paste these in cell A1 on each worksheet in the workbook.

4 Place a **thick box border** around cells A1:E2 and cells B4:C4 on each worksheet.

5 Save the workbook.

In Exercises 1 and 2 you have:

1 Entered a formula to work with data values.

2 Deleted errors on specific worksheets.

3 Inserted new rows.

4 Created **named range**.

5 Copied and pasted labels.

6 Created new labels.

7 Used the Function Wizard to enter the three database arguments necessary for this task item.

8 Viewed the database arguments **syntax**.

9 Used **text** and **cell address** as the **field** argument value.

10   Entered or selected **criteria** arguments **with** operators.

To create the **entries** on the **DMin**, **DMax**, and **DCount** worksheets only the following new information will be provided:

1 New **Label** to be entered.

2 Lookup **criteria** to enter in cell.

3 **Database** argument.

4 **Field** argument.

5 **Criteria** argument.

Select the **DMin** worksheet.

The **DMIN** Function. Find the lowest number specified in your criteria.

Creating a results area

Method

1 Enter **Minimum Places Booked** as a **label** in **cell B4.**

2 Cell C4 is where your results will appear.

   On the **DMin** worksheet you want to create a function in cell C4 to display the **minimum places booked on all courses**.

Task 3.9 Using available database functions

3 In cell D2 enter the greater that operator **>** followed by the figure 0 (zero).

4 Select cell C4. Start the Function Wizard and use the **DMIN** function to extract the minimum Figure for bookings.

5 Enter or select the following as arguments in the **DMIN** function window.

    a The database argument is **MinFigure**, the database named range.
    b The field argument is cell D1, the criteria cell label address.
    c The criteria argument is cell D1:D2, the criteria and cell label.

6 Select **OK** to apply the function and to close the DMin window.

7 **Format** the resulting figure **4** in cell C4 as Number, 0 decimal places.

8 Save and review your work before you move to the next exercise.

Select the **DMax** worksheet.

The **DMax function**. find the largest number specified in your criteria.

Method

You want to know the **maximum numbers booked on any courses**.

1 Enter the label **Maximum Course Places** in cell B4.

2 In cell D2 enter **>0**.

3 Select cell C4.

4 Start the Function Wizard and use the **DMAX** function to extract the **Maximum number of places** booked for a course.

5 The database argument is **MaxFigure**, the database named range.

6 The field argument is cell D1.

7 The criteria argument is cell D1:D2.

8 **Format** the resulting figure 20 in cell C4 as number, 0 decimal places.

9 Save and review your work before you move to the next exercise.

Select the **DCount** worksheet.

The **DCOUNT function**. Count cells that contain number specified in your criteria.

Method

1 Enter the label **Count of Separate Total Figures** in cell B4.

2 In cell E2 enter **>0**.

3 Select cell C4.

4 Start the function wizard and use the **DCOUNT** function to extract how many separate figures appear in the **Total** column.

5 The database argument is **DCountFigure**.

6 The field argument is cell E1.

7 The criteria argument is cell E1:E2.

8 **Format** the resulting figure **17** in cell C4 as number, 0 decimal places.

The **DCOUNT** function is used to count numbers, so anything else is not counted. There are **20** records in the database but the **count** of separate **total** figures shows **17**.

The DCount function does not count the **three error values** in the total column. These have been treated as text entries and therefore not included in the column count.

Note: You used the **cell label text** 'Total' in the first exercise as the **field** argument value. In all other exercises in this section you used the cell reference address as the **field** argument value.

For the **field** argument value, the **cell label** or **reference address** can be used.

EXERCISE *3 – Practice*

Method

To total new figures edit the operator and figure in cell E2 on the **DSUM** worksheet or use the Function Wizard.

1 Select cell E2 on the **DSUM** worksheet and find the answer to the following questions:

Question	Answer
The **total** figure for all course >2000	
The **total** figure for all course >6000	
The **total** figure for all course >10000	
The **total** figure for all course >12000	

2 Select cell E2 on the **DMIN** worksheet and find the answer to the following questions:

Question	Answer
Minimum Places Booked>5	
Minimum Places Booked >9	
Minimum Places Booked >12	

Save and review your work before you move to the next exercise.

Section 4: Analysis

All files for this section can be located on the accompanying CD-ROM.

Pivot Tables are used to produce different views of data contained in a spreadsheet, such as comparing sales between teams.

4.1 Creating a pivot table from spreadsheet data

EXERCISE 1 – Create a pivot table

Open the workbook **PivotTable**.

The workbook contains the sales figures for a group of dance promoters. The data you will use to create the pivot table is on the **PivotList** worksheet in cells A2:H18.

Method

1 Click cell A2 in the **PivotList** worksheet.

2 On the **Data** menu, click **PivotTable and PivotChart Report** to start the **PivotTable and PivotChart Report Wizard**.

Figure 4.1 Data menu

Pivot table and PivotChart Report Wizard – Step 1 of 3

In this step you tell the system where the data is that you want to use, and the type of report you want to create.

Figure 4.2 Step 1 window

3 Select the following options from the upper and lower sections shown in Figure 4.2, if these are not selected by default:

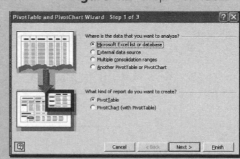

   a **Where is the data that you want to analyze?** Microsoft Excel list or database.

   b **What kind of report do you want to create?** PivotTable

4 Click **Next** to move to step 2.

PivotTable and PivotChart Report Wizard – Step 2 of 3

In this step the **data range** is set, to let the system know where in the spreadsheet the data that you want to work with is. The system should select and suggest cells A2:H14 on the worksheet when the **Step 2** window opens, see Figure 4.3 below.

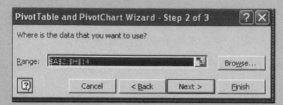

Figure 4.3 Step 2 window

To create absolute references, the system has added **dollar symbols** to the cell references to be used in the PivotTable.

If the cells selected are incorrect, use the collapse window icon to minimise the window, and the mouse to select an alternative **range of cells**.

You can also enter the cell range via the keyboard.

The **Browse** button can also be used to select an alternative worksheet from which to create the PivotTable.

5 Accept the suggested range A2:H14, by clicking the **Next** button.

PivotTable and PivotChart Report Wizard – Step 3 of 3

Figure 4.4 Step 3 window

Figure 4.5 The Pivot Table and PivotChart Wizard Layout window

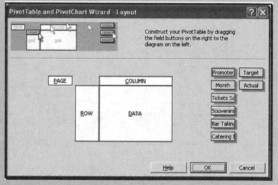

In Step 3 of the Wizard you can do the following:

a Design the **layout** of the PivotTable.
b Select **options**.
c **Decide** where to place the PivotTable.

6 Click the **Layout** button.

Designing your Pivot table

To design the Pivot table, you drag and drop **field buttons** (Figure 4.7) on the right of the window, onto the Pivot table layout diagram (Figure 4.6).

Figure 4.6 Layout diagram area

Figure 4.7 Field buttons

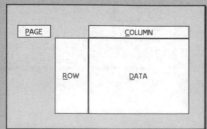

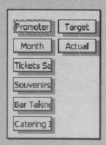

Task 4.1 Creating a pivot table from spreadsheet data

7 Drag and Drop the following field buttons:

   a The **Promoter** field on to the **Row** section.

   b The **Month** field on to the **Column** section.

   c The following fields on to the **Data** section:

      i **Tickets Sales**.

      ii **Souvenirs Purchases**.

      iii **Bar Takings**.

      iv **Catering Income**.

      v **Target**.

      vi **Actual**.

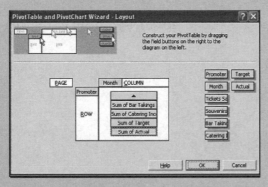

Figure 4.8 PivotTable and PivotChart Wizard layout window after drag and drop

8 Click **OK** to close the **Layout** window.

9 Click the **Options** button.

You will not be setting any additional options, but it is useful to have a look at the options available and **defaults** that you will be accepting.

Info

Figure 4.9 Options window with default options selected

10 When you are ready to continue, click **OK** to close the Options window and return to the wizard step 3 main window.

PivotTable and PivotChart Report Wizard – Step 3 of 3

Figure 4.10 Step 3 window

Deciding where to place the pivot table

11 Accept the suggested **New worksheet** by clicking the **Finish** button

The PivotTable will be created and placed in a new worksheet. The **PivotTable toolbar** (Figure 4.10a) will also be visible on screen.

Manipulating the pivot table

3			Month ▼			
4	Promote ▼	Data ▼	January	November	December	Grand Total
5	CHI	Sum of Tickets Sales	11724	2639	6524	20887
6		Sum of Souvenirs Purchases	2271	2315	1743	6329
7		Sum of Bar Takings	7168	4982	7234	19384
8		Sum of Catering Income	2500	2824	1371	6695
9		Sum of Target	18000	12000	15000	45000
10		Sum of Actual	23663	12760	16872	53295
11	ELIZ	Sum of Tickets Sales	15267	5991	7000	28258

Figure 4.11 The created pivot table

To add or remove **data items** from the PivotTable, click the black arrow next to the field name, e.g. **Month**.

In the example below, all data Items are visible (selected) in the PivotTable. To **deselect** an item, click the box beside the item to remove the tick. The data Item will not then be visible in the PivotTable.

Figure 4.12 All Month data PivotTable items visible

Figure 4.13 Only two Month data items visible in PivotTable

2 – Modify the pivot table data range

1 Enter the data in the table that follows on the **PivotList** worksheet:

		Data				
JR	February	4500	1500	7987	3890	18000
CHI	February	1500	150	689	300	20000
JBIRD	February	5500	2500	4000	2590	16000
ELIZ	February	8560	3000	9580	4000	20000

2 Copy the formula in cell H14 to cells H15:H18 to produce **Actual** figures if your system does not automatically display these.

3 Copy the fill colour formatting to these cells from the existing rows.

Adjusting the data range using the PivotTable toolbar (Figure 4.14).

4 Select the worksheet containing the pivot table.

Figure 4.14 Inactive PivotTable toolbar

Task 4.1 Creating a pivot table from spreadsheet data

If the toolbar is inactive, select any cell in the pivot table to activate it (Figure 4.15).

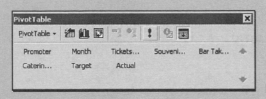

Figure 4.15 Active PivotTable toolbar

5 Hover the mouse over each toolbar button to see a screen tip of the button function.

When new data is added, this changes the **data range** of the pivot table.

Altering the existing data range

6 Click the **PivotTable Wizard** toolbar button on the PivotTable toolbar (the Wizard will open at Step 3).

7 Click the **Back** button, to **edit** the range in Step 2.

8 Edit the range, by clicking in the range box and changing the entry to: **PivotList!$A$2:$H$18**

Figure 4.16 Editing the range

The data is now contained in the cell range A2:H18.

9 Click **Finish** to close the Wizard. The new data will be added to the pivot table.

Making data changes to the pivot table

A data entry error has occurred for one of the Promoter's figures.

1 Select the **PivotList** worksheet.
2 Edit the **Souvenirs Purchases** figure for the Promoter **CHI** for **February**, from **150** to **300**.

To see data changes in a pivot table

1 Select the pivot table.

2 Click the **Refresh** button on the PivotTable toolbar, to refresh the data in the PivotTable.

Note: For pivot tables, be aware of the difference between **data range** changes and **data source** changes.

Displaying specific data in the pivot table

Task A – Display all data for the promoter CHI

How do you display the defined criterion?

Method

1 Click the black arrow next to the field name **Promoters**.

2 **Deselect** promoters **ELIZ**, **JBIRD** and **JR** by clicking in the box beside the item to remove the tick.

3 Click **OK** to close the list box.

3			Month ▼				
4	Promote ▼	Data ▼	January	November	December	February	Grand Total
5	CHI	Sum of Tickets Sales	11724	2639	6524	1500	22387
6		Sum of Souvenirs Purchases	2271	2315	1743	150	6479
7		Sum of Bar Takings	7168	4982	7234	689	20073
8		Sum of Catering Income	2500	2824	1371	300	6995
9		Sum of Target	18000	12000	15000	20000	65000
10		Sum of Actual	23663	12760	16872	2639	55934
11	Total Sum of Tickets Sales		11724	2639	6524	1500	22387
12	Total Sum of Souvenirs Purchases		2271	2315	1743	150	6479
13	Total Sum of Bar Takings		7168	4982	7234	689	20073
14	Total Sum of Catering Income		2500	2824	1371	300	6995
15	Total Sum of Target		18000	12000	15000	20000	65000
16	Total Sum of Actual		23663	12760	16872	2639	55934

Figure 4.17 The pivot table displaying the defined criterion for CHI

Task B – Display data for November and February for the promoter JBIRD

Method

1 **Deselect** all other **Promoters**, and the months **January** and **December**.

3			Month ▼		
4	Promote ▼	Data ▼	November	February	Grand Total
5	JBIRD	Sum of Tickets Sales	5724	5500	11224
6		Sum of Souvenirs Purchases	2971	2500	5471
7		Sum of Bar Takings	5168	4000	9168
8		Sum of Catering Income	2815	2590	5405
9		Sum of Target	18000	16000	34000
10		Sum of Actual	16678	14590	31268
11	Total Sum of Tickets Sales		5724	5500	11224
12	Total Sum of Souvenirs Purchases		2971	2500	5471
13	Total Sum of Bar Takings		5168	4000	9168
14	Total Sum of Catering Income		2815	2590	5405
15	Total Sum of Target		18000	16000	34000
16	Total Sum of Actual		16678	14590	31268

Figure 4.18 The pivot table displaying the defined criterion for JBIRD

Note: If you remove any of the data field items by mistake e.g. sum of target, you will need to drag and drop the item back onto the pivot table.

Save and review your work before moving to the next section.

Close the workbook.

1 – Create the worksheet DeptList

Method 1: Import a text file

Method 2: Enter the list via the keyboard

Before working through each method:

1 **Open** a new workbook.

2 **Save** the workbook as **PivotDept**.

3 Rename Sheet1 as **DeptList**.

4 In cell **A1**, enter the title **Department Sales**.

You decide how you want to create the **DeptList** worksheet using one of the two methods below

Import a text file

Method 1

1 Open a new workbook.

2 Import the text file **ImportPivot**.

3 To accept all default options, click the **Finish** button in Step 1 of the Text Import Wizard.

4 **Copy** the imported data in cells **A1:A17**

5 **Paste** the imported data into cell **A2** of the **DeptList** worksheet.

6 Save the workbook.

7 **Close** the imported text file **ImportPivot** workbook without saving the changes.

Enter the list via the keyboard

Method 2

1 **Select** the **DeptList** worksheet.

2 Enter the data from the table that follows into cells A2:F18:

Data					
Department	**Year**	**1st Quarter**	**2nd Quarter**	**3rd Quarter**	**4th Quarter**
Accessories	1998	2000	1500	1000	3000
Perfume	1998	1600	1000	900	2000
Leather Goods	1998	3000	4000	1500	5500
Kitchen Shop	1998	2500	1500	1982	3000
Accessories	1999	2997	2000	1500	2994
Perfume	1999	1000	1500	1000	2503
Leather Goods	1999	1500	1000	600	850
Kitchen Shop	1999	2500	2000	1900	3000
Accessories	2000	800	1500	1000	2000
Perfume	2000	2000	2500	2990	1500
Leather Goods	2000	3000	3500	2890	5000
Kitchen Shop	2000	2500	2000	2985	3000
Accessories	2001	1000	1500	1890	2500
Perfume	2001	800	999	1500	1980
Leather Goods	2001	4500	3000	2000	1500
Kitchen Shop	2001	1928	2289	1429	3685

3 Format the **DeptList** worksheet as follows:

   a **Merge** and **centre** the title **Department Sales** across cells A1:F1.

   b **Embolden** the Title and change the font size to Point 14.

   c **Format** cells C3:F18 as **currency**, zero decimal places.

2 – Create a pivot table from the data on the DeptList worksheet

Method 2

1 In Step 1 of the Wizard, check the defaults are as follows (if they are not as shown below, adjust them, following the steps in Exercise 1):

   a Microsoft Excel list or database.
   b PivotTable.

2 Click on **Next**.

3 In Step 2 of the Wizard, accept the **default range** of **$A$2:$F$18**, then click **Next**.

4 In Step 3, click on the **layout** button.

5 Drag and drop the following field buttons:

   a The **Department** field onto the **Row** section.
   b The **Year** field onto the **Column** section.
   c The following fields onto the **Data** section:
      i **1st Quarter**
      ii **2nd Quarter**
      iii **3rd Quarter**
      iv **4th Quarter**

6 Close the Layout window.

7 Click the **Finish** button to accept all other defaults of the **PivotTable and PivotChart Report Wizard**.

   The completed pivot table should look something like the one in Figure 4.19.

	A	B	C	D	E	F	G
3			Year ▼				
4	Departmen ▼	Data ▼	1998	1999	2000	2001	Grand Total
5	Accessories	Sum of 1st Quarter	2000	2997	800	1000	6797
6		Sum of 2nd Quarter	1500	2000	1500	1500	6500
7		Sum of 3rd Quarter	1000	1500	1000	1890	5390
8		Sum of 4th Quarter	3000	2994	2000	2500	10494
9	Kitchen Shop	Sum of 1st Quarter	2500	2500	2500	1928	9428
10		Sum of 2nd Quarter	1500	2000	2000	2289	7789
11		Sum of 3rd Quarter	1982	1900	2985	1429	8296
12		Sum of 4th Quarter	3000	3000	3000	3685	12685

Figure 4.19 DeptList PivotTable

8 Practice manipulating the pivot table by removing and adding items.

9 Save and close the workbook.

3 – Show selected data in a pivot table

Method

1 Reopen the workbook containing the sales figures for Dance Promoters.

2 Display the data in the PivotTable **data column** so that only the **target** and **actual data items** are visible in the **PivotTable** for the Promoters **ELIZ** and **JR**.

Figure 4.20 The result of the above defined criterion

1			Drop Page Fields Here				
2							
3			Month ▼				
4	Promote ▼	Data ▼	January	November	December	February	Grand Total
5	ELIZ	Sum of Target	30000	16000	18000	20000	84000
6		Sum of Actual	27386	15993	16052	25140	84571
7	JR	Sum of Target	30000	15000	20000	18000	83000
8		Sum of Actual	25056	13855	18283	17877	75071
9	Total Sum of Target		60000	31000	38000	38000	167000
10	Total Sum of Actual		52442	29848	34335	43017	159642

Task 4.3 Displaying specific data in the pivot table

When **data field** items are removed, the pivot table displays unused fields, such as the **page** field, which was not used when the **pivot table** was originally created.

3 Display all data for the promoter **CHI** for February. (Before you can display the defined criterion, you must drag and drop the data items back onto the pivot table.)

Figure 4.21 Data items

Drag and drop data items

When you click the data column arrow, having removed the four data items in the previous exercise, the window will only display the two that remain (see Figure 4.21).

To replace the data items

To add the data to the data column, drag a data item from the toolbar and drop it just under the **January** column, as shown in Figure 4.22.

3			Month ▼				
4	Promoter ▼	Data ▼	January	November	December	February	Grand Total
5	CHI	Sum of Target	18000	12000	15000	20000	65000
6		Sum of Actual	23663	12760	16872	2789	56084
7	ELIZ	Sum of Target	30000	16000	18000	20000	84000
8		Sum of Actual	27386	15993	16052	25140	84571
9	JBIRD	Sum of Target	22000	18000	20000	16000	76000
10		Sum of Actual	27075	16678	14394	14590	72737
11	JR	Sum of Target	30000	15000	20000	18000	83000
12		Sum of Actual	25056	13855	18283	17877	75071
13	Total Sum of Target		100000	61000	73000	74000	308000
14	Total Sum of Actual		103180	69286	65601	60396	288463

PivotTable ✕

PivotTable ▼

Promoter   Month   Tickets...   Souveni...   Bar Tak... ▲

Caterin...   Target   Actual   Drop here   ▼

Figure 4.22 Pivot table drop zone

If you drop the item in another area, use the **Undo** toolbar button on the standard toolbar to undo the changes and try again.

Below is an example of the pivot table after all data items have been replaced, showing data displayed by a **defined criterion**, for the Promoter **CHI** for February.

3			Month ▼	
4	Promoter ▼	Data ▼	February	Grand Total
5	CHI	Sum of Target	20000	20000
6		Sum of Actual	2789	2789
7		Sum of Tickets Sales	1500	1500
8		Sum of Souvenirs Purchases	300	300
9		Sum of Bar Takings	689	689
10		Sum of Catering Income	300	300
11	Total Sum of Target		20000	20000
12	Total Sum of Actual		2789	2789
13	Total Sum of Tickets Sales		1500	1500
14	Total Sum of Souvenirs Purchases		300	300
15	Total Sum of Bar Takings		689	689
16	Total Sum of Catering Income		300	300

Figure 4.23 pivot table for the promoter CHI for February

Save and review your work before moving to the next section.

Close the workbook.

In this section you have covered the following items:

● Create a pivot table using defined field names.

● Modify the data source and refresh the pivot table.

● Group/display data in a pivot table by a defined criterion.

You have also had the opportunity to import a text file or create the data manually.

4.4 Creating scenarios using specific cells

Scenarios is one of the many tools you can use for data analysis in a worksheet. It changes the contents of cells to produce new values. You can also produce summary reports of a scenario.

Open the workbook **MotelGroup**. All files for this section can be located on the accompanying CD-ROM.

The spreadsheet in the workbook calculates the quarterly operating profits of the Cedar Valley Motel Group. You will use **scenarios** to ask questions and produce results based on the data contained in the spreadsheets.

EXERCISE

1 – Find out occupancy rates/profit in a spreadsheet

What occupancy rate is needed to achieve an operating profit of ≥ £40,000 in cell E12? To solve this question, we are going to create a scenario.

Method

1 On the **Tools** menu, click **Scenarios**.

Figure 4.24 The Scenario Manager window

The **Scenario Manager** window is empty, as no scenarios have been created for this workbook; an application message confirms this in the window.

2 Click **Add** to open the **Add Scenario** window.

Figure 4.25 The Add Scenario window

3 In the **Scenario name** text box, key in the name **Occupancy Rate**.

4 In the **Changing cells** text box, enter the cell references that you want to change, by using the mouse to select cells B6:D6 in the spreadsheet. The **absolute** cell references **$B$6:$D$6** should appear in the text box.

Info

Comment section

By default, the registered user name of the software and the date are entered by the system. You can change or add to the system comment.

Accept the default comment

There are two Protection options:

1 Prevent changes

This option prevents any changes to the named scenario. To enforce the protection you must also use the **Protection → Protect Sheet** options on the **Tools** menu.

2 Hide

Selecting this option will hide the scenario. To enforce this choice you must also use the **Protect Sheet** option on the **Tools** menu.

Note: To edit or delete a scenario that has been protected, you need to remove both levels of protection.

5 On this occasion **do not** select a protection option. If an option is already selected, deselect it.

Figure 4.26 Completed Edit Scenario window

Did you notice when the **Add Scenario** window changed to the **Edit Scenario** window?

Next time you are in the **Add Scenario** window and *select* **Changing cells**, watch the window title bar.

6 Click **OK** to close the **Edit Scenario** window and to open the **Scenario Values** window.

7 In the **Scenario Values** window (Figure 4.27), key in the new values you want for the changing cells.

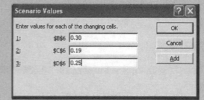

Figure 4.27 Scenario Values window

Info

The number of **Changing cells** text boxes presented in the **Scenario Values** window, is dependent on the number of cells selected or entered in the **Add Scenario** window changing cells text box.

8 Using the data in the table that follows, key in the *new values* for the changing cells:

			New Values		
Motel	Cell	Old Value	Old Operating Profit	New Value	Enter New Operating Profit
Morant Bay	$B$6	12%	£7,300	**0.30**	
Port Morant	$C$6	15%	£14,546	**0.19**	
Morant Point	$D$6	22%	£7,758	**0.25**	

9 To create your scenario, click **OK** (you will be returned to the **Scenario Manager** window).

Figure 4.28 Completed Scenario Manager window

If you want to create another scenario now:

a Click **Add**, and repeat the procedure of **naming** the scenario.

b **Select** cells to apply new values to.

c **Enter** the new values.

10 To apply the scenario you have just created (**Occupancy Rate**), click the **Show** button.

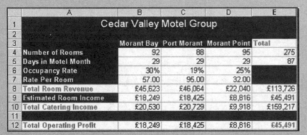

Figure 4.29 New scenario

Note the new contents of cells **B6:D6** and **B12:E12** (Figure 4.29).

11 Click the **Close** button to close the **Scenario Manager** window.

Generating a scenario summary

When you create a scenario summary report, the report is inserted as a new worksheet in the workbook.

1 Open the **Scenario Manager** window (Figure 4.30).

Figure 4.30 Scenario Manager window

2 If you have created several scenarios, choose the one you want by clicking on it, then click the **Summary** button.

3 Click the **Summary** button to open the **Scenario Summary** window (Figure 4.31).

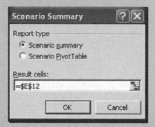

Figure 4.31 Scenario Summary window

4 In the Scenario Summary window, ensure that the **Result cells** text box reflects the cell reference that contains the total calculation figure(s), i.e. cell E12.

If the system has selected the wrong cell, click on the collapse window icon to minimise the window, and the mouse to select the correct cell(s).

5 Click **OK** to create a **summary** of the occupancy rate scenario.

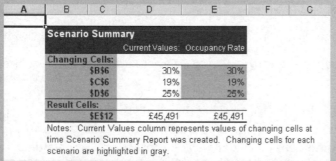

Figure 4.32 Occupancy rate scenario summary

When the summary has been created, it will be placed on a separate worksheet and presented with the outline buttons. You can use these outline buttons to create different views of the summary.

Save and review your work before moving to the next exercise.

Close the workbook.

2 – Practice

The RYC Netball Club team want to know how many goals they need to score in each quarter, to achieve 94 goals per game.

The table that follows shows the goals per quarter that they appear to be averaging at the moment:

RYC Goals per quarter

Data		
	A	**B**
1	RYC Goals	
2	Quarter	Goals
3	1st Quarter	22
4	2nd Quarter	11
5	3rd Quarter	16
6	4th Quarter	10
7	Total	=SUM(B3:B6)

Preparation

Method

1 Open a new workbook in cells A1:B7, and create a spreadsheet using the layout in the table above.

2 Save the workbook as **RYCScenarios**.

3 Rename Sheet1 as **Goals**.

In this exercise, two scenarios will be created.

The **first** will record original values on the spreadsheet, so that these can be replaced at any time.

The **second** scenario will suggest the **targets** the team has to achieve in each quarter, to aim for 94 goals per game.

Use the data in the two tables that follow, to create two named scenarios:

Scenario Name	Changing Cells	Cells	Protection	Values
Original Values	B3:B6	B3		22
		B4		11
		B5		16
		B6		10
			None	

Scenario Name	Changing Cells	Cells	Protection	Values
GoalOne	B3:B6	B3		24
		B4		23
		B5		24
		B6		23
			None	

Info

If you want to keep a record of the original values in your spreadsheet, create a scenario called **Original** that uses the original cell values, before you create scenarios that change the values.

Task 4.5 Generating a scenario summary

Applying the scenario

4 To apply the scenario **GoalOne**, click the **Show** button in the **Scenario Manager** window.

Note the new contents of cells B3:B6 of the spreadsheet (Figure 4.33).

	A	B
1		RYC Goals
2	Quarter	Goals
3	1st Quarter	24
4	2nd Quarter	23
5	3rd Quarter	24
6	4th Quarter	23
7	Total	94

Figure 4.33 New contents

5 Create a summary report for the **GoalOne** scenario by following the steps in Exercise 2.

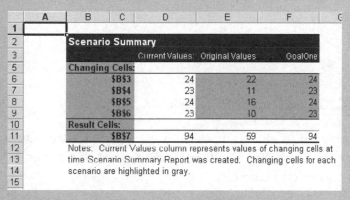

Figure 4.34 GoalOne summary

6 Create a summary report for the **original values** scenario.

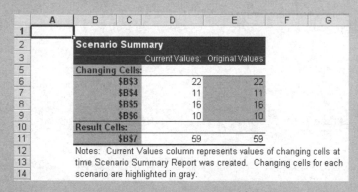

Figure 4.35 Original values summary

7 Return the spreadsheet to the original values using the scenario **Original values**.

	A	B
1		RYC Goals
2	Quarter	Goals
3	1st Quarter	22
4	2nd Quarter	11
5	3rd Quarter	16
6	4th Quarter	10
7	Total	59

Figure 4.36 Original values

8 Close the Scenario Manager window.

Save and review your work before moving to the next section.

Close the workbook.

4.6 *Using the auditing toolbar*

To understand the make up of a spreadsheet after it has been created, on the **Tools** menu point to **Auditing** to display the sub-menu.

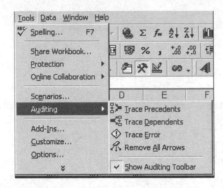

Figure 4.37 Tools menu – Auditing

Using the auditing options on the sub-menu, you can trace **Precedent** or **Dependent** cells. You can also select to show the **Auditing toolbar** by clicking on this option, so that all available audit options are shown on screen.

Info

Auditing worksheets using the auditing toolbar

The **Auditing** toolbar displays how cells on a worksheet are related, by giving a visual **display** of the **relationship** between them. Cell relationships are either **precedents** or **dependents**.

Figure 4.38 Auditing toolbar

The **Auditing** toolbar will **trace** and **display** how a formula or function relates to other cells within worksheets.

The two toolbar buttons on the **Auditing** toolbar that perform these functions come in pairs, **Trace** and **Remove**.

Clicking the **Trace** toolbar button once **adds** a single arrow to the worksheet.

Clicking the **Remove** toolbar button once **deletes** a single arrow from the worksheet.

Figure 4.39 Precedents button   **Figure 4.40** Dependents button

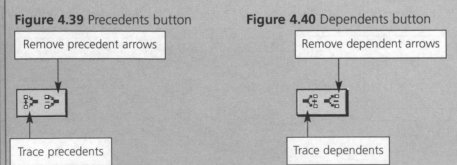

On any worksheet, to get a true picture of cells that **directly** and **indirectly** supply values to the cell you are tracing from, you may need to click either of these buttons several times.

If you need to remove all arrows added, use the Remove All Arrows toolbar button .

Open the worksheet **Auditing**. This file can be located on the accompanying CD-ROM.

Opening the auditing toolbar

Method

1 Point to **Auditing** on the **Tools** menu.

2 From the sub-menu, click **Show Auditing toolbar** to open the **Auditing toolbar**.

Figure 4.41 Auditing toolbar

Rest the mouse over each toolbar button to see a screen tip description of the button function.

EXERCISE

1 – Trace precedents

Method

1 Click cell D13.

2 Click the **Trace Precedents** toolbar button to display cells that supply values **directly** to the **formula** in cell D13.

Info

Direct values:

o Cells D9 and D11 supply values directly to the formula in cell D13.

o Cell D13 contains the total sum of the figures in cell D9 and D11.

This is a precedent as the two values precede the total.

3		JAN	FEB	MAR
4	Rooms			
5	Days	31	28	31
6	Occupancy Rate	0.7	0.6	0.65
7	Rate Per Room	40	40	40
8	Total Room Revenue	0	0	0
9	ERP - Rooms	0	0	0
10	Food Revenue	0	0	0
11	ERP - Food	0	0	0
12				
13	Total Operating Profit	0	0	0

Direct values cells D9 and D11

Figure 4.42 The Trace Precedents arrows – direct values

3 To see cells that **indirectly** supply values to cell **D13**, click the **Trace Precedents** button again.

3		JAN	FEB	MAR	TOTAL
4	Rooms				0
5	Days	31	28	31	90
6	Occupancy Rate	0.7	0.6	0.65	
7	Rate Per Room	40	40	40	
8	Total Room Revenue	0	0	0	0
9	ERP - Rooms	0	0	0	0
10	**Food Revenue**	0	0	0	0
11	**ERP - Food**	0	0	0	0
12					
13	Total Operating Profit	0	0	0	0

Indirect values, first tier, with trace arrows

Figure 4.43 Trace Precedents arrows – indirect values

Info

The indirect values are in cells D8 and D10.

4 Click the **Trace Precedents** button again. All cells that **indirectly** supply values to cell D13 will show the trace precedents arrows.

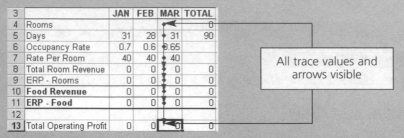

3		JAN	FEB	MAR	TOTAL
4	Rooms				0
5	Days	31	28	31	90
6	Occupancy Rate	0.7	0.6	0.65	
7	Rate Per Room	40	40	40	
8	Total Room Revenue	0	0	0	0
9	ERP - Rooms	0	0	0	0
10	Food Revenue	0	0	0	0
11	ERP - Food	0	0	0	0
12					
13	Total Operating Profit	0	0	0	0

All trace values and arrows visible

Figure 4.44 Trace Precedents – all indirect values

Info
The system will beep if you click the **Trace Precedents** button again, as there are no further traces.

EXERCISE

2 – Practice

Method
1 Trace all **precedents** for cell **E13**, **direct** and **indirect**.
2 **Remove** all arrows.

EXERCISE

3 – Trace dependents

Method
1 Click cell B6.

Info
The formula in cell **B8** is **directly** dependent on the figures in cell **B6**. Trace dependents arrows will be drawn form cell **B6 to** cell **B8** to indicate this.

2 Click the **Trace Dependents** button.

3		JAN	FEB	MAR	TOTAL
4	Rooms				0
5	Days	31	28	31	90
6	Occupancy Rate	0.7	0.6	0.65	
7	Rate Per Room	40	40	40	
8	Total Room Revenue	0	0	0	0
9	ERP - Rooms	0	0	0	0
10	Food Revenue	0	0	0	0
11	ERP - Food	0	0	0	0
12					
13	Total Operating Profit	0	0	0	0

Direct values, cell B8

Figure 4.45 Trace direct values

3 To see any **indirect** values, click the **Trace Dependents** button again.

3		JAN	FEB	MAR	TOTAL
4	Rooms				0
5	Days	31	28	31	90
6	Occupancy Rate	0.7	0.6	0.65	
7	Rate Per Room	40	40	40	
8	Total Room Revenue	0	0	0	0
9	ERP - Rooms	0	0	0	0
10	Food Revenue	0	0	0	0
11	ERP - Food	0	0	0	0
12					
13	Total Operating Profit	0	0	0	0

Indirect values, cells B9:B10 and E8

Figure 4.46 Trace indirect values

4 – Practice

1 **Trace** all dependents for cell B8, **direct** and **indirect**.
2 Click the **remove all arrows** button.

5 – Practice

1 Click cell B13.
2 Trace **precedents** and **dependents** for this cell.
3 **Remove** all arrows.

6 – Practice

Figure 4.47 shows a copy of the **Audit** worksheet with all formulas displayed. Now that you can see the underlying formulas, and to help you understand the worksheet, use the Auditing toolbar to trace precedents and dependents for cells not already audited.

	A	B	C	D	E
1	FIRST QUARTER				
2					
3		JAN	FEB	MAR	TOTAL
4	Rooms				=SUM(B4:D4)
5	Days	31	28	31	=SUM(B5:D5)
6	Occupancy Rate	0.7	0.6	0.65	
7	Rate Per Room	40	40	40	
8	Total Room Revenue	=B4*B5*B6*B7	=C4*C5*C6*C7	=D4*D5*D6*D7	=SUM(B8:D8)
9	ERP - Rooms	=B8*0.4	=C8*0.4	=D8*0.4	=SUM(B9:D9)
10	Food Revenue	=B8*0.45	=C8*0.45	=D8*0.45	=SUM(E8:E9)
11	ERP - Food	=B10*0.45	=C10*0.45	=D10*0.45	=SUM(B11:D11)
12					
13	Total Operating Profit	=B9+B11	=C9+C11	=D9+D11	=SUM(B13:D13)

Figure 4.47 Audit worksheet

7 – Practice

1 Open the **IsErrorAudit** workbook.
2 Display the Auditing toolbar and trace **precedents** or **dependents** for the following cells: **K37**, **J45**, cells in the range **A4:A18**, **L37**, **K41** and **G45**.

The Auditing toolbar can also be accessed by clicking **Customize** on the **Tools** menu, selecting the **Toolbars** tab, then placing a tick in the **Auditing** box.

Displaying all formulas

1 – Use the Go To dialogue window

In this exercise you will use this dialogue window to view the location of formulas in a spreadsheet.

Info

Go To is a Microsoft Office tool that you can use to move around a spreadsheet and to view specific elements, based on the option selected.

Method

1 Open the workbook **ViewFormulasTask1**.

All files for this section can be located on the accompanying CD-ROM.

2 Press the **F5** function key on the keyboard to open the **Go To** dialogue window (Figure 4.48).

Figure 4.48 Go To dialogue window

3 Click the **Special** button to open the **Go To Special** window (Figure 4.49).

Figure 4.49 Go To Special window

The **Comments** option button is selected by default when the window opens.

4 Select the **Formulas** option button to select all formulas within the worksheet, then click **OK** to view the formula locations in the **ViewFormulasTask1** workbook (Figure 4.50).

	A	B	C	D	E
E2		=	=SUM(B2:D2)		
1		January	February	March	TOTAL
2		72	66	75	213
3		31.00	28.00	31.00	90.00
4		0.70	0.66	0.65	2.01
5		42.00	40.00	40.00	122.00
6		65620.80	48787.20	60450.00	174858.00
7		26248.32	19514.88	24180.00	69943.20
8		29529.36	21954.24	27202.50	244801.20
9		13288.21	9879.41	12241.13	35408.75
10	Total Profit	39536.53	29394.29	36421.13	105351.95

Figure 4.50 ViewFormulasTask1 workbook with formulas highlighted

5 **Save and close** the workbook, then reopen it. The workbook should open with formulas highlighted as in Figure 4.50, so that you can view their location.

Note: to deselect highlighted formulas, click in any cell. **Save and Close** the workbook with formulas highlighted. If you have deselected the highlighted formulas, reapply steps 2 to 4 before saving the workbook.

2 – Use the edit menu to access the go to dialogue window

EXERCISE

In this exercise you will use the above method to select and view the location of formulas in a spreadsheet.

Method

1 Open the workbook **SecondViewFormulasTask**.

2 Click **Go To** on the **Edit** menu to open the **Go To** dialogue window.

3 Click the **Special** button to open the **Go To Special** window.

4 To select all formulas within the worksheet, click the **Formulas** option button (Figure 4.51).

Figure 4.51 Go To Special window with the Formulas option selected

Info

When the formulas option button is selected, the **Numbers**, **Text**, **Logicals** and **Errors** tick boxes are activated. These tick boxes help you to determine the type of formulas you want to select and view.

If you do not want to view the location of all formulas, deselect any that describe the formula you **do not want** to view.

If there are no formulas within a spreadsheet, an error message will be displayed (Figure 4.52):

Click OK to close the message box.

Figure 4.52 Error message

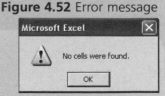

5 **View** any formula locations in the **SecondViewFormulasTask** workbook.

6 Close the workbook without saving any changes.

3 – Viewing functions and/or formulas syntax

Method

1 Open the workbook **LastViewFormulasTask**.

2 Locate the cell containing a **Text** formula.

3 What is the cell reference address?

4 Select **Options** from the **Tools** menu.

5 **Select** the **View** tab (Figure 4.53).

6 Under the windows **options** section, click the **Formulas** tick box to place a tick in it.

7 **Close** the Options window.

Figure 4.53 Options window – View tab

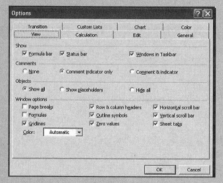

Info

Keyboard shortcut to View/Hide formulas:

Ctrl + ⌐

This key is located towards the top left hand corner on the main keyboard, under the Esc key and to the left of the numeric number 1 key.

4 – Practice

Method

1 **Display** the formulas/functions entered in the **LastViewFormulasTask** workbook, using one of the methods outlined above.

2 **Print** a copy of the spreadsheet with the formulas/functions displayed.

3 Close the workbook without saving any changes.

5 – Practice

Method

1 Locate the file **DataTableNewPC** that you created as part of the 'Use one-input or two-input data table' exercises.

2 **Display** and **Print** a copy of the following formulas/functions located in the workbook:

a The **PMT** function used on the **OneInputTable** worksheet.

b The **PMT** and **Multiplication** functions/formula used on the **OneInputCont** worksheet.

c The **ABS/PMT** function used on **TwoInputTable** worksheet.

3 Open the **Auditing** workbook and display and print all formulas on the **Audit** worksheet.

4 Open the **StockOrderFruitsFormula** workbook and display and print a copy of the **3D reference formula** used for the **grand total**.

Review your work before moving to the next task.

Close all workbooks without saving any changes.

In this section you have covered the following items:

- Display all formulas or view location of all formulas in a worksheet.

Use the Go To Special window to:

- Locate all formulas/functions
- Locate a specified type of function
- View the system error message when no formulas/functions are located in a worksheet.

View functions and/or formulas syntax:

- Using Options from the Tools menu or the keyboard shortcut.

4.8 Using comments

Comments are useful for providing feedback while you are working on a spreadsheet, or to remind you when you revisit a piece of work after a period of time, what your thought process was or why you calculated a formula/function in a particular way.

In the following exercises you will view the menu bar options to **insert**, **delete** or **edit** a comment, and to perform a task based on the task item. A shortcut menu option is also shown for inserting, deleting or editing a comment.

When undertaking each exercise, the choice is yours as to which method to use, menu bar or shortcut menu.

EXERCISE

1 – Insert a comment using menu bar options

Method

1 Select the cell where you want the comment to appear by clicking on it.

2 Select **Comment** from the **Insert** menu.

Figure 4.54 Comment window

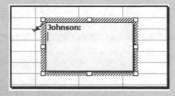

Info

Depending on your system configuration, the comment window will have the application user name already inserted. The cursor is usually in the window when first opened.

3 Type in your comment via the keyboard, then close the window by clicking anywhere on the worksheet, **outside** the comment selection handles.

EXERCISE ## 2 – Insert a comment using shortcut menu options

Method

1 Right click the cell where you want the comment to appear.

2 From the pop-up menu, click **Insert Comment**.

3 To close the window, click anywhere on the worksheet, **outside** the comment selection handles.

Open the **Comments** workbook. The files for this section can be located on the accompanying CD-ROM.

EXERCISE ## 3 – Practice

Method

1 **Insert** the comment '**The New Database Area'** in cell R100.

2 **Insert** the comment ' **Calculate Net Figure'** in cell A11.

3 Save the workbook.

Info

To view comments

Cells containing a **comment** have a **red triangle** in the top right corner of the cell (Figure 4.55).

Third	Total
6	#NAME?
9	#VALUE!

Figure 4.55 Cell containing a comment

Rest the mouse over the cell containing the comment; you do not need to click the cell. The comment will appear (Figure 4.56).

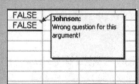

Figure 4.56 Visible comment

Move the mouse away from the cell containing the comment. The comment will disappear.

4 View the two comments you have entered in cells **R100** and **A11**.

EXERCISE ## 4 – Edit comments using menu bar options

Method

1 Select the cell by clicking on it.

2 Click **Edit Comment** from the **Insert** menu.

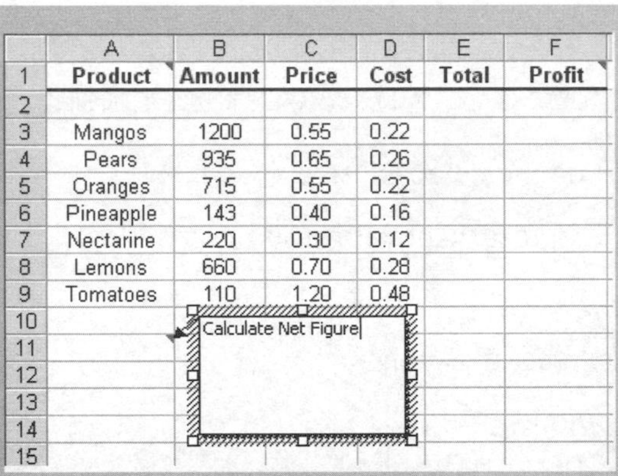

Figure 4.57 Edit comment window

	A	B	C	D	E	F
1	Product	Amount	Price	Cost	Total	Profit
2						
3	Mangos	1200	0.55	0.22		
4	Pears	935	0.65	0.26		
5	Oranges	715	0.55	0.22		
6	Pineapple	143	0.40	0.16		
7	Nectarine	220	0.30	0.12		
8	Lemons	660	0.70	0.28		
9	Tomatoes	110	1.20	0.48		
10		Calculate Net Figure				
11						
12						
13						
14						
15						

The Comment window will open with the I-Beam cursor flashing at the end of the existing contents, ready for editing.

3 To close the Edit comment window, click anywhere on the worksheet **outside** the window.

EXERCISE

5 – Edit comments using shortcut menu options

Method

1 Right click the cell containing the comment.

2 From the pop-up menu, click **Edit Comment**.

EXERCISE

6 – Edit comments: practice

Method

1 Open the **Comments** workbook.

2 Edit the comments:

a In cell **A1**, 'We need to find a supplier for organic', to read 'We need to find a supplier for organic and tropical fruits'.

b In cell **F1**, 'Profit formula is', to read 'Profit formula is =D3*B3'.

EXERCISE

7 – Delete comments using menu bar options

Method

1 Select the cell containing the comment by clicking on it.

2 Point to **Clear** on the **Edit** menu.

3 Click **Comment** on the sub-menu to delete the comment.

EXERCISE

8 – Delete comments using shortcut menu options

Method

1 Right click the cell containing the comment.

2 From the pop-up menu, click **Delete Comment**.

9 – Practice

Method

1 Delete the comment in cell M45 'This will be the database area'.

2 Delete the comment in cell H1 'Format the spreadsheet with style Classic 2'.

Review your work.

Save and close the workbook.

Other shortcut menu options for comments:

1 To make a comment **always visible on screen**:

   a Right click the cell containing the comment.

   b From the pop-up menu, click **Show Comment**.

2 To **hide** a comment that is **always visible on screen**:

   a Right click the cell containing the comment.

   b From the pop-up menu, click **Hide Comment**.

10 – Inserting comments

Open the workbooks **CCSO2**, **CPCPO2** and **CLARO2**. The files can be located on the accompanying CD-ROM. These workbooks were used in the 'Link data/chart between spreadsheets' exercises in section 2, data handling.

Task A

Method

1 Select **Sheet1** in the **CCSO2** workbook.

2 Insert the comment 'First Aid Training' in cell B14.

3 Select **Sheet1** in the **CPCPO2** workbook and insert the following comments:

   a 'Pool Bronze Training' in cell D11.

   b 'First Aid or Fire Officer Courses' in cell D12.

4 Select Sheet1 in the **CLARO2** workbook.

5 Insert the comment 'First Aid Training' in cell B12.

6 Save and close all workbooks.

Task B

Method

In this task you will add a comment to the **ANDFunction** worksheet in the workbook **MyAndFunction**, to give you some feedback at a later stage.

1 Locate and open the file **MyAndFunction** workbook, that you created and saved in the **AND** function exercise in section 3.

2 Select the ANDFunction worksheet.

3 Insert the comment 'This is the wrong type of question for this function' in cell H9.

4 Save and close the workbook.

Task C

Method

1 Open the workbook **IsErrorComments**. The file can be located on the accompanying CD-ROM. (This is a back-up copy of the workbook IsError that you used in Section 3, to practise inserting the function **ISERROR**, to test the value of cell contents.)

Cell K36 contained the value #NAME?

When you tested the cell, the system returned **False?** This response indicates that a name used in the formula syntax does not exist, such as a named range.

2 Insert the comment 'a name used in the formula syntax does not exist, such as a named range' in cell K36, to remind you of this.

3 Copy and paste special the comment in cell K36, into cell I29.

4 Save and close the workbook.

Task D

Method

1 Open the **AuditingComments** workbook. The file can be located on the accompanying CD-ROM.

2 Using the **New Comment** button on the Auditing toolbar, insert the comment 'Precedents values come from cells D9:D11 and Dependents values from cell E13' in cell D13 as a reminder of where the values comes from.

3 Save and close the workbook.

Task E

Method

1 Open the workbook **DataTableComments**. The file can be located on the accompanying CD-ROM. (This is a back-up copy of the workbook DataTable that you used to practise creating one- and two-input tables in Section 1, Editing.)

2 On the **TwoInputTable** worksheet, insert a comment in each of the following cells, to remind you of their activity on the worksheet:

   a D5: 'Column Input cell'.

   b D6: 'Row Input cell'.

   c A9: 'Nested Function'.

3 Save and close the workbook.

Task F

Method

1 Open the workbook **4_NoPasswordComments** (location as for Task 5).

2 Delete the comment in cells A1 and F1.

3 Save and close the workbook.

Task G

Method

1 Open the workbook **CreateQueryComments** (location as for Task 5).

2 Edit the comment in cell A43 'Why upturn?', to read 'Upturn New Section Created'.

3 Save and close the workbook.

Save and review your work before moving to the next section.

Section 5: Special Tools

5.1 Recording a macro

Info

Macros can be used to automate the routine tasks that are involved in creating and manipulating spreadsheets.

A macro should be considered as a low-level programming tool, which is available in the user interface of the spreadsheet application.

A **saved** macro represents a recording of all the keystrokes used to complete a task, such as applying formatting to data or cells, that you can replay at a later stage to recreate the original spreadsheets.

In this context, formatting can be interpreted as:

- Font style.
- Applying fill colour.
- Applying borders.
- Currency style.

In this main task you will cover the following macro topics:

- View the menu bar options to record and save a macro.
- Names and Naming conventions for macros.
- Work through exercises based on the three main tasks.

EXERCISE 1 – How to record a new macro

Method

1   Point to **Macro** on the **Tools** menu.

Figure 5.1 Tools menu

2   Click **Record New Macro** on the sub-menu, to open the **Record macro** window.

Figure 5.2 Record Macro window

Record macro options

Macro names

This name will uniquely identify the macro for you. You could accept the default name of Macro1, but at a later stage when you may need to use the macro in another situation, will the name Macro1 mean anything to you?

When you create macros, give them meaningful names that reflect their actions.

Macro naming conventions

Macro names should follow the style of the default name. The default name has no spaces between the word 'macro' and the number following the name. If you attempt to create a macro name that contains spaces, the system will return an error message (Figure 5.3).

Figure 5.3 Macro name error message

Programming languages follow specified conventions. One of these conventions is that objects such as macros must have their names structured in a certain way.

General naming conventions

When naming objects such as macros and individual worksheets, you should get used to giving them names that do not include any spaces. The default worksheet name **Sheet1** also follows the macro naming convention, but the convention is not obligatory for worksheet names.

Apart from being an industry convention, if you decide to use a programming language to develop a sheet at a later stage, spaces within names may cause you problems within the chosen programming language code.

Letters or figures, or a combination of the two (known as alphanumeric data), can be used, but the following characters **should not** be used in a name: (.) (!) (') (') ([ ) (]).

Storing a macro

You can choose where to store a macro, by selecting the location. As you gain more experience you may decide to use one workbook for storing macros. **Store in This Workbook** is the default location if you have not activated the personal macro workbook stored on your system. If you are working on a network, speak to the system administrator about changing your personal system settings if the personal macro workbook is the default when you save a macro.

Shortcut Key

Macros can also have a shortcut key, but ensure that you don't use one already in use, or it will be overriden. The vast majority of shortcuts in use start with **Ctrl+(letter)**. When creating your own, use **Ctrl+Shift+Letter**. Also, remember that (A) and (a) are not the same shortcut key!

Description

By default, the date and current user name will be included. You can edit and/or add additional information to personalise the description.

3 After entering the Record Macro options, click **OK** to close the Record Macro window.

The **Stop Recording Macro** button will be visible onscreen while you are recording the macro.

4 After recording your steps, click the Stop Recording Macro button to complete a recording.

2 – Create a macro

The macro will:

a Change the page orientation to landscape.

b Change top and bottom margins to 1.5.

c Change the data font to Arial.

d Turn on row and column headings for printing.

1 Open a new workbook and save it as **FormatPage**.

2 Enter the **labels** and **data** from the following table, within cells A1:D4 on **Sheet1** of the **FormatPage** workbook:

	A	B	C	D
1	North	South	East	West
2	100	75	98	369
3	55	98	875	258
4	685	753	159	854

3 Total each column in cells A5:D5, using the AutoSum toolbar button.

4 Save your work.

3 – Recording a macro

1 Open the Record Macro window.

2 Name the macro as **MyPageSetUp**.

3 Select the option 'store macro in this workbook' if this is not your system default. Accept all other defaults in the Record Macro window by clicking **OK**.

4 Carry out the following steps to create the macro in the Page Setup window (Figure 5.4):

   a Click **Page Setup** from the **File** menu.

   b From the **Page** tab under the **Orientation** section, select **Landscape** (Figure 5.4).

Figure 5.4 The Page Setup window – Page tab

   c On the **Margins** tab, select the following figures by keying them in, or by using the spin buttons (the up and down arrows to the right of the figure boxes) (Figure 5.5):

    i Set the top margin as **1.5**.

    ii Set the bottom margin as **1.5**.

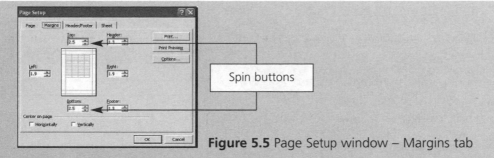

Figure 5.5 Page Setup window – Margins tab

d From the **Sheet** tab under the **Print** section select:
   i   **Gridlines**.
   ii **Row and column headings**.

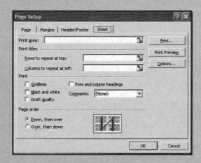

Figure 5.6 Page Setup window – Sheet tab

5 When you have selected all the options, click **OK** to close the Page Setup window.

6 Highlight cells A1:D1, then change the font to Times New Roman, and centre the labels.

8 Highlight cells A2:D4 and left align data.

9 Highlight cells A5:D5 and centre and embolden the totals data.

10 Click the **Stop Recording** button.

That completes recording a macro.

11 In the **FormatPage** workbook, print preview **Sheet1**, which should look like the example in Figure 5.7

	A	B	C	D
1	North	South	East	West
2	100	75	98	369
3	55	98	875	258
4	685	753	159	854
5	**840**	**926**	**1132**	**1481**

Figure 5.7 Worksheet with macro applied

12 Close print preview.

What does a macro look like?

4 – Viewing the make up of a macro

To do this, you need to access the Visual Basic Editor window, where you can see (and alter if necessary) a complete text of the steps that make up the macro.

1 Point to **Macro** on the **Tools** menu.

2 Click **Macros** from the sub-menu, to open the macro window.

3 Select the name of the macro you want to **edit** (**MyPageSetUp** in this exercise), so that it appears in the **Macro name** box.

4 Click the **Edit** button; the macro will open in the Visual Basic Editor window (Figure 5.9).

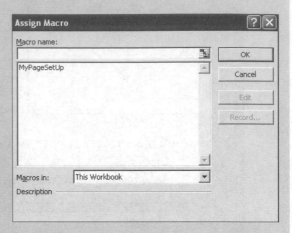

Figure 5.8 The Macro window

Info

Your macro will be stored in what is known as a module. The default name is usually Module(1); the number on your computer may be different.

```
Option Explicit
Sub MyPageSetUp()
' MyPageSetUp Macro
' Macro recorded 30/07/02 by Johnson

    With ActiveSheet.PageSetup
        .TopMargin = Application.InchesToPoints(0.
        .BottomMargin = Application.InchesToPoints
        .PrintHeadings = True
        .PrintGridlines = True
        .PrintQuality = 360
        .Orientation = xlLandscape
        .PaperSize = xlPaperA4
        .FirstPageNumber = xlAutomatic
        .Order = xlDownThenOver
        .Zoom = 100
    End With
```

Figure 5.9 The Visual Basic Editor window, showing part of the MyPageSetUp macro

5 From the **File** menu, select **Close and Return.** to close the Visual Basic Editor window and return to the worksheet.

Info

When creating macros, it may be helpful for you to walk through the steps you want to use, before attempting to record the macro. Make sure that you use the mouse to select an option you want to use, for example, if you want to use Sheet2, you must select the Sheet2 tab using the mouse pointer.

If you find that your macro is not being created properly, e.g. some commands get missed in the recording, try using the keyboard rather that the mouse, to select the options you want to include (some systems 'prefer' the keyboard method).

5.2 Using a macro

Task A – Preparing the worksheet

Method

In this exercise you will use the macro you have created to format Sheet2 in the **FormatPage** workbook.

1 In cells A1:D5 on **Sheet2**, enter the **labels** and **data** from the following table, to test the **MyPageSetUp** macro:

	A	B	C	D
1	Qrt1	Qrt2	Qrt3	Qrt4
2	150	752	990	379
3	559	981	475	238
4	689	653	359	824

2   In cells A5:D5, total each column using the AutoSum button.

3   **Copy** and **paste** cells A1:D5 into cell A1 of **Sheet3**.

Task B – Running the macro

Method

1   Point to **Macro** on the **Tools** menu.

2   From the sub-menu, click **Macros** to open the Macro window (Figure 5.10).

3   Select the name of the macro you want to **run** so that it appears in the **Macro name** box.

4   Click the **Run** button.

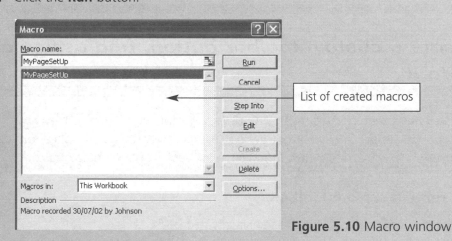

Figure 5.10 Macro window

Task C – Applying the macro

Method

1   Select **Sheet2**.

2   Using the commands above, apply the **MyPageSetUp** macro to Sheet2 of the **FormatPage** workbook.

3   Save and close the workbook.

Task D – Checking the macro has been applied

Method

1   Reopen the **FormatPage** workbook.

Info

When you reopen the workbook, you will be advised by the system that the workbook now contains macros (Figure 5.11).

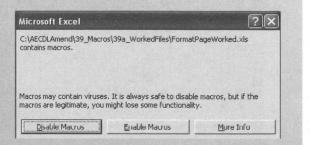

Figure 5.11 System macro Information window

2 **Click** the **Enable macros** button, to ensure that you can use the macros in the workbook.

If you click the **Disable macros** button and attempt to run any macros in the workbook, the system will advise you with the following error message (Figure 5.12):

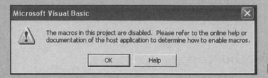

Figure 5.12 System error message

3 Close and reopen the workbook, and select the **Enable macros** button.

4 **Save** the workbook.

Do not close the **FormatPage** workbook.

Customising a macro

1 – Create a custom toolbar button, and assign a macro to it

Info

Now that you have created a macro, if you always go through, **Tools**, **Macro**, **Macros…** etc. to run the macro, you may not use it very often, as it takes longer to access, compared to other tools that are available direct from a toolbar button.

Task A – Create a custom toolbar

Method

1 Re-open the **FormatPage** workbook if not already open.

2 Point to **Toolbars** on the **View** menu.

3 Click **Customize** to open the window (Figure 5.13).

Figure 5.13 Customize window

4 Click the **New** button to open the **New Toolbar** window (Figure 5.14).

Figure 5.14 New Toolbar window

5 Delete **Custom 1** and enter **MyFormat** as the toolbar name.

6 Click **OK** to close the **New Toolbar** window.

Do not close the Customize window.

Info If you cannot see your new toolbar, drag the Customize window left or right; the toolbar will be behind this.

Task B – Assign a macro to a custom button

Method

1 Click the **Commands** tab in the Customize window (Figure 5.15).

2 In the **Categories** Box list, select **macros**.

3 In the **Commands** Box list, select **Custom Button**.

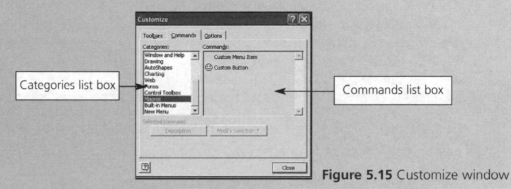

Categories list box →

← Commands list box

Figure 5.15 Customize window

4 Click the **Description** button (Figure 5.15) to see a pop-up window describing the button function.

5 Click on the window to close the description.

Info If the custom button is now unselected, reselect it by clicking on it in the commands box list.

6 Drag and drop the custom button onto your new **MyFormat** toolbar.

MyFormat toolbar with Custom Button icon

Task C – Selecting options for a custom button

Options can include the **Name** or **Picture** displayed on the button.

Method

1 Right click on the new toolbar, to display the custom button Formatting pop-up menu (Figure 5.16).

Setting the Name Option

Figure 5.16 Custom Button formatting pop-up menu

2 **Delete** the **&Custom Button** text and replace this with **HouseStyle**.

3 Press **Enter** (the pop-up menu will close and the Customize window should remain open).

Task D – Assigning a macro to a new toolbar

Method

1 Right click the new toolbar to display the Toolbar Formatting pop-up menu again.

2 Click the **Assign macro** option to open the Assign macro window with available macros (Figure 5.17).

Figure 5.17 Assign Macro window

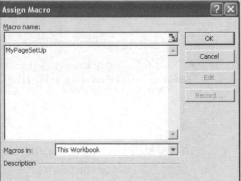

Info

At this stage you should only have one macro, provided you have not added any others. If your macro name is not visible, ensure that the **Macros in** box is displaying **This workbook** (click on the down arrow and select from the list if necessary).

3 **Click** the name of the macro you want to **assign** so that it appears in the **macro name** text box.

4 Click on the macro name **MyPageSetUp**.

5 Click **OK**, to assign the macro to the new toolbar button.

6 Close the Customize window.

7 Drag and drop the new toolbar next to the Standard or Formatting toolbars.

8 Using the new toolbar, apply the **MyPageSetUp** macro to **Sheet3** of the **FormatPage** workbook.

Save and review your work before moving to the next Exercise.

Close the workbook.

---

2 – Create a macro to move data to a named range on a spreadsheet; assign a macro to a toolbar button

Task A – Creating the workbook

Method

1 Open and save a new workbook as **ChequeEntry**.

2 Enter the following labels on **Sheet1** in cells A1:E1 –

   a **Client No**.
   b **Cheque No**.
   c **Ccard No**.
   d **Date In**.
   e **Amount**.

3 Copy and paste the labels into cell P28 (the range will cover cells P28:T28 when pasted).

4 Rename Sheet1 as **Cheques**.

5 **Delete** Sheets 2 and 3.

6 Create a named range from cells P28:T28, called **ChequesIn**; this will be your database area.

7 Enter the following data in cells A2:E2 (you will use this data when creating the macro):

   a A2: **011**.
   b B2: **980147**.
   c C2: (leave blank).
   d D2: **11/04/02**.
   e E2: **350**.

Task B – Creating the macro

In this task the macro is created, to transfer the data from cells A2:E2 to the area under the named range in cells P28:T28.

In Task 5.1, review exercise 1 – How to record a new macro – then read through the steps below, before starting to record the macro.

When following the steps below, use the menu bar options, **not** the toolbar button alternatives.

Method

1 Open the **Record Macro** window.

2 **Name** the macro **TransferData**.

3 Click **OK** to accept all other defaults in the Record macro window, and to start recording the macro.

Task C – Recording the macro

Method

1 Select **Row 29** by clicking on the row heading; this will highlight the entire row.

2 Click on **Rows** from the **Insert** menu.

3 Press **Ctrl+Home** on the keyboard, to move to cell A1.

4 Highlight cells A2:E2.

5 Select **Cut** from the **Edit** menu.

6 Click cell P29.

7 Click on **Paste** from the **Edit** menu.

8 Press **Ctrl+Home** on the keyboard.

9 Click cell A2.

10 Stop the Macro Recorder.

After you have entered details of a single cheque or of credit card payments in cells A2:E1, when you then run the macro TransferData, the macro performs the following functions in your ChequesEntry workbook:

a A new row is inserted below row 28.

b After highlighting cells A2:E1, the data in these cells is cut and pasted in the new row under the named range **ChequesIn**.

c Cell A2 is selected for you, to enter a new record.

The **TransferData** macro then ends.

Task D – Viewing and testing the macro

1 View the **TransferData** macro in the Visual Basic Editor window, to see how closely this matches the example below (Figure 5.18).

```
Option Explicit
Sub TransferData()
''  TransferData Macro
'  Macro recorded 23/07/02 by Johnson
    Rows("29:29").Select
    Range("P29").Activate
    Selection.Insert Shift:=xlDown
    Range("A2:E2").Select
    Selection.Cut
    ActiveWindow.SmallScroll ToRight:=7
    ActiveWindow.SmallScroll Down:=15
    Range("P29").Select
    ActiveSheet.Paste
    Range("A2").Select
End Sub
```

Figure 5.18 Visual Basic Editor – TransferData macro

Depending on your system configuration you may have additional code in your macro. As long as the macro performs as expected ignore these additions.

2 Close the Visual Basic Editor window.

3 Test the **TransferData** macro by entering the following data in cells A2:E2:

a A2: **072**

b B2: (leave blank)

c C2: **cc800100**

d D2: **12/04/02**

c E2: **200**

4 Run the macro:

a Point to **Macro** from the **Tools** menu.

b Click on **Macros** from the sub-menu.

c Select the **TransferData** macro.

d Click **Run**.

Did the macro perform as expected?
If the macro is not working correctly, try one of the following:

a Check the code against the example in Figure 5.18.

b Delete the macro and start again.

How do I delete a macro?

1 Point to **macro** on the **Tools** menu.
2 Click **macros** from the sub-menu.
3 Select the name of the macro you want to **delete** so that it appears in the **macro name** box.
4 Click the **Delete** button.

A system message box (Figure 5.19) will ask you to confirm the name of the macro you are deleting.

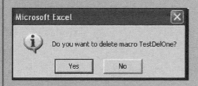

Figure 5.19 Delete macro – system message box

5 Click **Yes** to delete the selected macro.

Task E – Create a custom toolbar and button, and assign the macro to them

After completing this task, you will then have easy access to the macro.

1 Point to **Toolbars** on the **View** menu, then click **Customize**.

2 In the **Customize** window, click the **New** button to open the **New Toolbar** window.

3 In the text box, enter **UpdateCheques** as the toolbar name then click **OK** to close the window.

New **UpdateCheques** toolbar

If the new toolbar is not visible, drag the Customize window left or right; the toolbar will be behind it.

4 Click the **Commands** tab in the Customize window then select **Macros** in the **Categories** box list.

5 In the **Commands** Box list, select **Custom Button**.

6 Drag and drop the custom button onto the new **UpdateCheques** toolbar.

UpdateCheques toolbar with custom button

7 Right click the new toolbar to display the toolbar formatting pop-up menu (Figure 5.20).

8 Set the properties by following the steps below:

a Delete the default name **&CustomButton**, and replace it with **EnterCheques**.

b From the selection available, change the **UpdateCheques** button image to something more appropriate.

c Point to **Change Button Image** on the toolbar properties pop-up menu. A sub-menu of graphics will be displayed. Click an image to select this as the new image for your toolbar button.

Figure 5.20 Toolbar Formatting pop-up menu

Task F – Assign the TransferData macro to the UpdateCheques toolbar

Method

1 Right click the toolbar and click **Assign Macro**, to open the Assign Macro window with available macros (Figure 5.21).

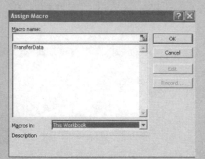

Figure 5.21 Assign macro window

2 Click the name of the macro you want to assign so that it appears in the **Macro name** text box.

3 Click the **OK** button to assign the macro.

4 Drag and drop the new toolbar next to the standard or formatting toolbars.

EXERCISE

3 – Password protection: investigation

Method

1 Add the password **Cheques** to open the **ChequesEntry** workbook.

2 Save and close the **ChequesEntry** workbook.

Should you add a password to modify the workbook?

Info

Before adding this type of password you need to think about the work that the macro in the workbook carries out.

Would the option **Password to modify** be practical for this particular workbook? Read the the author's view on this, in the Info box at the end of the next exercise.

3 Open the workbook **ChequesEntry** (ensure that you select the **Enable Macros** button).

4 Format the **Cheques** worksheet as follows:

   a Add an all border to cells A1:E1.   **b** Add a thick box border to cells B2:E2.
   c Cells A1:E1, fill colour black.   **d** Cells A1:E1, font colour white.

5 Using the **Format Painter**, copy the formatting from cells A1:E1 to cells P28:T28.

6 To test the **TransferData** macro, add one record to cells A1:E1 from the list that follows:

7 Using the **UpdateCheques** toolbar button, run the **TransferData** macro to move the data to the database area.

8 Repeat this procedure until all records have been added to the database area.

Client No	Cheque No	Credit CardNo	Date In	Amount
011	852470		11/04/02	350
072		cc800100	12/04/02	200
048	852140		01/04/02	750
011	992570		12/05/02	350
072		cc800100	14/05/02	200
048	892574		16/05/02	750
011		cc69874	13/06/02	350
072		cc800100	14/06/02	200
048	869852		17/06/02	750

Info

Having used the **TransferData** macro to enter a number of records, you have now had an opportunity to work with this repetitively.

Should you add a password to modify the **ChequesEntry** workbook?

The **TransferData** macro would need to lock and unlock cells. A macro is not flexible enough for that purpose.

In this situation, to ensure that only authorised users access, update or amend a workbook:

a Add a password to open the workbook.
b Protect the workbook **structure** with a password.

EXERCISE

4 – Viewing and hiding toolbars

The new **MyFormat** and **UpdateCheques** toolbars are now available each time you open a workbook, but this could cause a problem if they are used in the wrong situation.

Method

1 Right click any toolbar to select or deselect a toolbar name on the pop-up menu. In Figure 5.22, toolbars that have a tick beside their names are currently visible on screen.

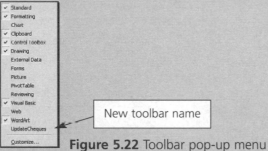

Figure 5.22 Toolbar pop-up menu

2 If the toolbar you want is not visible on the pop-up menu, click on **Customize**, select the **Toolbars** tab in the Customize window, then place a tick in the box beside the toolbar you require.

Info

If you are the only one that uses your system, then you can leave the toolbar visible all the time. If you share the system, then you can close the toolbars and open them as and when you need to use them.

Save and review your work.

In this section you have covered creating, using and customising macros.

You also named cell range(s) in a worksheet, and added password protection to a spreadsheet to facilitate the exercises being undertaken.